Information Security Roles & Responsibilities Made Easy

CHARLES CRESSON WOOD
CISA, CISSP

Information Security Roles & Responsibilities Made Easy

by Charles Cresson Wood, CISA, CISSP

© 2000-2002 PentaSafe Security Technologies, Inc. All rights reserved.
Printed in the United States of America.

Published by PentaSafe Security Technologies, Inc., 1233 West Loop South #1800, Houston, TX 77027.

Editor:	Ken Camerino	
Cover Design:	Krista Kirkland	
Printing History:	June 2001:	First Edition.
	January 2002:	Second Edition.

This book is sold on an individual copy basis. An organization-specific license to copy, modify, and republish parts of this book as in-house documentation is granted only to registered purchasers for internal use only. This material is for internal use only at licensee organizations, and may not be remarketed or redistributed. Consultants, VARs, OEMs, and other third parties using this material on behalf of another organization must purchase separate licenses for each organization where this material is used.

No part of this material may be reproduced or transmitted in any form or by any means, electronic or mechanical, including photocopying, recording, or by any information storage and retrieval system, without the written permission of the copyright owner, except where permitted by law.

The information in this reference book and accompanying storage media (CD-ROM and the like) is provided as a service to the business community. At the time of its preparation, the job descriptions, mission statements, and other materials found in this book are believed to be current, relevant, useful, and appropriate for organizations concerned about information security. Such information is nonetheless subject to change without notice. Although every reasonable effort has been made to ensure the accuracy, completeness, and relevance of the information contained herein, Pentasafe Security Technologies, Inc., InfoSecurity Infrastructure, Inc. and its affiliates (including the author) cannot be responsible for any errors and omissions, or any party's interpretations or applications of the ideas contained herein. Readers preparing job descriptions, mission statements, and other information security documentation are advised to seek the expert advice and guidance of lawyers familiar with computer issues, information systems security specialists, and human resources specialists. Neither, Pentasafe Security Technologies, Inc., the author, nor InfoSecurity Infrastructure, Inc. make any warranties, guarantees, or representations about the fitness for any purpose of the information security materials found in this book.

ISBN: 1-881585-08-5

Dedication

To Tony, Pat, and Andrea for their
insightful perspectives and many good works.

CONTENTS

Chapter 1 INTRODUCTION

The total cost of ownership (TCO) models developed by industry analysts such as the Gartner Group indicate that labor represents anywhere from two-thirds to three-quarters of the on-going cost associated with information technology (system set-up, administration, maintenance, etc.). Information security is just one of many subspecialties within the information technology field, but its costs are also dominated by labor. In spite of what information security vendor sales representatives may tell you, the information security field is still in an embryonic state, and many of the essential activities have not yet been automated. This means that all organizations, no matter how sophisticated they happen to be, will be critically dependent on the work of people to achieve a truly secure information technology environment.

Management in many organizations doesn't yet appreciate how important the labor of many different people is to achieving information security goals. This book is intended to provide the specific roles and responsibilities that every organization needs to wake-up management, to get management to pay more attention to information security, and for management to start allocating realistic budgets for information security staffing. In the process, I hope to engender more discussion about the many contributions that an Information Security Department regularly makes. With this book, I also seek to generate greater respect for and understanding about the information security function by pointing out the many—often behind-the-scenes —ways that the information security team adds value to a business. I furthermore hope that you will be surprised to see that information security staff do so much, or at least could do so much, in so many ways working to make sure that things turn out right.

In the real world, the typical organization's information security efforts are characterized by a surprising amount of chaos and unnecessary internal politics. At an excessive number of organizations, lack of clearly articulated roles and responsibilities has become the number one impediment to information security progress. Confusion and ongoing arguments about roles and responsibilities distract and deter workers from attending to the time-consuming work that needs to be done. Such confusion and ongoing arguments prevent both departments and individuals from creating the strong cooperative relationships that are needed for a successful information security effort. With this book, you can change all of this for the better.

If your organization has not yet clarified roles and responsibilities, then the organization is much less likely to be successful with other tasks related to information security. For instance, if the responsibility for information security training and awareness has not been assigned, chances are this job is not being done or is being done in an inadequate manner. Workers at your organization may wonder whether this work should be done by the Human Resources Department, the Training Department, or the Information Security Department. It is not an exaggeration to say that clear roles and responsibilities are an essential prerequisite for all information security activities. To genuinely be effective in the information security arena, every organization needs to consciously specify and coordinate the activities of a team of people, each with different information security roles and responsibilities (the reasons why a team is needed are covered in Chapter 3, "Persuasion").

As another example, consider the development of an innovative new Internet business application system. The programmers involved may be concerned about security, and may even know a thing or two about how best to implement security. Yet, the performance evaluations of most programmers today do not directly deal with how well the programmers build secure systems. Other factors, such as how fast they write code that works, receive much greater emphasis. In the absence of clear roles and responsibilities for building security into this application, and feeling deadline pressure, the programmers most likely will decide that serious security will be incorporated into a future version of the application. Thus important security decisions will be made by default, but they may not be what's best for the organization. To have security-related decisions that are truly in the best interests of an organization, definitive roles and responsibilities documentation is required.

This book is intended to provide you with all the content you need to immediately develop or update mission statements, job descriptions, organizational reporting relationship diagrams, and other documentation dealing with information security roles and responsibilities. The book assumes that you must quickly compile roles and responsibilities documentation—that you do not have the time or budget to hire consultants, go to classes, or perform extensive research. To this end, this book provides the most comprehensive collection of practical ideas and ready-to-use documentation about information security roles and responsibilities available anywhere.

My intent has been to give you a compendium of the best standard practices found in successful organizations operating in industrialized nations. You are expected to pick and choose practices that best match the needs of your organization. My information security document development consulting practice has proven that it's a lot faster to choose items from an already-developed list than it is to develop a new list from scratch. You will, of course, need to tailor the material that I provide so that it fits in with your organization's documentation standards (format, length, graphics, topics, etc.).

There is no need for you to worry whether you have the requisite technical expertise to understand and use the material in this book. The book is written for a newly-appointed information security manager who has only a cursory knowledge of information systems concepts, and no particular technical information security expertise. Because the material is written with a management perspective, the book can also be used by technical staff, users, consultants, auditors, and others who find themselves in a position where they need to quickly prepare information security roles and responsibilities documentation. Although the language will be oriented towards managers, seasoned information security specialists will nonetheless discover that this book provides many useful tips and templates.

The entire process of developing and/or revising information security roles and responsibilities documentation has been scripted for you. The chapters in this book are sequenced to step you through all the important tasks on the road to developing professional, relevant, and effective information security roles and responsibilities documentation. The book provides you with all the detailed information you will need to prepare credible and meaningful memos to management to advance an information security roles and responsibilities project. Accordingly, you are urged to at least skim the material found in each of the chapters to identify material that could be used within your organization. After this skimming process has been completed, you can determine which materials should be used at your organization. Then you can start modifying the files provided on the accompanying CD-ROM. This modification process typically involves changing organization names, department names, and job titles to be consistent with existing organizational structures. The

process could also include the addition of references to relevant laws, industry specific regulations, and other external requirements that are unique to your organization. The process should additionally involve the provision of references to other relevant documents at your organization, such as a Human Resources Manual. Also advisable during the modification process is the addition of introductions or prefaces that will help to integrate the material found in this book into the documentation found at your organization.

One of the easiest ways to proceed is for you to go through the hardcopy book using a highlighter, pen, or pencil. As you read or skim, you should mark the material that seems relevant for your organization. Then, using your web browser, you should open the relevant chapter's file on the CD-ROM and copy and paste information into a word processing document to edit so that it is uniquely tailored to your organization. Besides following the specific directions found in each chapter and getting management approval, that's really all there is to it.

Under great pressure to produce roles and responsibilities documentation, you may use the materials found in this book without anything more than changing organization names and department names. Although this approach may sound attractive at first glance, I discourage it. You are instead advised to prepare a project justification memo, a project schedule, a list of interviewees, and related planning documents. These topics are discussed in Chapter 2 through Chapter 10. By spending some time to plan the project, you can help ensure that the material that you develop dovetails nicely with the organization's business activities, the so called "corporate culture," and other circumstances at your organization.

Before submitting roles and responsibilities documents to management for approval, you should also have the material reviewed by a human resources specialist, an intellectual property lawyer, and a seasoned information security specialist. Chapter 7, "Review and Approval" discusses the best ways to get management approval and support for your roles and responsibilities documents, so this will not be explored further here. Suffice it to say that a considerable amount of your time on a roles and responsibilities project will be devoted to justifying and explaining the reasons why certain words were included in memos that you issued. This book is intended to provide all the necessary ammunition not only to fight these battles successfully, but also to staunchly and resolutely defend the importance of the information security function.

Since all of the material in this book is provided on the accompanying CD-ROM in a Web Help format, you do not need to retype anything. Topics of interest can be quickly located using the Contents, Index, and Search tabs. I have done everything that I could think of to speed your development of professional and credible information security role and responsibility documentation. Nonetheless, there is always room for improvement. If you have suggestions for the next version of this book, please contact me at the electronic mail address shown in "About the Author" on page 177.

The scope of the material licensed with this product should be mentioned. The legal words can be found on the inside title page to the hardcopy book. You must be aware that this material is licensed on an organization-wide basis (based strictly on organizational name). A perpetual and worldwide license to edit, copy, and internally republish the derivative material at your organization is extended to all registered and licensed individuals. This license is for a single organization only; if more than one legal organizational name is involved, then a multi-organization license is required. If you take a job at a different organization, then a new organization-wide license is required to use this material. Consultants and other third parties must likewise obtain a separate license for each organization using this material (as evidenced by the letterhead on letter stationery).

Chapter 2 JUSTIFICATION

This chapter discusses the reasons why you should establish clear role and responsibility statements for all people involved with information security. If management support for a role and responsibility clarification project is still missing, you might want to write a project justification memo using the material found in this chapter. If you seek a quick-and-dirty justification memo, you may simply want to copy the bullets in "Summary of Reasons to Establish Clear Roles & Responsibilities" on page 9.

Having specific documented role and responsibility statements is advisable for every organizational unit, not just information security. Those organizational units with fully developed role and responsibility statements will enjoy greater respect and greater resources. At many organizations, information security is a new organizational unit or function. As a result, a formal Information Security Department at many organizations is still in development. This means that these same organizations are often missing documents that cover information security job descriptions, mission statements, and reporting relationships. When these roles and responsibilities are documented and approved, the information security function will be increasingly recognized as a legitimate and on-going organizational function, worthy of respect and its own share of organizational resources.

One of the most important reasons to document role and responsibility assignments is to demonstrate top management support. Information security specialists often feel as though many people oppose what they are trying to do. Occasionally information security specialists must take an unpopular position, for example, postponing the release of a new software package until appropriate controls can be included. If the information security specialists aren't going to be outvoted, outmaneuvered, and otherwise overruled, a clearly documented mandate from top management must be in place. With documented and approved roles and responsibilities, information security specialists can prevent or resolve many arguments and then get on with their work.

At many organizations, the information security function has been moved from department to department. Many of these departments may not have known what to do with the information security function. These departments often treat the information security function like an unwanted foster child that really never had a home. As a result, management may not have seriously considered the recommendations offered by information security specialists. Consequently, management may have postponed or failed to fund a number of important information security projects. But when roles and responsibilities for the information security function are specified and approved by top management, all this can quickly change. Then the information security function will have a real home, in other words, it will know where it fits into the organizational structure. Then the information security function will have formal communication channels with top management that can be used to get important projects underway.

Information itself knows no individual or organizational boundaries. It travels around at the speed of sound, light, or electricity, and ends up distributed to those who are interested in it, those who request it, and those who don't know how to stop it from coming. Intangible and by its very nature difficult to corral, information can only be secured adequately when all the people who have access to it consistently observe certain policies, standards, procedures, and other requirements. In other words, information security is a team effort that requires extensive interpersonal coordination. The coordination has long since gone beyond a team within the Information Technology Department; now this coordination must include end-users, contractors, consultants, outsourcing firm personnel, customers, suppliers, and business partners. This coordination should include clearly documented information security roles and responsibilities. This critically important topic is addressed at length in Chapter 3, "Persuasion," and so will not be expanded upon here. Only through roles and responsibilities documentation can all of the individuals and organizations on this team work in both unison and harmony.

Many Internet Service Providers (ISPs), Application Service Providers (ASPs), hosting firms, facilities management firms, outsourcing firms, and other third parties have not paid adequate attention to information security. Organizations that rely on these third parties may be lowering their short-term costs, but unless information security roles and responsibilities are crystal clear, the organizations are also significantly increasing their *reputation risk*. Reputation risk is a new term that refers to the adverse publicity, loss of customer confidence, and even loss of customers that can accompany a major information security problem. If information security roles and responsibilities are included in negotiations with third parties, then the initial cost will typically go up, but the issue is really "pay me now, or pay me later—either way you've got to pay." When negotiations with third parties include a detailed examination of information security roles and responsibilities, management will be indirectly notified that there is a significant reputation risk associated with a decision not to specifically assign critical information security tasks to certain persons, groups, or organizations. These specific tasks are covered in Chapter 17, "Outsourcing Firms."

Information security is inherently inter-disciplinary and inter-departmental, and at many organizations, it is fast becoming inter-organizational. For example, an effective encryption system requires a mix of human resources ideas (such as training), computer science ideas (such as mathematics to determine key length), and management ideas (such as procedures for key recovery when a key is lost). To implement an encryption system, a variety of people are needed including: systems administrators, technical information security staff, physical security staff, EDP auditors, and networking technologists. In addition, to have an encryption system such as a virtual private network (VPN) work with business partners, these same people must work with their counterparts at other organizations. All this complexity requires a great deal of coordination if it's going to be effective. The roles and responsibilities of these individuals and organizational units must be clearly delineated if significant confusion and serious security lapses are going to be avoided.

Rather than eliminating the need for human involvement, the new information systems that organizations are using today (such as Internet commerce systems) are increasing the reliance on certain types of people with specialized skills. For example, if a critical technical person were to abruptly leave his or her employer, the organization might be hard pressed to continue operations without this person. The increased reliance on people with highly specialized skills and training can be reduced by backup personnel, cross-training, sharing job responsibilities, documenting the work, and other tasks associated with the development of clear information security roles and responsibilities (these topics are discussed in Chapter 18, "Smaller Organizations"). This book assists you in an effort to reengineer the information security function so that the people working within information security do not themselves become a single point of failure.

The information security field is still embryonic when compared to the marketing or accounting fields. While some interesting new technological solutions to information security problems are now on the market, in most organizations the achievement of effective information security critically depends on people. At this point in the evolution of the technology, there are many information security problems that can only be handled by people. For example, there is no commercially-available technological solution to the social engineering (masquerading) threats that all organizations face. All too often the people within organizations don't understand what management expects them to do, and this in turn will prevent the achievement of information security goals. Only after roles and responsibilities have been clarified and documented, and after selected people are then appropriately trained, can these same people participate as an essential component of the solution to information security problems.

Management at many organizations has never clearly stated its intentions about the work it wanted an information security function to perform. For example, does it expect the Information Security Department or the EDP Auditing Department to do compliance checks to make sure that user departments were operating in a manner consistent with information security policies and standards? Likewise, does it expect the Information Security Department or the Business Contingency Planning Department to do information systems contingency planning work? These and other turf battles can consume an excessive amount of time and money, which would be better spent addressing pressing information security vulnerabilities. When clear role and responsibility documentation is in place, staff can refocus their efforts on those things that truly advance the organization's goals. When this documentation is in place, departments will not "step on each other's toes" (anger one another because they are doing something that the other is expected to do), just as they will not duplicate work already done in another department.

It's hard to do a "good job" if you don't know what your job is supposed to be. As perverse as this situation may sound, many information security specialists have been asked to do just that. When things go wrong, they often get blamed even though they didn't know these same things were important. Besides increasing the chances of coming down with an ulcer or a heart attack, this situation demoralizes and discourages staff. But when roles and responsibilities are clarified, when management clarifies its expectations for the individuals working in the Information Security department, workers will be much more likely to be focused, motivated, and working in accordance with management's intentions.

The entire information security field is shot through-and-through with denial. Some people deny that there is an information security problem, while others deny its importance. No doubt you have come across individuals who claim that doing something "is not my job." The latter type of individuals are often unwilling to find out whose job it is when they notice an information security problem. With all this denial, it's very hard to get people to view information security as their own personal responsibility. But when roles and responsibilities are documented they can't avoid it any longer. When this type of documentation exists, workers are a lot more serious about incorporating information security into their regular job activities. When this type of documentation has been prepared, workers can also readily determine who is responsible for specific tasks related to information security.

A voluntary approach to information security is not generally effective. If organizational structure defining the required activities related to information security are not specified, the work simply will not get done. This is because information security is in competition with other business objectives such as low cost, high performance, ease-of-use, and compressed time-to-market for a new product or service. Because worker performance is generally evaluated with these other factors and not with information security, there is a tendency for information security to be compromised in favor of other objectives. Stated differently, workers must be explicitly instructed how to act in ways that maintain information security. Some of the most effective ways to accomplish this are through specific words appearing in job descriptions and organizational unit mission statements. Even in those rare and progressive organizations where worker performance evaluations include consideration of information security, there is still a need to be clear about just what workers should be doing. When management is clear about roles and responsibilities, the proper balance between security and competing objectives will also be much easier to strike.

Roles and responsibilities documentation will also help a great deal with disciplinary actions up to and including termination. These intermediate disciplinary actions include denial of pay raises, denial of bonuses, denial of promotions, denial of transfers to other organizational units, denial of special training, and forced time off without pay. Besides providing a reference point for the worker performance review process, clearly documented roles and responsibilities show what people should be doing, how they should be doing it, and when they should be doing it. This documentation may be essential when there is a so-called wrongful termination lawsuit (where an employee alleges that he or she was fired for inappropriate reasons). For example, if a worker is fired for not performing a certain job described in his or her job description, then sufficient basis for the termination has not only been previously communicated to the employee but documentation supporting the termination has been established. In a broader sense, role and responsibility documentation supports fair and efficient management decisions that in all well-managed firms include a disciplinary process.

Experienced information security specialists are currently in great demand. According to recent market research studies, the demand for information security services is growing at a 70-100% compounded annual rate. In other words, organizations will need to offer an attractive pay and benefits package if they are going to be successful with efforts to hire experienced information security specialists. These much-sought-after specialists will want to know what the prospective job entails. Nothing quite communicates the answer to that question as well as a job description and an Information Security Department mission statement. Having clear role and responsibility documentation will additionally let you accurately match an organization's needs with the skills and knowledge of people who have applied for a job. If your organization is using temporaries, consultants, or contractors rather than employees, having documented roles and responsibilities will also speed the selection of appropriate people.

If your organization has operations in the United States, be sure to discuss the implications of documenting roles and responsibilities with your accounting manager. The Internal Revenue Service (IRS) has a twenty question test that it uses to determine whether consultants and contractors are really employees (and whether the employer owes additional taxes). These questions include the lack of instructions how to accomplish a job and the lack of a continuing relationship. If contractors or consultants are used, there is still significant merit to documenting clear roles and responsibilities; this documentation should, however, be prepared so as to be consistent with IRS requirements.

Many organizations are now turning to outsourcing firms to handle their information security needs. While some management responsibilities such as making final decisions about information security policies should ultimately rest on the shoulders of internal management, a considerable amount of the security work can be outsourced. If roles and responsibilities are not clearly established at the time that a contract is negotiated, the organization that contracted the outsourcing firm may find itself in a difficult spot. The outsourcing firm may claim that the requested service (such as tracking down a hacker) is not in the contract, and that the customer must pay additional fees, assuming that the outsourcing firm does have technically-competent people available at the time. Of course, other consulting firms can also be called in, but with any of these options, precious time will be wasted negotiating fees, defining the work to be done, etc. While all of these ad-hoc business arrangements are being made, a hacker could be on the loose inside the internal network at your organization. To keep losses to a minimum, it is absolutely essential that roles and responsibilities for all important information security activities be defined in advance in outsourcing contracts (this topic is explored at length in Chapter 17, "Outsourcing Firms").

While many of the people working at your organization are likely to be concerned about information security issues, such as viruses, they often don't know whom to contact. Imagine an ordinary end-user who has just inadvertently infected his personal computer with a virus thanks to downloaded software from the Internet. If he doesn't know whom to contact, he may try to eradicate the virus himself. In the process, he may destroy data or spread the virus to other computers. On the other hand, if he knows whom to contact for immediate expert assistance, these negative consequences can be minimized. Thus clear statements of roles and responsibilities facilitate communications that are needed to promptly resolve information security problems.

Another good reason to document roles and responsibilities is to demonstrate compliance with internal policies as well as external laws and regulations. Auditors and government examiners are impressed with documentation. It gives them the feeling that things are under control. In addition, with clear documentation defining information security roles and responsibilities, an organization can show that it is operating in a fashion which is consistent with the standard of due care. Being able to demonstrate this consistency may be very important in terms of reducing or eliminating management liability for losses and other problems. Such documentation may help with a variety of liability concerns including computer professional malpractice and breach of management's fiduciary duty to protect information assets. Having such documentation may also be useful in showing business partners that any confidential information they disclose to your organization will be handled in a secure manner.

Another important reason to document information security roles and responsibilities involves the provision of assurance to management that people are doing their jobs. This is one of the primary tasks of an Internal Audit Department, but this task cannot be adequately performed unless auditors have a reference point against which to compare current worker activities. Without clearly documented roles and responsibilities, auditors will not be in a position to provide an opinion whether individuals or departments are doing the work that management intends them to do.

Yet another reason to document information security roles and responsibilities involves the capture of organizational knowledge to prevent mistakes from happening again. If roles and responsibilities are documented, an organization can codify what it knows. If this information is not captured, new staff members are bound to repeat the mistakes of their predecessors. Consider the common mistake where an Information Security Manager reports directly to the Chief Information Officer (CIO). This hierarchy involves an inherent conflict of interest. The CIO is likely to give the information security function inadequate resources and attention because he or she is measured with competing objectives (response time, new application development time, etc.). The CIO and Information Security Manager may have had several discussions about this problem, but may not have written anything down. If both the CIO and the Information Security Manager were then to leave for other jobs, this problem may not be appreciated by those who remain, and the dysfunctional reporting relationship may be continued. Reporting relationships are discussed at length in Chapter 13, "Reporting Relationships."

In management circles, it is fashionable to talk about the Japanese concept of *kaizen* (continuous improvement). While the quality assurance and quality control disciplines have been around for a long time, the move towards ISO 9000 certification is relatively new and clearly an effective way to achieve competitive advantage. If information security roles and responsibilities are clearly documented, then a starting point for a process of continuous improvement has been created. Over time, staff can upgrade and refine the roles and responsibilities to better suit the organization's needs. The very act of writing these things down often illuminates important distinctions that were never previously considered.

Recent research on the criteria for organizational success and growth indicates that both tension and disequilibrium are vital. This tension and disequilibrium helps to encourage rapid evolutionary changes in response to changes in both the business and the technological environments. As the research of Margaret Wheatley in Leadership And The New Science indicates, the tension and disequilibrium that leads to change and growth is dependent on a certain organizational order. I strongly argue that the necessary order is supported by clarifying information security roles and responsibilities in a manner that meets organizational objectives. The tension and disequilibrium in turn can be created via separation of duties, dual control, supervisory checking of the work of others, and other tactics that are further explained in Chapter 18, "Smaller Organizations."

The process of periodically updating roles and responsibilities documentation also helps to move an organization in the direction of accepting information security as a legitimate business function such as accounting and marketing. In far too many organizations, the information security function is perceived as a project, and when it is done, people get back to "business as usual." To the contrary, information security needs to be an ongoing organizational unit that serves the organization by performing recurring tasks like risk assessments. Having job descriptions, mission statements, and reporting relationships in writing and signed by top management helps to make this point with those who still resist it.

Some managers will want to start an information security training and awareness effort as a way to get the ball rolling in the information security area. While their motivation may be laudable, this approach often produces less than stellar results. A training and awareness effort that is not built on an underlying statement of roles and responsibilities, as well as a current set of policies, is bound to have little impact. This is because the recipients of the training and awareness effort will naturally ask: (1) "Who's our contact point?", (2) "What should I do?", and (3) "How should we be using information systems in a more secure fashion?" Any training that lacks answers to these roles and responsibilities questions is likely to be ineffective and also tarnish the image of an information security function for years to come. To ensure that a training effort illuminates the activities that an Information Security Department performs, as well as illuminates the participants' own information security responsibilities, written roles and responsibilities must first be prepared.

Perhaps the most significant reason to establish and document clear roles and responsibilities involves increasing worker efficiency and productivity. The information security field is an new area and there is still great confusion about who should be doing what. For example, when a worker has his or her laptop computer stolen, who should this event be reported to? Should a notice be sent to the Information Security Department, the Physical Security Department, or the Insurance Department? Maybe the notice should go only to the worker's manager? Without clear roles and responsibilities, users will unnecessarily spend time figuring out the answers to these questions. Likewise, if roles and responsibilities are clarified and documented, employees will not waste their time trying to figure out whom to invite to certain meetings, who needs to sign-off on certain proposal, etc.

Summary of Reasons to Establish Clear Roles & Responsibilities

- Garner greater respect and greater resources for information security function

- Establish demonstrable top management support for information security

- Establish formal communication channels with top management

- Foster coordinated team effort to safeguard information as it travels around

- Lower the risks to the organization's reputation due to security problems

- Manage the complexity of modern information systems and networks

- Reduce chance that information security staff will be single point of failure

- Clarify exactly what information security activities management expects

- Motivate and focus the work of specialists and rank-and-file staff

- Force staff to view information security as their personal responsibility

- Eliminate or reduce turf battles and related problems with internal politics

- Strike an appropriate balance between security and competing objectives

- Leverage performance reviews to get people to take security seriously

- Support a variety of disciplinary actions up to and including termination

- Speed selection of appropriate workers including contractors and consultants

- Allow outsourcing firms to handle incidents without contract renegotiation

- Facilitate communications that are needed to resolve security problems

- Demonstrate compliance with internal policies, laws, and regulations

- Shield management from negligence and related liability claims

- Assist auditors in determining whether people are doing necessary work

- Capture organizational knowledge to prevent mistakes from being repeated

- Provide starting point for a process of continuous improvement (ISO 9000)

- Establish the required order needed to grow and change the organization

- Foster acceptance of information security as a legitimate business function

- Lay a foundation for an information security training and awareness effort

- Increase worker efficiency and productivity by eliminating confusion

Chapter 3   PERSUASION

If you or others involved with information security at your organization have not yet had a discussion about roles and responsibilities with top management, one perspective probably prevails. Top management probably believes that the scope of information security roles and responsibilities is confined to the Information Security Department. If that old-fashioned view is used to determine information security roles and responsibilities, then the organization will be prevented from creating a truly effective information security organizational structure. If this happens, the resulting roles and responsibilities will leave major areas without sufficient attention and resources, and this will most likely lead to serious information security related losses.

With the intention to change top management's perceptions, this chapter discusses the reasons why information security has become a team effort rather than simply an activity performed by a relatively isolated department. To acquaint top management with the true nature of modern information security, you should at least write a memo such as the one provided. This memo is intended to open management's eyes to the need for not just a team approach, but a multi-organizational team approach.

The memo provided seeks management's approval to discuss roles and responsibilities with interested parties within your organization. While this may at first appear unduly conservative to you, there is merit to going through the proper management channels and in advance making sure that all involved managers are aligned with the project's objectives.

As this memo implies, the development of new roles and responsibilities should be done in accordance with, and in a manner that is respectful of existing organizational structures. The roles and responsibilities discussed in this book seek only to augment existing organizational structures so that information security objectives can be appropriately met. Unlike a reengineering project, the roles and responsibilities provided in this book are not intended to achieve any other organizational design objective besides the establishment of a strong and effective information security function.

Beyond a memo, a meeting to discuss the project scope and the involvement of other groups is also recommended. At such a meeting, you can solicit management's ideas about all the different job titles and departments that in one way or another have something to do with information security. A good agenda for such a meeting would be:

1. Impediments to information security progress (see Chapter 4, "Preparation" for further details)

2. Benefits from clarifying information security roles & responsibilities (see Chapter 2, "Justification" for further details)

3. Potential participants in an information security team (see the "Memo To Management" in this chapter)

Throughout this book the words "Company X" are intended to be replaced with your organizational name (whether that be a partnership, a corporation, a government agency, a non-profit agency, or some other entity).

MEMO TO MANAGEMENT

Regarding: Information Security Has Become A Team Effort

To: *[insert your manager's name]*
From: *[insert your name]*
Date: *[insert today's date]*
Classification: Internal Use Only

Thank-you for authorizing me to develop new roles and responsibilities for the information security function at Company X. This memo describes the reasons why job descriptions (and perhaps mission statements and reporting relationships) outside the information security department need to be modified to achieve effective information security. This memo ends by seeking your permission for me to work with individuals in other functional groups besides information security, to concretely and responsively define appropriate information security roles and responsibilities.

Two or three decades ago, the only people who worked with computers were in what was then called a Data Processing Department. As local area networks, minicomputers, departmental servers, and personal computers became widespread, information was dispersed away from a central data processing organizational function and away from an isolated "computer machine room." This distribution of information continues with the spread of the Internet, telecommuting, and dial-up remote access. Over the last few decades, the number of people who have access to Company X sensitive, critical, and valuable information has grown tremendously. The information handling activities of these people must be coordinated if security is going to be achieved.

As the technology evolved, the ability to locally capture and manipulate information has grown exponentially. The computer terminals with no local storage capabilities and local connections to a mainframe that were common several decades ago, for the most part, have been replaced by small portable computers (such as the Palm Pilot) with local storage capabilities and international networking connections. This local storage and manipulation of information has placed much greater reliance on users as the key to achieving information security goals. For example, now a user can steal Company X trade secrets simply by making a copy on a floppy disk and removing it from Company X offices. This type of easy removal of sensitive information could not have taken place in the mainframe world. Because users are now in a significant position of power when it comes to information security, they need to be enlisted as motivated participants on an information security team.

In some respects, technology itself is now dictating organizational structure, especially to the degree that it is dictating increased communication, for example, with groupware (like Lotus Notes) and teleconferencing. There is much more interaction between people than in years gone past, and with this has come an expectation that resources in other departments will be used to achieve certain organizational goals and objectives. For example, e-mail is now used to notify all workers about new viruses distributed over the Internet, and each user is expected to play some role in the prevention of damage from viruses. To coordinate these increased communications with a larger number of people, there needs to be an associated clarification of information security roles and responsibilities.

While the original focus of attention in the information security field was on the technology, that has also changed, and now the focus is on information and information systems. For example, the information security field used to be called "computer security" but now that anachronistic term is rarely encountered. While an isolated organizational function could handle the technical aspects of computer security, Company X now needs an organizational unit which deals with the technical, the business, and the human relations sides of information management. Company X information is now in the hands of nearly every worker at the organization, not to mention in the hands of a number of third parties, and it is therefore necessary to enlist the support of all of these people in the achievement of information security goals.

The increasing focus on information has shown up in the recent emphasis on knowledge management systems. These systems capture, store, and appropriately disseminate critical information to those insiders who need the information to do their jobs. In an age where global competition is heating up, when just about every other aspect of an organization (people, technology, buildings, etc.) can be replaced, it is the critical working knowledge, the reputation, and the relationships that have been built up over the many years of business that sets one business apart from another. This working knowledge is often expressed as patents, copyrights, and trade secrets. A fine reputation is often attached to a trademark or service mark. The relationships are often captured in customer databases and supplier agreements. These examples show how information is pervasive throughout the organization, and by implication why responsibility for information security should also be pervasive throughout the organization.

Information itself frequently changes form as it is used for various purposes. To make a decision, a manager may read a computer-generated hardcopy report and then discuss the numbers appearing in the report via telephone with a specialist at a remote site. In the process information will have morphed from paper form to verbal form. The dynamic manifestations of information mean that people outside the Information Systems Department must be involved with information security. For example, the Telecommunications Department needs to assist with voicemail security, and the Corporate Records Manager needs to assist with paper records storage and retrieval.

Over the last several decades, the workplace has changed and there are many fewer full-time employees. Now many organizations have contractors, consultants, temporaries and outsourcing firms. To do their jobs, these non-employee workers must also understand their information security roles and responsibilities. Unlike employees, many of these non-employee workers cannot simply be instructed to do things in the moment. For example, an information systems facilities management outsourcing firm must be very explicitly told what to do in a contract. Likewise, consultants cannot have their activities changed without a contractual revision. Other regulations, such as the US Internal Revenue Service stipulations on the relationship between a contractor and a client may further erode an organization's ability to define roles and responsibilities dynamically. For example, IRS regulations indicate that contractors should have the ability to determine where, when, and how to perform certain duties. Unless the specific roles and responsibilities are clear in advance, these laws and regulations can interfere with the successful accomplishment of information security objectives by non-employee workers.

The discipline of information security has also changed dramatically over the last few decades. While it used to be primarily focused on computer access control and contingency planning, it now includes a wide variety of issues such as web site privacy, credit card fraud prevention, and identity theft detection. This expansion of the information security field has meant that specialists in areas like criminal investigations, employee training, and internal auditing must assist to achieve effective information security. Information security has become, now more than ever, multi-disciplinary. The multi-disciplinary aspects of the new information security field have in turn meant that individuals must specialize to effectively and efficiently achieve information security goals. These new specialists in turn need clear roles and responsibilities documentation to properly work together.

Information security has also become multi-departmental and multi-organizational in nature. Extranets and electronic data interchange (EDI) systems provide good examples of how modern information systems must incorporate a clear understanding of the roles and responsibilities of people in several organizations. Just to handle problems within a single company, it is now clear that cooperation between multiple departments is required. For example, to investigate a hacker break-in, organizations often need cooperation from the Information Security Department, the Legal Department, and the Physical Security Department. To investigate security incidents such as Internet fraud, the participation of multiple organizations such as an Internet Service Provider (ISP) and the Federal Bureau of Investigation may be required.

Just as specialists are needed in the information security area, so too they are needed in other functional domains such as insurance and risk management. The increased division of labor, and the division of organizations into specialized subunits, unfortunately brings with it a tendency for specialists to see only their own activities, and fail to see how what they do fits in with other activities throughout the organization. This in turn erodes the ability of specialists to make decisions that include an organization-wide perspective. Often called "sub optimization," this process often occurs in the information security area, for example, where user departments make local decisions without considering the impact on others who share the same computer network resources. A project to clearly define information security roles and responsibilities across the organization will reduce sub optimization problems and will encourage a broader understanding of the ways that various specialists work together to achieve common information security goals.

Information security is also dynamic because every change in an information system or even the way an existing information system is used has information security implications. It is no longer sufficient for information security to be handled as a project, where vulnerabilities get examined from time to time. In most organizations of medium to large scale, a full-time staff composed of knowledgeable, trained, and motivated people needs to be supported by clear definitions of their roles and responsibilities.

If one examines the statistics of information system related crime and abuse, it is clear that the majority of the losses are caused by errors and omissions, and not by high profile hacker intrusions that often get reported in the newspapers. Frequently those responsible for these losses failed to pay attention to the mundane details associated with information systems management. Often those responsible failed to understand that they must perform certain tasks, such as backup a database. Clearly specified roles and responsibilities are the one and only approach that can be used to ensure that necessary information systems management activities are taking place and being performed by those who should be doing them.

If management believes that information security can be adequately dealt with by a single department working largely alone, the scope of an information security roles and responsibilities project will be unduly restricted. This in turn will mean that the Information Security Department will have an extraordinary and unrealistically large set of duties, which inevitably will lead to disappointing results. There is simply too much work to be accomplished by a single department. The Information Security Department in today's organizations doesn't have the political power, the organizational vantage point, or the technical tools to be in all the places where it needs to be to ensure effective information security throughout an organization. Only by an orchestrated definition of an information security team can an Information Security Department achieve the information security goals sought by management.

Over the years, many organizations have tried to organize the information security function with an all volunteer army. At the same time they skimped on training and awareness efforts, so it should be no surprise that the all volunteer army was not motivated, and when it came time to do something important, they did not fight as management hoped they would. Information security has become too important to modern business to continue with this informal and uncommitted approach. What Company X needs now is a team of motivated individuals who understand the roles each member of the team plays and how they all work together. What Company X needs now is accountability for information security as reflected in clearly defined roles and responsibilities.

I have provided below a list of the job titles that I believe have some role or responsibility in the information security area. Please authorize me to speak with these people, either in person or by phone, so that I can get their perspective about the roles and responsibilities that they should have in the information security area. While I will do my best to incorporate their comments about the unique ways in which Company X does business, the specific roles and responsibilities that I will recommend will primarily be a function of best industry practices.

The specific job titles at Company X which I believe have an important contribution to make to the Company X information security effort are:

- Information Security Department Manager
- Access Control System Administrator
- Internal Information Security Consultant
- Information Security Engineer
- Information Security Documentation Specialist
- Information Systems Contingency Planner
- Local Information Security Coordinator
- Chief Information Officer
- Information Systems Analyst/Business Analyst
- Systems Programmer
- Business Applications Programmer
- Computer Operations Manager
- Computer Operator
- Information Systems Quality Assurance Analyst
- Help Desk Associate
- Archives Manager/Records Manager
- Telecommunications Manager
- Systems Administrator/Network Administrator

- Web Site Administrator/Commerce Site Administrator
- Database Administrator
- Data Administrator
- Physical Security Department Manager
- Physical Asset Protection Specialist
- Building And Facilities Guard
- Office Maintenance Worker
- Internal Audit Department Manager
- EDP Auditor
- Internal Intellectual Property Attorney
- Human Resources Department Manager
- Human Resources Consultant
- Receptionist
- Outsourcing Contract Administrator
- In-House Trainer
- Insurance And Risk Management Department Manager
- Insurance And Risk Management Analyst
- Business Contingency Planner
- Public Relations Manager
- Chief Financial Officer
- Purchasing Agent
- Chief Executive Officer

Please sign (with a date) below indicating your approval that I proceed to contact these individuals to discuss information security roles and responsibilities.

_____

[insert your manager's name here]

Chapter 4 PREPARATION

There are many dependencies in the information security field, and this chapter describes those that relate to the development of roles and responsibilities documentation. This chapter discusses the efforts which should be completed to ensure that information security roles and responsibilities documentation will be read by those involved, will be taken seriously, will be used appropriately, and will be updated periodically. This chapter also discusses the efforts that will lay the foundation for a successful information security roles and responsibilities development project. These will, for example, ensure that interviewees will be cooperative, that middle management will review draft documents, and that top management will be willing to approve the final documents.

One essential prerequisite to any information security documentation effort is top management appreciation that information itself has become an asset or an organizational resource. Sometimes called Information Resource Management (IRM), this way of looking at modern business activity (including the activity in governments and non-profits) suggests that the factors of production have been expanded to include information. Traditional factors of production included labor, land, and capital. People were added to this list recently. Most recently, progressive managers are coming to appreciate that information itself is used to produce whatever products and/or services an organization offers. This perspective is essential because it implies that special tools and techniques are needed to manage information, just as special tools and techniques are required to manage people. When management adopts this modern perspective, an information security roles and responsibilities effort will naturally follow.

Another important prerequisite to information security documentation efforts is management appreciation that they could be held personally liable for information security problems. In America, laws such as the Foreign Corrupt Practices Act define circumstances under which managers can be held personally responsible for lapses in internal controls, including information security problems. This type of discussion is perhaps the single most influential way to get top management support for information security projects that you may propose. Putting together a presentation on management liability is also a great opportunity for you to establish a good working relationship with internal legal counsel, if that relationship does not already exist. Legal issues are addressed in Appendix E, "Responsibility and Liability."

Although popular publications will have partially done it already, you should also get management to appreciate that the old techniques for managing information security are no longer sufficient. For example, the use of locking file cabinets and shredders is no longer sufficient to achieve true information security. More sophisticated tools like virus screening software and web site surfing blocking software are necessary. To get management to admit this critical point, you may need to talk about recent cases, particularly cases that dealt with problems in the organization's industry, organizations in the same geographical area, and organizations with similar information systems technology. Clippings from newspapers and magazines with hand-written notes like "Could it happen here?" are additionally recommended if management still does not understand information security.

Information security roles and responsibilities should be documented as soon as possible after management support is obtained. Management support typically goes up and down over time in a fairly predictable fashion. Figure 4-1 on page 18 illustrates this phenomenon graphically. Over time, management awareness will die away because information security awareness unfortunately is often an "out of sight, out of mind" situation. Then an information security incident occurs that causes management to become concerned; this might be an internal computer fraud, a hacker break-in to a competitor's system, or simply a widely-publicized information security problem. Shortly after things have been brought under control, management should be approached with a proposal to document information security roles and responsibilities. In Figure 4-1, a security related incident occurred at points A and C, and therefore a good time to initiate a roles and responsibilities project would be at points B and D.

Figure 4-1: Level of Management Awareness Over Time

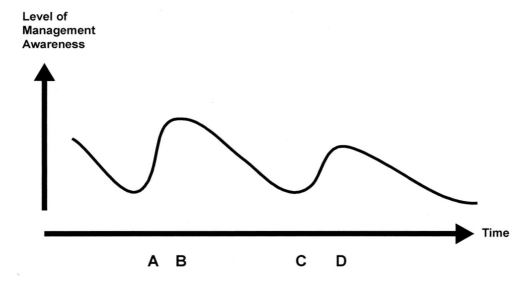

While serious information security incidents are happening with greater frequency these days, they are a mixed blessing. For example, not knowing what else to do after a serious security incident, senior management at some organizations will terminate the Information Security Department Manager. Each incident will make it look like the information security unit is not doing its job. If there are no recent incidents, management will wonder whether they should cut back on the information security function. Rather than relying on unpredictable incidents, many Information Security Department Managers are hiring independent consultants to perform penetration attacks. Using technical information security consultants whose ethics are clearly aligned with those of the organization, you can cause the level of management concern to increase rapidly. In effect, a risk assessment can take the place of an incident in terms of raising the level of management awareness. For instance, a penetration attack could show how easily a disgruntled ex-employee or a competitor could gain system access, and then you will be in a good position to propose to write information security roles and responsibilities documentation. Of course, other less dramatic ways to perform a risk assessment will also be effective in raising the level of management awareness. These techniques include scenario analysis, standard of due care comparisons, as well as quantitative estimates of threat probabilities and the associated expected losses.

After management support has been obtained (through an incident, a risk assessment, or some other method), management must buy into a centralized initiative to formalize roles and responsibilities. A centralized initia-

tive is necessary because the defined roles and responsibilities will be issued by a certain executive, a certain committee, or a certain department. While a centralized focus for a role and responsibility development project is necessary, in no way does this prevent or discourage the establishment of a decentralized information security organizational structure. For example, distributed information security coordinators may be an important part of the proposed organizational structure. Similarly, having a centralized group put together a clear definition of roles and responsibilities in no way prevents or discourages input from workers in other groups. In fact, the role and responsibility statements that you develop are much more likely to be successful if they have been reviewed by all the people at your organization who have a vested interest in information security. The issue of centralization is discussed at length in Chapter 19, "Organizational Structure."

Before an information security role and responsibility documentation effort gets underway, other roles and responsibilities critical to the organization's mission should already be documented. For example, within a software company, the roles and responsibilities for the Chief Executive Officer, the Chief Technologist, and the Chief Information Officer will need to be clear before the roles of information security staff are developed. Information security is a support and service function, and with the exception of companies specializing in information security, it is not the main focus of business activity. The nature of the information security roles and responsibilities will vary from organization to organization, and these roles and responsibilities cannot be adequately defined unless the roles and responsibilities that they support have been previously clarified. An exception should be made in the case of a brand new organization, such as a so-called "dot-com" firm, in which case all roles and responsibilities can be defined at the same time.

The performance of an information security function is critically dependent on the fit between its organizational structure and the organizational structure of the larger organization. For example, if top management has been intent on empowering individuals, and has distributed decision-making to many different workers, then a completely centralized approach to information security is likely to be problematic (this topic is further explored in Chapter 19). To ensure that the information security roles and responsibilities you propose will fit with the larger organizational structure, you should research the existing information security roles and responsibilities. In the process of conducting this research, you are likely to encounter certain patterns that are likely to be reflection of management's vision for the organization, of the organizational culture, and of other unique circumstances affecting the organization. For example, one increasingly common pattern is the preferred use of consultants and contractors over full-time employees whenever possible. These patterns should in most cases then be used to modify the templates provided in this book (outsourcing is discussed in Chapter 16, "Product Vendors" and Chapter 17, "Outsourcing Firms"). In some cases the patterns will be dysfunctional from an information security standpoint, in which case they should be changed and not used to modify the templates provided in this book. For example, if users are permitted to buy their own computer hardware and software, without any standardization or approval process, this is likely to be dysfunctional from an information security standpoint, and most likely should not be carried forward into a new information security organizational structure.

Also needed before an information security roles and responsibilities project gets underway is an organizational method to capture, store, and disseminate roles and responsibilities documents. These days this is accomplished most often through an intranet server that provides roles and responsibilities for all authorized users to view. In organizations that don't yet have an intranet, there may be a documentation repository where this information is filed, and there may be a group whose job it is to archive, index, and otherwise manage this type of information. If you are not yet familiar with your organization's approach to documenting and

handling organizational design documents, you should become acquainted with that process before a roles and responsibilities development project begins.

Another thing needed before a roles and responsibilities project is initiated is a clear and documented management approval process. Roles and responsibilities documentation that is prepared only for the consumption of those within the Information Security Department will be very much less effective than documentation that is widely dispersed throughout the organization and contains the approving signature of a top manager. Most often this approval process will have been defined by others who have gone through similar initiatives, but occasionally you will be required to clarify who approves and at what step in the process. This topic is addressed at greater length in Chapter 7, "Review and Approval."

Before roles and responsibilities related to information security are documented, it is advisable for you to get a clear picture of what happened to the information security function in the years gone past. If the people working in information security made fools out of themselves because they took an unsupportable stand, that should be known by you. If the people working in information security were generally viewed as technically incompetent, that too should be known. If these same people did a great job, but were lured away to other firms offering higher salaries, this should also be known. In general, you should learn how the information security function is viewed by the rest of the organization, the extent to which the internal information security function has been a success, and the extent to which management supports the information security function. This political information should be kept in mind and subtle changes reflecting this information should be made to the roles and responsibilities templates included in this book (factors affecting changes to the templates are discussed in Chapter 14, "Customization Factors"). While some of this political information can come to light when conducting data gathering interviews, it is far better to have it before the project begins (interviews and related data gathering activities are discussed in Chapter 8, "Required Resources").

Last but perhaps most important in terms of necessary prerequisites to a successful roles and responsibilities project is the availability of personnel who have the knowledge and skills to do the work defined in the roles and responsibilities documents. While an excellent set of roles and responsibilities documents can be prepared, if the workers who must perform according to these documents don't have or cannot readily obtain the training, technical reference material, or experience they need to do their jobs, the work on roles and responsibilities will provide very little benefit. Information security is a very complex field that requires the work of bright and experienced people if it is going to be adequately addressed. See Appendix B, "Personal Qualifications," Appendix C, "Performance Criteria," and Appendix D, "Professional Certifications," for further discussion on this topic.

Chapter 5   MODIFICATION

Since it is fundamental to so many other activities related to information security, writing role and responsibility documentation should be one of the first things that an organization does in the information security area. Having proper roles and responsibilities documentation is part of the foundation for information security—something on which all other tasks will be built. This documentation will be useful background for information security policy projects, information security awareness and training projects, information security architecture projects, and other initiatives. A list of internal documents that are supported by clear information security roles and responsibilities can found in Chapter 10, "Current Documents."

In most organizations, some information security efforts have already taken place and information security roles and responsibilities have not yet been sufficiently clarified. Perhaps management has noticed that the efforts were not as successful as they could be. Perhaps some of the problems described in Chapter 2, "Justification" are beginning to be noticeable (these problems included confusion about who should be doing what jobs). When these problems become evident, it's time to write the initial version of, or update the existing version of information security roles and responsibilities.

If the problems discussed in Chapter 2 are not yet painful enough to get management to allocate sufficient resources to develop clear roles and responsibilities documentation, often a security related event will raise management's awareness to the point where they take action. These events include a major computer fraud written up in the newspaper, a serious hacker intrusion that disrupted operations, a massive computer virus infestation, or a serious privacy related customer relations problem. The larger the financial loss, the more the adverse publicity, and the more the liability exposure that is associated with such an event, the more effective it will be when it comes to raising the level of management awareness. You should exploit the times when management awareness is high, and if needed, make a proposal to revise or update information security roles and responsibilities at that time.

If management is considering the outsourcing of any significant portion of information systems activities, this is also a great opportunity to revisit the existing information security role and responsibility documentation. Before any outsourcing agreements are struck, the specific roles and responsibilities of the two firms need to be very specifically defined. I have direct knowledge of a number of horror stories where outsourcing firms did not respond well to break-ins, virus infestations, and other pressing information security problems because these services were not specifically defined in the contract. The risk to your organization goes beyond a slow response to security relevant events—now experts in the information security industry are talking about the *reputation risk* associated with outsourcing contracts. This issue of outsourcing information security is discussed in detail in Chapter 17.

Another important time to revisit and formalize information security roles and responsibilities is when new business partnerships are being considered or when they are actually being established. Suppose your organization is building a new product or service with an outside firm, and management wants to establish linked firewalls with encrypted channels over the Internet (alias Virtual Private Networks). Management may also want to establish a certain level of trust between the computers found in both firms, perhaps through file/directory loading mechanisms like NIS used for UNIX. Before all this gets implemented, management needs to clarify not only network security policies, but also information security roles and responsibilities. For example, who is going to administer the user privileges associated with the communications link between the two organizations?

Information security roles and responsibilities are most useful for repetitive tasks that are performed on an ongoing basis. There are a large number of repetitive tasks that workers perform to achieve a satisfactory level of information security. These tasks, however, often require creativity and innovative approaches to problems that have never before been encountered at your organization. One example involves determining what applications should be allowed to tunnel through an Internet firewall; even when the roles, responsibilities, policies, procedures, and other aspects of this activity are documented, there will still be a variety of new challenges and questions. When repetitive tasks change, you will need to change the associated roles and responsibilities. If organizations don't promptly make these changes, there is a risk that workers will engage in what's called *malicious compliance*. Malicious compliance takes place when a worker knows that inappropriate results will be achieved if he or she is in compliance with documented roles and responsibilities, but he or she proceeds as documented to cause trouble for management. This abusive behavior points to the need to emphasize that results are more important than compliance. Some professional judgement should be involved to avoid *trained incompetence* where workers blindly follow orders, not thinking about what they are doing. This notion of trained incompetence was used widely as a war crime courtroom defense strategy. If there is a reasonable chance that workers will engage in malicious compliance or trained incompetence, then roles and responsibilities must be changed immediately after the underlying business processes change.

Unlike information security policies, role and responsibility documentation does not need to be modified every 12 to 18 months as business activities and information systems technology change. On the other hand, role and responsibility documentation will often need to be modified in response to organizational changes whereas information security policies often will not. You should expect your information security role and responsibility documentation to be modified every few years. You shouldn't think that the first set of documentation must last forever, or that it must cover every conceivable situation and every question that someone might ask. As your organization adopts to the initial assignment of roles and responsibilities, it is customary and expected that adjustments will be made.

In general, if there are no significant changes within an organization, information security roles and responsibilities should be reviewed and most likely modified once every two years. In the business world, many significant changes are happening at an accelerating pace. Organizations with recent documents that describe information security roles and responsibilities may need to have these documents reviewed and most likely updated if any of the following events have taken place since the documents were prepared:

- The organization has gone through a merger or acquisition process, or has gone through a major reorganization (such as a significant layoff or a multi-departmental reengineering project),

- The organization has had a significant change in the nature of products or services currently offered (for example, a major new product was introduced),

- The methods used to market the existing products or services have gone through a major change (such as a shift of marketing efforts from direct mail into Internet commerce),

- Laws or regulations have changed that are related to information security and are applicable to the organization,

- It is clear that those working in the information security area are not doing what needs to be done (for example, a major hacker penetration has demonstrated the need for better access controls),

- A third-party EDP audit or risk assessment has indicated that changes in information security roles and responsibilities are necessary,

- A new working arrangement with a business partner, customer, or supplier has been established (such as electronic data interchange or an extranet),

- A member of the top management team has decided that he or she will become personally involved (in an intensely focused way) in a matter related to information security,

- There has been a dispute over who is responsible for certain aspects of information security,

- Those responsible for aspects of information security have complained about inadequate roles and responsibilities documentation,

- Internal legal counsel has openly expressed concerns about the potential liability of management to information security related claims,

- The way in which the worker performance evaluation process is performed internally has gone through a major change (for example, project completion bonuses have been widely adopted),

- Those working in the information security area have taken jobs elsewhere in part because they didn't feel that they could meet management's expectations as reflected in current role and responsibility documentation,

- A new manager has taken over the Information Security Department, and he or she wants to ensure that the Department's performance will be evaluated according to realistic goals and objectives.

Chapter 6 DOCUMENTATION

From the start of any roles and responsibilities project, you should be clear about who will write the first and subsequent drafts, who will review these drafts, who will make modifications in response to comments received, and who will approve the final draft. If you fail to do this from the project's inception, you are running the risk of being accused of not "practicing what you preach" (because you may advocate the need for clear and defined roles and responsibilities, but not take the time to do them yourself). So before interviewing interested parties, before writing the first draft document, and before doing anything else described in this book, you should make sure that the project roles and responsibilities are clear and documented. This chapter discusses who should write the documents, while Chapter 7, "Review and Approval," discusses the review and approval process.

As is discussed in Chapter 11, "Mission Statements," an Information Security Management Committee is a group, typically composed of middle level managers, which prioritizes and supervises information security projects as well as provides policy guidance. While this committee may sound like a logical group to develop role and responsibility documentation, the use of any committee to write such documentation is strongly discouraged. Those who have attempted it before will acknowledge that writing with a committee, no matter how smart and motivated the participants may be, is very difficult, unnecessarily time consuming, and generally a waste of organizational resources. An information security management committee should, of course, review, modify, and approve of roles and responsibilities documentation that has been developed.

Instead of a committee, a single individual who knows the organizational structure and the organizational culture at your organization should write the first draft. This individual should also have significant business experience so that the resulting document will be clearly grounded in practical day-to-day business activities. This person should furthermore have an overall understanding of information security including generally accepted practices found at other organizations in the same industry. These qualifications will help ensure that the resulting roles and responsibilities document is realistic and grounded in the real world.

At first blush, some people may think it to be prudent to have a professional writer compile the roles and responsibilities documentation. While the first draft of the documentation should certainly be sent to a professional writer for polishing, a professional writer is not the appropriate person to generate the first draft. To have a professional writer compile the first draft would be like asking an automobile mechanic to design a new car. An auto mechanic, like a professional writer, doesn't have the appropriate background to do the job in question. If a professional writer does compile the first draft, it will probably be too high-level as well as contain a number of impractical ideas and inadvertent inconsistencies.

The person who generates the first draft roles and responsibilities document should nonetheless be a decent writer. For example he or she should be able to quickly generate clear and direct sentences. Being a good writer in this case will require that the individual also be able to envision the big picture, as well as separate the essential from the irrelevant. The individual should ideally be able to sense what is best for the organization as a whole, and then write the roles and responsibilities document from that perspective rather than be swayed by internal political pressures.

The best person to write the first draft is most often a senior member of the Information Security Department at your organization. Nonetheless, sometimes this is not feasible or appropriate. For example, if an information security function is just getting underway, there will be no senior member to write the initial roles and responsibilities documentation. Likewise, if the current members of an existing Information Security Department are all relatively new to the field, then it may be best to use an experienced external party to write roles and responsibilities documentation.

If an employee is not going to write the first draft, it is preferable to have an external technical consultant (or contractor) prepare information security role and responsibility documentation. Such a consultant should go through all the same steps that an employee would, such as interviewing interested parties within your organization. While a consultant should not skip any steps, a consultant often works faster and in a more focused way because he or she has significant experience in this area. A consultant may also be able to produce a result faster than an employee would because the consultant can devote all of his or her working hours to this task. A consultant may additionally be able to work more independently with many different groups throughout an organization than internal information security staff can due to existing relationships and internal politics.

Another advantage to having a consultant do this work is that he or she doesn't have a conflict of interest, or at least a perceived conflict of interest. If an information security specialist who is also an employee prepares roles and responsibilities documentation, he or she stands to benefit through the resulting assignments. In spite of potential conflicts of interest, many organizations designate employees who are senior information security specialists to write roles and responsibilities documentation. If employees write the documentation, they should be ready to justify the choices they made based on best practices for the industry in question, published standards, as well as existing laws and regulations. If you, who are an employee, keep this justification in mind, and hopefully keep notes that can be referenced at a later date, then any future accusations of conflicts of interest will quickly be dispensed.

Some organizations may believe that it is prudent to use an outsourcing firm to prepare roles and responsibilities documentation. Although there are some excellent outsourcing firms that can do this type of work, this approach introduces a number of potential problems. In the first of these, management should be concerned about delegating too many tasks associated with information security to an outsider. There are some tasks that should always be performed only by the management at your organization. For example, the final approval of methods to protect and conserve organizational assets (including the definition of roles and responsibilities) should always be performed by internal management.

In the second of these problems involving outsourcing firms, management needs to look at potential conflicts of interest. For example, by structuring roles and responsibilities in a certain way, an outsourcing firm may directly or indirectly give itself more business when top management never intended to send the business to that particular outsourcing firm. In a similar fashion, an outsourcing firm that writes roles and responsibilities could create an organizational structure which places undue reliance on outsourcing firm personnel, and not enough on internal management. This could be a problem after a hacker break-in takes place; outsourcing firm personnel may be designated as the decision makers when internal management should instead be the ones calling the shots. Likewise, in an effort to keep costs down, outsourcing firms may not incorporate

sufficient cross-training, technical expert back-up, and separation of duties into the roles and responsibilities that they write-up.

A provocative study performed by the Meta Group in 1996 indicates that 48% of the information systems budget is currently controlled by departments other than the Information Technology Department. This percentage was expected to grow to 70% by the year 2000. These statistics point to a major shift of power that is now underway. The statistics indicate that user departments are increasingly calling the shots when it comes to information technology. This does not, however, mean that someone from a user department should put together documentation for information security roles and responsibilities. A clear definition of roles and responsibilities should instead come from a centralized organizational unit such as the Information Technology Department (alias the Data Processing Department or Information Systems Department). Since the roles and responsibilities will apply to many different departments across the organization, they should be developed by a centralized group with clear authority to specify roles and responsibilities. The merits of centralization over decentralization are discussed in greater detail in Chapter 19, "Organizational Structure."

It is very important that the person who is writing the new and/or revised information security roles and responsibilities be recognized as the designated person to perform this task. Out of frustration, memos will often be prepared in an attempt to clarify the often-murky domain of roles and responsibilities. These memos typically come from a wide variety of people including the Chief Information Officer (CIO) and EDP auditors. While these memos may help or hinder, they will not be definitive unless top management recognizes the author as the designated person to write information security role and responsibility documentation. While clarifying the person to write roles and responsibilities may seem obvious to some, it is woefully missing in many organizations.

Top management recognition of responsibility to develop information security roles and responsibilities can be implied, for instance with the title Senior Vice President of Information Security. Alternatively, this recognition can be explicit, for example, through a project memo. If you do not have responsibility for roles and responsibilities implied by your title, a project memo is strongly recommended (see Chapter 4, "Preparation" for more details). A project memo simply defines what will be done, who it will be done by, how it will be reviewed and approved, the schedule, and the resources to be consumed. The memo should be issued by the Chief Executive Officer, the Chief Information Officer, or another member of the top management team. To save time, you, in many cases, should prepare a draft of this project memo and then submit it to the executive in question for signature. If you cannot get these members of the top management team to issue the memo, it will often suffice to have top management approve a memo that you develop.

Whoever it is that will be compiling the draft documentation should not chop up the work and dole it out to various groups. This task segmentation approach inevitably leads to inconsistent material that must be extensively rewritten to get material that is consistent

and professional looking. The task segmentation approach is furthermore ill advised because it involves a significant amount of time to facilitate communications and resolve disputes between the parties involved, and thus will often seriously delay the delivery of a first draft. Instead, you should go out and interview the people who have a vested interest in information security (EDP auditors, systems administrators, etc.) and get their ideas about roles and responsibilities. Then these notes should be merged with the templates provided in this book to yield a customized document that is truly responsive to the unique needs of your organization.

Chapter 7   REVIEW AND APPROVAL

Chapter 6, "Documentation," discussed the best individuals to write the initial draft (or a revised draft) of information security roles and responsibilities documentation. That same chapter discussed a project memo that defines what will be done, who it will be done by, how it will be reviewed and approved, the schedule, and the resources to be consumed. This chapter provides input to that memo, specifically addressing the document review and approval process.

Because so many different people are involved with information security, it is important to understand the different perspectives of these people. You should interview a good number of them to get their perspectives on the work that should be done, who it should be done by, and related considerations. This type of initial data gathering is also advisable because it gives these interviewees an opportunity to indicate whether they would be interested in the subsequent review and editing process. This interviewing approach is additionally advisable because it can be used to generate "grass roots" (widespread) support for the project. This support will be important when the time for implementation of these roles and responsibilities comes around. As a by-product of a roles and responsibilities effort, the interviewing process can additionally be used as an opportunity to increase the level of awareness about information security.

Just who should be interviewed is most often a straightforward task. A simple review of the Contents to this book will reveal the job titles (see Chapter 12, "Job Descriptions") and the department names (see Chapter 11, "Mission Statements") that would make good interview candidates. Beyond these lists, there will always be other people who have a thing or two to say about information security. These people often work in user departments that rely on one or more information security measures (for example the Telemarketing Department may rely on access controls to maintain the integrity of the sales contact manager database). In some other cases these people have prior experience with information security activities in other organizations, but are disturbed that your organization is not employing generally accepted practices.

To identify these supplementary interviewees, you should prepare a brief announcement of the project and have it issued by a member of the top management team via broadcast e-mail or traditional paper memo. The announcement should identify the project manager and should solicit support for the activity. This alone will help you to get interviewees to give you the time for an interview. The announcement should also ask interested parties to get in touch with the project manager. After an e-mail exchange or a telephone conversation, the project manager can readily determine whether it is advisable to interview those who have expressed an interest. For those people who expressed an interest but did not get an interview, there can still be an opportunity to respond to the first draft roles and responsibilities document.

To conserve time, you should only interview those who express an interest if they would offer an important perspective that no other interviewee could provide, if they have significant management roles, or if they have hands-on experience with information security activities. More than any other aspect of the project, the interviewing process has the potential to significantly extend the project completion date into the future, and also to significantly inflate project expenses. Accordingly, the number of interviews should be strictly limited, and a list of interviewees should be approved by your manager prior to embarking on the interviewing process. For an organization of over 1000 employees, 15-20 interviews, each lasting 20-30 minutes, should be sufficient.

Questions to ask during these interviews include:

- Are you currently playing any role in the information security area (a definition of information security may be necessary)? If so, what is that role?

- If the answer to the previous question is yes, for information security purposes, what other people do you interact with and what is the role of each?

- With respect to information security, what other roles are you aware of within Company X, and who plays those roles?

- What would you say are the essential information security tasks that need to be performed?

- Are there some information security tasks that are not currently being done, but should be done?

- Are there some information security tasks that are currently being done, but should be abandoned?

- Which departments or other organizational units should be primarily responsible for information security, and why?

- Which information security tasks should be performed by outsiders such as outsourcing firms, consultants, contractors, and temporaries?

- Where in the organizational hierarchy do you think the information security function should report?

- To what extent do you think that information security responsibility should be decentralized or centralized? How would you manifest your opinion in terms of organizational roles and responsibilities?

- Have there been any major incidents that show that information security work is not being adequately handled here at Company X? (This might include a hacker intrusion, a virus infestation, or other security relevant events.)

- Are you aware of any major law or regulation that specifies the information security work that Company X must perform? If so, what are these responsibilities?

- Are you aware of any contract with a supplier, a customer, or a business partner that dictates that certain information security responsibilities must be performed? If so, what are these responsibilities?

- Are you familiar with the information security distinctions called owners, custodians, and users [*see Chapter 15 for details*]? If so, do you think that these distinctions could work well here at Company X? Why or why not?

- Are there any other organizational design models or structures that you think Company X should be using to organize its information security roles and responsibilities?

- Would you like to review an initial copy of the roles and responsibilities document?

- Who else should we interview regarding information security roles and responsibilities, and why are they important to this effort?

- What documentation are you aware of that defines existing information security roles and responsibilities here at Company X? If you know of any information security roles and responsibilities documentation whatsoever, where could I go to get a copy of that documentation?

- How do you see the roles and responsibilities of the information security function changing over the next five years here at Company X? For example, do you believe that information security will become something that is viewed as a competitive advantage or even a competitive necessity? If so, what would be the organizational design implications of this new attitude?

- What methods do you suggest for communicating these roles and responsibilities once they have been developed, edited, and approved?

After the interviewing process is complete, you will want to use the information that you have gathered to customize the templates in Chapter 11, "Mission Statements," Chapter 12, "Job Descriptions," and Chapter 13, "Reporting Relationships." This editing process ordinarily involves only a word processing program such as MS-Word, and optionally a graphics program such as Visio. After you have edited the templates in light of specific Company X information gathered via the interviewing process, a review and approval process begins. Note that the specifics of the review and approval process should have already been specified in the project memo mentioned in both this chapter and Chapter 6.

To save time, a bottom-up review and approval process is recommended. This involves obtaining the support and feedback of people on the lower levels of the organization and then submitting the roles and responsibilities document to the middle level of management for review and approval. After the middle level of management has approved, then the material is submitted to top management for final review and approval. In smaller organizations, engagement with the middle level of management can be eliminated. The bottom-up approach allows you to gather important technical details about information security roles and responsibilities earlier rather than later in the documentation development process. The sooner these technical details can be integrated into the draft documentation, the faster the final product will be produced and approved.

Review of the first draft roles and responsibilities document by the managers in certain departments is mandatory. These departments include Internal Audit, Information Security, Information Technology (Information Systems), Human Resources, Legal, and Physical Security. Managers in other departments are optional but often useful. These departments include Accounting & Finance, Training, Sales & Marketing, Public Relations, Risk Management, and Strategic Planning. These department managers are the bottom level approvals of the organization and their support is very helpful when making a case for approval with the members of the middle and top management teams. Often no formal documented approval is required at this level; it is often sufficient to get some feedback and to incorporate some of this feedback into the documentation.

For a medium to large-scale organization, the next review process typically involves selected members of the middle management team. These include Chief Operations Officer, Chief Information Officer, Chief Marketing Officer, and Chief Financial Officer. To provide background and to answer any questions they may have, a brief presentation may be given at a monthly meeting of the middle managers. If it can be shown that the support and acquiescence (if not approval) of many other managers at lower levels of the organization has already been obtained, then review and approval at this level is accelerated significantly. If the organization already has an Information Security Management Committee, then the review and approval of this committee should be obtained before submission of any draft to middle managers. This step in the review and approval process constitutes the middle level approvals of your organization.

Assuming that all required changes have been made, and that the resulting documentation has been approved at both the bottom and middle levels, it is now time to submit the documentation to the upper levels of management. This may involve the Chief Executive Officer, the President, and members of the Board of Directors Audit Committee. A presentation is often necessary to explain why the project has been initiated and why top management support is needed. The existence of support and input from both lower level and middle level managers will make approval at the upper levels move along rapidly. In many cases, top managers will trust the other managers who are after all closer to the issues, and will then approve of the roles and responsibilities with only perfunctory review. I am not encouraging top managers to deal with this important topic in a perfunctory manner. I am only acknowledging the many other pressing issues that top managers must deal with on a regular basis.

The signature of one or more of the top managers is needed to bring credibility and influence to those people and groups that will be performing the tasks defined in the roles and responsibilities documentation. Top management should be asked to go beyond a signature, to support the project in other ways, such as mentioning the new document in its quarterly speech to employees.

Top management will also be asked to allocate resources to support the work defined in the roles and responsibilities document. A warning should be extended to you: a specific budget may also be needed before top management approves of the roles and responsibilities document. Prerequisites for a roles and responsibilities document are further discussed in Chapter 4, "Preparation."

The whole area of roles and responsibilities is fraught with internal politics. Certain managers will, for example, want the function to be within their division. Other managers will want nothing to do with it, fearing that it is a thankless task and not part of their path to the executive suite. To have a roles and responsibilities document that is truly in the best interests of the organization, it will often be necessary for the person writing the policies to politely say no to influential and powerful managers. This should not be taken lightly because there may be personal repercussions associated with saying no. A *no* such as this needs to be well-justified and documented, not to mention communicated in a polite and respectful manner. If this approach is adopted, you may later be surprised how the managers who received such a *no* are strong supporters later in the project.

Another important aid that you should employ to protect yourself from an internal political standpoint is a log of all suggested modifications accompanied by the reasons why these modifications were adopted or abandoned. To make this log work effectively, you should only accept written suggestions. This log should also indicate the date when memos were sent back to those people who submitted suggestions, explaining what was done with each of their suggestions. These memos can also be good way to thank people for taking the time to review the roles and responsibilities documentation. Such a log will enable you to effectively defend yourself from later being accused of forgetting an important topic that a manager supposedly suggested some time ago. The log can also be an important way to organize the review and revision process, making sure that there has been some action taken for each suggestion received.

Even if a log of all suggested modifications and their disposition isn't maintained, it is advisable to be sure that the working papers include notations explaining why changes were made to previous versions of the documentation. These working papers may be important to auditors looking over your work, as well as to lawyers defending against allegations of management negligence. Most importantly, these working papers will be useful a year or two in the future, when someone needs to update the documentation. Perhaps the best reason to keep a log or detailed working papers is that this someone may be you.

Given the politicized environment surrounding the clarification and documentation of roles and responsibilities, it should come as no surprise that some people will attempt to sabotage the process. Perhaps the most insidious way to do this is to hold up the process by not approving or reviewing a certain version of the document. To prevent this type of abuse, and to accelerate the project progress (perhaps there is no malicious intent, perhaps the reviewer is simply overwhelmed with other tasks), you can insist that all suggested changes be communicated by a certain date. If that date comes and goes, and feedback from certain parties was not received, then you should assume that there was no problem with the roles and responsibilities documentation.

Of course, the reviewers will need to be informed about this default approval process in advance. A reminder as the due date approaches is advisable. In highly political environments, you should send a note informing the reviewer that no response was received, and that the lack of a response by a certain date implies consent. Such a

reminder is also good practice because it allows any previous communications problems (such as lost snail mail or e-mail) to be overcome.

Another thing that people may do to sabotage or delay the process is to claim that they never got a copy of the draft document. An objection of this nature coming from a reviewer may mean that the reviewer wants the original project schedule to be abandoned and replaced by a schedule entirely dependent on them. A convenient way to prevent this type of manipulation and delay is to get an acknowledgement of receipt. Many electronic mail systems provide a return message indicating that a message has been examined. Likewise, couriers like Federal Express indicate that a package was received on a certain date and by whom.

In large organizations there may be a formal process for the generation of, review of, approval of, and dissemination of documents dealing with roles and responsibilities. Where this process exists, you should attempt to follow it as much as possible to help ensure rapid progress in the direction of a final approval by top management. The entire process often takes months, so you shouldn't take it personally if you get bogged-down in review, revision, and approval efforts. A variety of scheduling issues are discussed in Chapter 9, "Time Estimates."

Chapter 8   REQUIRED RESOURCES

Inevitably management will ask anyone who proposes to write information security roles and responsibilities how much it will cost. This query is really two questions that should be dealt with separately: (1) how much will it cost to develop, edit, and approve information security roles and responsibilities documentation, and (2) how much will it cost to implement the new ideas embodied in the documentation. This chapter can only do justice to the first of these because the second will always be a function of your organization, the extent of the changes that have been proposed, the time frame for implementing these changes, and other factors. This chapter also provides a detailed listing of the resources needed to develop, edit, and approve roles and responsibilities documentation, as well as a template for calculating the cost of the time involved in this same documentation process.

To compile professional-looking roles and responsibilities documentation that truly responds to the needs of a particular organization, very few resources are required. Specifically you will need:

- Personal computer that has a web browser, a word processing package, a printer, and a CD-ROM drive

- Access to a phone to conduct interviews with people at remote locations

- Access to an electronic mail system to schedule appointments with interviewees and to shepherd the document approval process

- Pens, pencils, and paper to take notes during interviews

- This book and CD-ROM containing role and responsibility templates

- The time of at least one information security specialist (you are assumed to be this person)

- The time of various interviewees to provide relevant background information and to review draft versions of the document

- The time of management to review and approve the document.

Before you attempt to estimate the costs of these resources, you should make a distinction between *incremental costs* and *sunk costs*. Incremental costs are costs that require an additional outlay, such as the retention of an information security consultant to help write roles and responsibilities documentation. Sunk costs are costs that would have been incurred anyway due to existing commitments, or that have already been incurred. Sunk costs are not relevant to a decision regarding the initiation of a role and responsibilities project because they do not change. An example of a sunk cost would be this book and CD-ROM. In most organizations, management is most interested in incremental costs because these are above and beyond the costs that have already been budgeted or committed. From an incremental cost standpoint, in most cases, all that is required to write roles and responsibilities documentation is the time of the individuals involved plus communications costs such as telephone and e-mail.

Another concept which is useful when answering management's question about costs is called *opportunity cost*. Technically, an opportunity cost is defined as the maximum alternative earnings or profit that might have been obtained if a productive resource was used for some other purpose. In this situation, the most important opportunity cost is associated with workers, because these people could be working on other projects which, hopefully, would benefit the organization. For example, middle and top management may have negotiated a deal with another supplier if they were not attending to a roles and responsibilities document development process. Just what this opportunity cost happens to be is difficult to estimate because it is based on speculation and subjective opinion rather than specific transactional data. If management in your organization is interested in opportunity costs, it is often sufficient only to provide the number of hours of the three types of people that are involved on the project: the information security specialist, various interviewees, and middle and top management. The rest of the items on this same list are inconsequential, or as the accountants would say "immaterial," when compared to the time of people in these three categories. Accordingly, the balance of this chapter will be devoted to a process for estimating the time required to develop (or revise), edit, and approve information security roles and responsibilities documentation.

Before specific estimates of the time required are presented, it is important to discuss a few factors that will reduce the average estimates. For example, if your organization already has information security roles and responsibilities documentation that has been formally approved by management, and this documentation has been prepared within the last five years, then the estimates can be reduced by approximately 20%. If this documentation exists, but has not yet been approved, the estimates can be reduced by approximately 10%. If the documentation is over five years old, whether or not it has been formally approved, then no discount on these estimates is warranted.

The size of the organization will have a lot to do with the complexity of the effort to develop, edit, and approve roles and responsibilities documentation. The following estimates are based on an organization with 1,000 full-time equivalent workers. This means that 1,000 people work full-time, or perhaps 2,000 people work half-time. The estimate of the number of workers on staff includes employees, outsourcing firm personnel, contractors, consultants, and temporaries. Table 8-1 provides a very rough estimate of how the hourly estimates can be modified to reflect the size of the organization. You can simply change the number of hours by the inflator or deflator factor to arrive at an estimate applicable to your organization. As is the case with all numbers in this chapter, these numbers are not based on statistical studies, but they are a reflection of my consulting experience. As a result, your actual experience may vary considerably from these estimates.

Table 8-1: Factors to Estimate Development Time

Full Time Equivalent People	Inflator or Deflator Factor
10,000	+50%
5,000	+30%
1,000	no change
500	-10%
100	-20%
50	-30%
25	-40%

Next you will find estimates of the number of hours required to work on roles and responsibilities documentation for the three categories of people involved on the project. The hours shown in Table 8-2 are broken into three specific phases of the work, respectively develop (or revise), edit, and approve.

If you are ambitious, you can multiply the hours for each type of worker by a certain hourly rate to develop estimates of the opportunity costs. The actual real world hourly rates will vary considerably by organization, and so are not presented here.

Table 8-2: Estimated Hours to Complete Roles & Responsibilities Documentation

Category of Person	DEVELOP	EDIT	APPROVE	TOTAL HOURS
Information Security Specialist	60	35	15	110
Interviewees	25	10	00	35
Middle and Top Management	05	05	02	12
Total by Phase of the Work	**90**	**50**	**17**	**157**

Table 8-3: Unadjusted Opportunity Cost to Complete Roles & Responsibilities Documentation

Category of Person	TOTAL HOURS	COST/HR	OPPORTUNITY COST
Information Security Specialist	110	$50	$5,500
Interviewees	35	$60	$2,100
Middle and Top Management	12	$100	$1,200
Total Personnel Opportunity Cost	**157**	**$56.05 (avg.)**	**$8,800**

To provide an integrated example how all of these numbers can be used to quickly come up with an estimate of opportunity costs, consider the situation at Company X. They have role and responsibility documentation that has been approved by management within the last five years, so we can reduce the time required by 20%. At the same time the organization has 10,000 full-time equivalent workers, so we need to increase the estimates by 50%. Combining these two adjustment factors, this means that in overall terms we need to increase the estimates by 20%. At this company, the fully loaded cost (including fringe benefits, income taxes, pension costs, etc.) for information security specialists is $50/hour, for interviewees is $60/hour, and for management is $100/hour. This means that the opportunity cost for developing, editing, and approving role and responsibility documentation is $12,780. The calculations are briefly sketched in Table 8-3.

Adding the totals for these three types of worker we have $8,800, which needs to be inflated by 20% for the reasons described in the last paragraph. Stated another way, multiplying $8,800 by 120% we come up with $10,560. Reflecting the fact that these calculations are only rough estimates, this number should probably be rounded to $10,500 and some sort of significant error factor should be attached (for example +/- 25%).

Before you get engrossed in detailed cost calculations, it's important to ask what is the opportunity cost of not writing or updating information security role and responsibility documentation? This will be significant in almost any organization. The numbers in most instances will be several orders of magnitude larger than the opportunity costs for the three types of workers described immediately above. If you have made a persuasive case about the need for formal information security role and responsibility documentation, the detailed numbers mentioned above in most cases will not need to be calculated. But if management at your organization insists on cost estimates, you can get more ideas for the opportunity costs associated with not writing roles and responsibilities documentation by reviewing Chapter 2, "Justification." The opportunity costs for not writing roles and responsibilities documentation can also be explored in an information security risk assessment project, a topic that is beyond the scope of this book.

Chapter 9 TIME ESTIMATES

This chapter discusses the schedule for an information security roles and responsibilities project including project tasks and milestones. The estimates assume that your organization is not going through a major internal change such as a major reorganization, a merger, a large acquisition, or an initial public offering (IPO). If a major internal change is underway, the elapsed time to complete the project must be extended by 50% or more.

Taking the opposite perspective, if management is especially motivated, perhaps due to a recently publicized system penetration, the project can be accelerated. Such motivation may also come from an audit report, a lawsuit in process, an upcoming government regulator investigation, or an imminent buyout. In these cases, the elapsed time to complete the project can be compressed 25% or more. Such an acceleration of the project requires that more people get involved, and these additional people must communicate with each other. This in turn imposes some additional overhead that would not ordinarily be required if only one information security specialist (assumed to be you) acts as project manager and document writer.

In general, you should allocate two and a half months for the completion of the whole project. Smaller organizations can move considerably faster, and larger organizations inevitably move more slowly. A two and a half month estimate for the entire roles and responsibilities project is based on an organization with 1,000 full-time equivalent workers (including employees, contractors, consultants, temporaries, etc.). This two and a half month estimate also assumes that no other internal information security roles and responsibilities documentation exists.

While at first two and a half months may sound like a long time, the majority of the elapsed time is consumed by the review and approval process. It is certainly advisable to prepare a schedule in advance, but in the real world, you are at the mercy of the schedules of both top management and middle management. The review and approval process can, however, be accelerated by periodic friendly reminders, by agreements about the dates when certain tasks will be completed, and by default approval mechanisms (if there is no word, then approval is implied).

A typical roles and responsibilities project schedule with tasks to be completed is presented in Table 9-1 on page 36. I suggest that you simply copy this set of tasks into a memo that discusses the project schedule. The list of milestones, which appears later in this chapter, can also be copied and used in this same manner.

All references to days involve business days rather than calendar days. The actual number of days that you work on the project will, of course, be considerably fewer than the total elapsed days. Typically a single project manager and document writer (assumed to be you) will need about 12-15 days of focused work to complete the project. This estimate assumes that you have no prior experience developing this type of material. This estimate also assumes that there will be three versions of the roles and responsibilities document, while some projects require fewer versions, others will require additional versions.

Milestones

- Complete project management memos
- Review related internal documentation
- Present talk to the committee
- Complete interviews
- Complete first draft of R&R document
- Complete second draft of R&R document
- Complete third draft of R&R document
- Deliver half-hour top management presentation
- Publicize R&R document

The estimates in this chapter assume that the prerequisites to a roles and responsibilities project, such as a risk assessment, have already been handled. These items were discussed in Chapter 4, "Preparation." If any of these tasks must still be accomplished, this will further delay the completion of a roles and responsibilities project because additional remedial work will be required. Similarly, the schedule presented above does not acknowledge any pressing projects that an Information Security Department might be currently engaged with, and these in turn are likely to further delay the completion of a roles and responsibilities documentation project.

Table 9-1: Estimated Days to Complete Project Tasks

Task Description	Elapsed Time (days)
Review this book and CD-ROM and prepare project memos	1
Gather and review related internal documentation	2
Prepare and deliver talk to Information Security Management Committee	2
Select interviewees and make appointments for interviews	2
Perform interviews and document/analyze results	5
Write first draft roles and responsibilities document	2
Circulate first draft for comments and feedback	15
Write second draft roles and responsibilities document	2
Circulate second draft for comments and feedback	15
Write third draft of roles and responsibilities document	1
Develop and deliver half hour presentation to top management	2
Make additional adjustments requested by top management	1
Internally publicize new roles and responsibilities document	3
Total number of elapsed business days (no holidays included)	**53**
Assuming an average of 20-business days per month, months required	**2.65 months**

Chapter 10 CURRENT DOCUMENTS

No matter how little work has actually been done in the information security area at your organization, and no matter how small the budget for information security happens to be today, every organization with over 50 workers should at the very least prepare three basic role and responsibility documents: job descriptions, mission statements, and reporting relationship diagrams. Words that you can use right now for each of these three documents are provided in Chapter 11, Chapter 12, and Chapter 13, respectively.

Moving beyond these three basic documents, this chapter assists you in identifying the other documents that should include mention of information security roles and responsibilities. These other documents may already exist within your organization, or they may still need to be compiled. In general, as the number of different documents containing information security roles and responsibilities rises, workers will view information security more seriously. The more seriously that workers take information security, the more they will perceive it to be a regular part of modern business, just like accounting and marketing. The more workers consider information security to be just a part of modern business, the greater the compliance, support, and alignment with information security objectives.

To prepare a list of other documents that should include information security roles and responsibilities, you can simply copy the list found in this chapter, delete those documents that do not seem appropriate at this point in time, and use the balance as the basis for a memo to management. A review of this list may also trigger a conversation about the merits of revisions to these documents—revisions above and beyond the inclusion of more specific information security roles and responsibilities.

When making a decision about the other documents that should include mention of information security roles and responsibilities, you should keep in mind that information security deals with many intangible matters—things that cannot be specifically touched and felt. For example, privacy is a psychological, social, and legal issue that cannot be tangibly manifested without some documentation in the form of laws, policies, and procedures. In many areas of the information security field, security cannot be said to exist unless it is reflected by a written document. For example in a court of law, the fact that management exercised due diligence can be

evidenced by an up-to-date information security policy manual. You are urged to consider the many ways in which the following documents may be needed to tangibly manifest an information security effort.

When looking over the list of documents, you should bear in mind that the number of different documents, the length of these documents, and the level of detail found in the documents is largely a function of the level of information security sophistication at your organization. For example, a bank will typically have more information security documents, of greater length, that provide more detail than a manufacturing firm. This situation is a reflection of the fact that a bank has typically spent considerably more time and resources focusing on information security than a manufacturing firm. Even within the same industry, two different organizations can have quite different levels of information security sophistication. Larger organizations are generally more sophisticated because the complexity of their operations requires more formal structure. Likewise, information intensive organizations (like a research institute) will tend to be more sophisticated than those that are not information intensive (such as a chain of restaurants). Similarly, those organizations that rely heavily on information systems as a mechanism to achieve competitive advantage will typically have a greater investment in information security, and accordingly will be more sophisticated.

When you review the list of information security documents that can include some mention of roles and responsibilities, you should consider just how sophisticated your organization is. If your organization is very sophisticated, roles and responsibilities will probably appear in a vast majority of these documents. If the organization is just beginning its serious information security work, it may have just a few of these documents. If the latter situation prevails at your organization, the first step should be to write the basic three role and responsibility documents: job descriptions, mission statements, and reporting relationship diagrams. Organizations that have less than everything on this list should consider how they can further the cause of information security by including role and responsibility words in the other documents on this list.

Although outside the scope of this book, it should be mentioned that there are a variety of dependencies between the documents. For example, it will be difficult to develop a systems administration procedures manual if an information security policies manual has not already been developed. This is because the latter document is a higher-level document, which establishes the general rules that are then in part implemented via the former document. In general, you are urged to write the general documents before the detailed documents are prepared. Beyond the basic three roles and responsibilities documents, the most important general document is an information security policy manual.

I acknowledge that, in the real world, the actual situation within a particular organization most often is not so clear-cut, and that you often inherit a hodge-podge of incomplete and conflicting documents with various degrees of obsolescence. Nonetheless, to economize your time, and also to provide the greatest contribution with limited resources, revisions to these existing documents can still follow the general to detailed approach. This general to detailed approach will also allow you to start with the big picture and then to apply this big picture in a consistent and logically straight-forward manner.

The following list of documents is meant to be illustrative rather than comprehensive. Within your organization there will undoubtedly be other documents where information security roles and responsibilities are mentioned. A brief discussion of the nature of each of these documents is provided below as well as an example of how information security roles and responsibilities could be included in these documents.

Information Security Department and Other Department Missions

An Information Security Department mission statement specifies, in overall terms, the charter of the Information Security Department (the reasons why management has created this organizational unit). The document will typically cover the objectives of the department and how it fits in with the organization's business or strategic objectives. The inclusion of information security roles and responsibilities information in this document is required, but information security responsibilities also need to be incorporated into the missions of other departments. Detailed words for all department mission statements can be found in Chapter 11, "Mission Statements."

Information Security Staff and Other Staff Job Descriptions

Job descriptions provide the specific tasks and duties of a certain job or position. For example, the activities of an Access Control System Administrator on a day-to-day basis would be specified in a job description. While there is likely to be little objection to including information security tasks and duties in the job descriptions for staff in the Information Security Department, these same tasks and duties need to be included in job descriptions for staff in other departments. Detailed words for both types of job descriptions can be found in Chapter 12. Job descriptions may also include verbal descriptions of reporting relationships, just as they may include standards of performance.

Information Security Department Reporting Relationships Diagram

This document graphically depicts the organizational units that report to the Information Security Department as well as the unit to which the Information Security Department reports. These reporting relationships can be dotted line (advisory) as well as straight line (manager/direct report). If specific roles and responsibilities information is included (perhaps in bulleted form), this document includes only a few words. In many cases reporting relationships are not diagrammatically represented, instead being described in words. In these cases, the words may be integrated with job descriptions or mission statements. Detailed words and diagrams for information security reporting relationships are found in Chapter 13, "Reporting Relationships."

Information Security Awareness Pamphlet

This booklet, pamphlet, or manual covers the basics that every employee should be aware of when it comes to information security. The organization's basic philosophy about information security is typically presented, as are some essential policies (such as never share a fixed password with any other person). Other topics include whom to contact when there is a question or a suspected information security problem. These contact points include the Help Desk (for trouble reporting), the Information Security Department (for security problem reporting, system access control, and contingency planning), Physical Security Department (for theft of equipment, access to buildings, and other physical security issues), and the Information Systems Department (for systems development, testing, and change control reasons). This pamphlet can also describe the distinctions between information owners, custodians, and users. The latter distinctions are covered in Chapter 15, "Ownership."

Information Security Awareness Reminder Memos

These brief memos are typically broadcasted to all workers via electronic mail or internal physical mail. They remind people to attend to a certain aspect of information security, such as backing-up data on portable computers. A contact point is always provided should a worker need additional information. URLs on an intranet may also be included. A brief mention of the roles and responsibilities of the Information Security Department is often included at the end of these memos. Such memos can also be provided on coffee mugs, on mouse pads, on log-in banners, and in other places.

Information Security Policy Manual

This manual defines the rules which will be used to manage information security throughout an organization. An example of such rules involves fixed passwords, which may be restricted to strings of characters that are at least eight characters long and composed of both numbers and alphabetic characters. This policy manual typically includes an introductory section which, in a high-level way, addresses who is responsible for information security, whom to contact if there are questions, and whom to contact if a security problem exists. A policy manual also covers who is responsible for implementing the rules (such as a systems development group within the Information Systems Department). Aside from job descriptions, mission statements, and reporting relationships, this document is one of the most likely places to find statements of information security roles and responsibilities. To help with the preparation of a policy manual, I have written a reference entitled *Information Security Policies Made Easy*, which contains sample policies.

Information Security Standards Document

This document specifies the technical standards for selecting, implementing, and configuring information security systems. In the encryption area, for example, a standards manual will typically cover algorithms and modes of operation. Brief comments about responsibility for enforcing these standards and the approval process for changing the standards are typically found in a document like this. Standards documents may also include mention of the authority for preparing and issuing such standards, and this may require a brief statement about information security roles and responsibilities.

Information Security Architecture Document

This document provides a broad overview of the control measures which will be observed throughout an organization or a multi-organization networked community. Examples include digital signatures and dynamic password access control. These control requirements will have no effect unless management specifically assigns responsibility for integrating these controls into systems, compliance checking, administering the controls, and the like. Mention of these responsibilities is recommended, although pointers to other documents may additionally be used. An architecture document may also include mention of the authority for preparing and issuing the document, and this may require a brief statement about information security roles and responsibilities.

Information Security Action Plan

Information security action plans are lists of projects to be accomplished in the near future. They often result from a risk assessment or an EDP audit. Action plans typically include mention of the results to be achieved, the person or group that will spearhead the projects, the persons or groups that will assist, the resources that will be required, and the estimated schedules. If the participating individuals and groups are not included in an action plan, management will still need to identify these individuals and groups before the work gets underway. These individuals and groups are sometimes discussed in an implementation details memo that goes along with an action plan. Whatever the documents needed to initiate these projects, management will need to work with existing mission statements and job descriptions. Reference to the relevant mission statements and job descriptions may reveal that they need to be modified or expanded. Until these changes to existing job descriptions and mission statements can be made, new roles and responsibilities may appear only in action plan memos.

Information Security Forms

Information security forms are paper or electronic memos with structured questions and answers. They are used to achieve a variety of results, such as request approval for a user-ID and approve certain privileges which go along with that same user-ID. Forms are increasingly being provided via html, and sent through the Internet or an intranet. Forms will often make mention of whom to contact if there is a question, as well as who is responsible for certain steps in a process. For instance, a form may indicate that the owner of the information in question must approve access before a systems administrator actually grants access. Forms may also provide emergency information security responsibilities. For example, on the "contact us" form provided with some web sites, there is a notice at the bottom that security problems or issues should be directed to the Web Administrator.

Systems Administration Procedures Manual

A systems administration procedures manual discusses the steps that Systems Administrators need to take to maintain the systems they have been charged with managing. These steps include running vulnerability identification software to quickly illuminate security weaknesses, as well as the process of installing the latest operating system release to minimize the threat of intrusions. Systems administration procedures manuals not only discuss the very important role that Systems Administrators play on the information security team, they also refer the Systems Administrators to other people on the team for assistance with a variety of circumstances. For example, if an intruder has compromised the security of an organization's network, the Physical Security Department will typically get involved with the investigation. The roles and responsibilities of these other people can be covered in abbreviated fashion to help ensure that these other people are consistently engaged when they are needed. "Systems Administrator/Network Administrator" on page 75 provides ideas for this manual.

Risk Acceptance Memos

A risk acceptance memo is evidence that management has approved a situation where a system, a department, or an individual is out of compliance with an information security policy or standard. The variance is approved for only a limited period of time, such as six months, at which point another memo is needed, or else the situation needs to come into compliance. Risk acceptance memos often mention who is responsible for compliance checking, issuing policies and standards, revising policies and standards, and approving variances from these same policies and standards. Typically a memo with standardized language is developed and used repeatedly, and this stock memo can include a variety of roles and responsibilities statements. A risk acceptance memo also involves an assumption of personal responsibility on the part of the requesting

manager (career risk at your organization, not financial risk), and this needs to be specifically described in the memo.

Information Systems Contingency Planning Manual

An information systems contingency planning manual provides a methodology for the development, testing, and revision of contingency plans. These plans typically focus on information systems, although sometimes they include business processes. Alternatively, a separate business contingency planning manual may be issued. Both of these manuals need to define who is responsible for writing, testing, and revising contingency plans, as well as who is responsible for auditing and approving of these same contingency plans. For example, many organizations specifically place responsibility for business contingency plans on the shoulders of user department managers. Separately, the manuals can include pointers directing you to various groups within the organization that can provide supporting goods and services. For example, the Information Security Department may provide consulting assistance in the development of contingency plans. These pointers typically summarize a variety of roles and responsibilities related to the preparation of, testing of, and revision of contingency plans.

Organizational Code of Conduct

An organizational code of conduct is an ethics statement which defines the ways that an organization will do business. Among other things, it covers conflicts of interest, such as a buyer who receives personal gifts from a supplier. Codes of conduct often overlap slightly with information security policy manuals, for example, in the area of disclosure of sensitive information only to those who have a demonstrable need to know such information. At the end of the code of conduct there may be mention of the internal departments that can answer questions. In this context, the Information Security Department may be mentioned as may the Legal, Internal Audit, and Human Resources Departments. Words in the code of conduct may also cover how violations will be handled, which group will perform investigations, which group will handle disciplinary actions, etc.

Standard Operating Procedures (SOP) Manual

A standard operating procedures manual covers the regular business procedures needed to conduct day-to-day activities. For example, an SOP manual will often define how to prepare and submit a travel expense reimbursement claim. As the number of internal processes that are computerized continues to increase for most organizations, the number of procedures that involve some aspect of information security will also rise. An SOP manual may reference an information security policy manual as well as procedures that deal with information security topics (such as a systems administration procedures manual). An SOP manual will also point you in the direction of internal groups that can assist with various tasks and processes, and these should include the Information Security Department. A brief mention of the roles and responsibilities of the Information Security Department can appear at this point.

Systems Development Process Manual

A systems development process manual discusses the steps that various people must go through to plan, analyze, develop, test, and deploy a new or modified business application system. This manual helps to ensure that serious errors are not made, that the application system will be responsive to business needs, and that it will be both reliable and stable. Ideally, this manual mentions specific points in the systems development process where the Information Security and/or Internal Auditing Departments will review the work done to date to ensure that adequate controls are being incorporated into the new or modified application system. Likewise, the Quality Assurance Department may be used to test the application system before it is moved into production. The responsibility of the user department manager who approves the final system is also typically described in this manual.

Application System Requirements Documents

Application system requirement documents define the functionality of a proposed business application system. The proposed application may be brand new or it may be a major revision to an existing application. In either instance, the role of the Information Security and/or Internal Auditing Department can be at the very least implied by approving signatures at the end of the document. A more specific statement, perhaps only a sentence or two, can define the roles of either or both of these departments in the development process. The information security role of the user department manager who approves the final system can also be defined in a sentence or two. For example, "I have performed a detailed review of this requirements document, and to the best of my knowledge, all required functionality, including security and privacy measures, has been described herein."

User and Computer Operations Application Manuals

These manuals provide specific instructions in the operation of a business applications such as an accounts payable system. The manuals define the detailed actions that both end-users and those in the computer operations group within the Information Systems Department must take to achieve certain business results. These manuals are application specific, and in that respect differ from Standard Operating Procedure (SOP) manuals. These manuals could include mention of the user's responsibility, such as never sharing a personal fixed password with others. They can also define the responsibilities of the computer operations group, for example, to back-up the application's database on a nightly basis. These manuals can also define the role of the Information Security Department (reporting suspected security problems), as well as other groups on the information security team (for example the Help Desk).

Records Management Policies and Procedures Manual

A records management policies and procedures manual will, among other things, discuss the rules for designating certain information as an official archival record, as well as the procedures for granting access to this information, and the procedures for safeguarding the information against unauthorized modification. The policies and procedures are meant for both those working in the Records Management Department as well as all other workers who must interface with these people. This manual discusses the responsibilities of users to pass along records that should be archived, as well as the responsibilities of other groups involved with the handling of this information. The roles and responsibilities of the Records Management Department and the Information Security Department are often mentioned in these manuals.

Worker Performance Reviews

Most organizations have worker performance reviews that ask a variety of questions, such as "Did this worker consistently show up for work on time?" Most do not make specific reference to information security. But those organizations which do ask questions like "Did the worker consistently observe information security policies and procedures?" are finding that workers take information security considerably more seriously. Even if no such broad question is included in the standard worker performance review form, much can be accomplished by modifying mission statements and job descriptions to include specific information security words. This is because the person reviewing another's performance will consider these specific words when writing the review. The net effect will be for workers to pay greater attention to information security, instead of saying "It's not my job." This topic is addressed in greater detail in Appendix C, "Performance Criteria."

Systems Usage Responsibility Agreements

Systems usage responsibility agreements, also known as user compliance agreements, are typically signed when a worker is first hired or when they are given a user-ID and password. Some organizations require that workers sign such an agreement annually, although many people consider this to be overkill. The implication of this agreement is that the worker gets a job and/or system privileges in return for agreeing to abide by the existing information security policies and perhaps other information security requirements as well. The user's information security roles and responsibilities are covered in outline fashion, but reference is made to a document that contains the full list of roles and responsibilities (perhaps the information security manual). A standard set of words for this agreement is provided in "Sample User Agreement" on page 175.

Outsourcing and Consulting Agreements

Outsourcing and consulting agreements define the work to be done by a third party such as a facilities management outsourcing firm, a management consulting firm, or a technical contractor. Sometimes these agreements incorporate specific standards for performance, also called service level agreements or SLAs. Outsourcing and consulting agreements define the ways in which a third party must protect the information belonging to your organization, as well as the specific tasks that the third party will perform. These tasks include backing-up the data, performing network management services such as monitoring for intrusions, and conducting risk assessments. It is very important that these agreements are explicit about information security because the third party may not perform anything that is not specifically stated in the contract, and may disclaim all responsibility for doing things that are not expressly mentioned therein. Note that explicit delineation of information security roles and responsibilities is typically not necessary for temporary workers, which are treated more like employees (and who should be subject to similar requirements as employees, as would, for example, be defined in the information security policies manual). Chapter 16, "Product Vendors" and

Chapter 17, "Outsourcing Firms" discuss the roles of outsourcing firms and other third parties in greater detail.

Confidentiality and Non-Compete Agreements

Confidentiality agreements (sometimes called non-disclosure agreements or NDAs) are legal agreements which define the way that sensitive information will be handled after it has been disclosed to trusted parties. Non-compete agreements also talk about how sensitive information will be handled, but are focused primarily on how the information must not be used to launch or support a business competing with the organization that disclosed the information. Both types of agreement can be used with employees as well as contractors, consultants, outsourcing firms, and temporaries. The role of these parties in terms of protecting the information in question is typically explicitly defined in these agreements (for example, sensitive information must not be disclosed to third parties without the express permission of the original source). If you are not satisfied with the specificity found in the current versions of these agreements, you can take this up with an Internal Intellectual Property Attorney. Further discussion about the roles and responsibilities of third parties can be found in Chapter 16 and Chapter 17.

Human Resources Manual

This document covers pension eligibility requirements, sick time policies, vacation policies, and other matters related to being an employee at your organization. Human resources manuals also typically discuss the information that the Human Resources Department keeps on each worker, how to access a copy of this information, and to whom this information will be disclosed. Other privacy issues related to worker-provided information (such as who can examine background check reports) may also be found in this manual. The information security responsibility of the Human Resources Department is accordingly covered as it relates to this information. The role of other groups who may become involved with an employee's situation, such as an ombudsman or internal legal counsel, may additionally be described.

Physical Security Pamphlet

This flier or pamphlet typically describes an identification badge system and a process for gaining access to buildings and other facilities after hours. It often also covers issues related to information security such as theft of computer equipment and use of shredders. The physical security responsibility of the worker will typically be covered, and so will the responsibilities of the Information Security and Physical Security Departments. For example, whom to contact in the event of a computer theft will typically be covered in this pamphlet. In many cases, also covered in this pamphlet are user department manager responsibilities pertaining to both physical and information security matters within a department's office area.

Chapter 11 MISSION STATEMENTS

This chapter provides specific words that you can use to quickly prepare mission statements (also called charters) that define the work that needs to be done in the information security area. A complete mission statement is provided for a centralized Information Security Department. Partial mission statements are provided for other organizational units that, in one way or another, play an important role on the information security team. When a partial mission statement is provided, it deals only with information security. All the other words that describe the objectives of these other organizational units have been omitted from this book to keep the focus strictly on information security. This non-information security material is likely to already exist in written form within your organization, and if it does not, then many organizational design textbooks can be consulted for suitable words.

As an example of this approach, the Legal Department's responsibility to deal with employment discrimination issues is not addressed in this chapter because it is not directly related to information security. Nonetheless, the Legal Department's responsibility to assist with investigations of hacker intrusions, computer frauds, and other information security problems is discussed in this chapter. As this illustration shows, to minimize the time required to affect appropriate organizational design changes, you should restrict your inquiry and work only to matters that directly relate to information security. This approach also prevents you from being placed in the awkward and dangerous position where you are making organizational design suggestions to experts in a certain area, but you do not know exactly what that functional area does on a day-to-day basis.

You should make sure that the draft mission statements that you develop are no longer than a single page, and preferably no longer than a half page. People throughout the organization will examine mission statements, and they don't have time to go through a long list of all the many activities that an organizational unit performs. In many cases these people will simply want to determine whether they should call members of the unit in question for help with their problem. Rather than being the subject for a mission statement, a detailed listing of activities should instead go into various job descriptions (see Chapter 12, "Job Descriptions"). If a mission statement goes beyond 250 words, chances are that it's becoming a job description, which is generally only examined by the involved worker, his or her manager, and occasionally an auditor.

At this point, a clear distinction between a mission statement and a job description should be drawn. A mission statement is a brief statement of objectives that describes what top management expects from the involved organizational unit. Although a broad-brush overview of activities is often helpful in a mission statement, specifics about these activities should instead appear in a job description. A mission statement should deal with a whole department or similar multi-person organizational unit, and should not talk about the objectives for a specific job title (the latter should be handled in a summary section appearing at the beginning of a job description). Likewise, a mission statement should not use any technical language, acronyms, or other jargon that will not be immediately understood by non-technical workers or top management.

Prior to publication within your organization, every new or revised mission statement must have received top management approval. Certainly drafts can and should be circulated for discussion, but the final version must not be released in any form until written top management approval is obtained. Many Information Security Departments seek only the approval of the Chief Information Officer, or the Manager of the Information Technology Department. Obtaining only the approval of only these managers is ill advised because information security is much more than just a technological issue. In a more general sense, stopping the management approval process after the approval of middle level managers has been obtained is not recommended because these middle level managers will have jurisdiction only over part of your organization. If the approval process has been stopped with middle level manager approvals, people in other parts of the organization can legitimately claim that their departments have not agreed, and this means that they need not observe the dictates of the new roles and responsibilities documentation. Mission statements are read by more people than any other roles and responsibilities document, and for this reason should be completely approved, at the highest levels of management, prior to posting on an intranet web page or distributed in any other form. The approval process is discussed at length in Chapter 7, "Review and Approval."

You are also warned that suggesting changes to the mission statements of organizational units other than the Information Security Department is a tricky and highly politicized process. Before suggested changes to information security roles and responsibilities are submitted to top management for approval, the managers in charge of the affected organizational units will need to approve of and support the suggested changes. Before they even consider these suggestions,

top management will often ask whether the approval of these lower level managers has been obtained. To ensure that the suggestions are well grounded and supportable by those who will be affected, the information gathering, decision-making, and approval processes should all move from the bottom of the organizational ladder to the top. This bottom-up approval process is further discussed in Chapter 7, "Review and Approval."

INFORMATION SECURITY DEPARTMENT

[Also known by a variety of other names including: Information Systems Security Department, Information Protection Department, Data Security Department, Computer Security Department (antiquated terminology), Systems Security Department, Information Technology Security Department, IT Security Department, InfoSecurity Department, InfoSec Department, and Information Resources Security Department.]

The Information Security Department is charged with identifying, assessing, and appropriately managing risks to Company X information and information systems. It evaluates the options for dealing with these risks, and works with departments throughout Company X to decide upon and then implement controls that appropriately and proactively respond to these same risks. The Department is also responsible for developing requirements that apply to the entire organization as well as external information systems in which Company X participates (for example, extranets) *[these requirements include policies, standards, and procedures]*. The focal point for all matters related to information security, this Department is ultimately responsible for all endeavors within Company X that seek to avoid, prevent, detect, correct, or recover from threats to information or information systems.

These threats include, but are not limited to:

- unauthorized access to information
- unauthorized use of information
- unauthorized disclosure of information
- unauthorized diversion of information
- unauthorized modification of information
- unauthorized destruction of information
- unauthorized duplication of information
- unavailability of information

Many organizations like to use the old-fashioned "CIA" terminology—confidentiality, integrity, and availability—but I discourage it because "integrity" is ambiguous. In support of these objectives, the Department additionally establishes, administers, and manages a variety of computer/network security systems that apply to the entire organization *[password-based access control systems are the most common example]*.

PHYSICAL (INDUSTRIAL) SECURITY DEPARTMENT

[Mission Statement Relevant to Information Security]

The Physical Security Department is responsible for protecting all Company X tangible assets including raw materials, finished goods inventory, company transportation vehicles, and office buildings. The Department is responsible for identifying, assessing, and managing risks to Company X tangible assets, no matter where these assets may be located, and no matter whose possession they may be in. In support of efforts to manage these risks, the Department is required to

establish and manage physical access controls to Company X offices and facilities *[these include closed circuit TV, magnetic card badge readers, etc.]*. The Department is additionally charged with investigating all violations of laws, regulations, and company policies, as well as acting as the liaison with the law enforcement community. *[Due to its importance to Company X and its technical nature, information security is handled by a separate group; note that the focus of the Physical Security Department is not on information but on tangible assets.]*

INTERNAL AUDIT DEPARTMENT

[*Mission Statement Relevant to Information Security*]

The Internal Audit Department is charged with providing the Board of Directors and top management with objective reports on the effectiveness of internal controls, the accuracy of records, the reliability of information, and the safeguarding of assets. The Department also provides compliance checking services where it determines not only whether workers are following management's instructions but also whether the organization employs the same generally accepted practices found at other firms in Company X's industry. The Department additionally reviews the efficiency and effectiveness of business activities performed by internal organizational units [*including the Information Security Department*]. The Department furthermore periodically follows up with various levels of management to determine the extent to which they have taken action in response to previously-delivered audit findings and reports.

EDP AUDIT UNIT

[*Mission Statement Relevant to Information Security*]

Located within Internal Audit Department, the Electronic Data Processing (EDP) Audit Unit provides specialized technical services in support of the performance of a wide variety of information systems audits. These technical services include reviewing the adequacy of controls accompanying business application systems in development, determining the adequacy of security measures provided with third-party software, checking that workers are performing their jobs in accordance with internal requirements (policies, standards, procedures, etc.), as well as performing statistical tests of computer-based records to determine whether they are accurate, up-to-date, and free from material error.

ETHICS AND COMPLIANCE UNIT

[*Mission Statement Relevant to Information Security*]

The Ethics and Compliance Unit is responsible for the development and implementation of an organization-wide program to ensure the consistent operation of Company X business in an ethical and moral manner that is compliant with all relevant laws and regulations. The Ethics and Compliance Unit regularly conducts reviews of Company X operations to ensure that it continues to be fully observant of these requirements. The Unit additionally drafts and proposes policies and procedures to ensure ethical and moral business operations as well as compliance with external requirements. [*An Ethics and Compliance Unit may deal with privacy violations, in addition to right-to-know issues, for example, workplace hazards.*]

EXTERNAL AUDITING FIRM

[*Mission Statement Relevant to Information Security*]

The External Auditing Firm is charged with testing the internal controls used to create financial records to ensure that the involved information systems are reliable and free from material error [*note that the External Auditing Firm is not responsible for doing a information security related risk assessment on these same systems unless separately engaged to do so*]. The External Auditing Firm is additionally responsible for bringing to management's attention those information systems control deficiencies that come to its attention. The Firm is additionally charged with delivering to management a professional opinion stating whether the financial records fairly represent the current financial status of Company X [*if an "unqualified opinion" (clean bill of health) is not obtained, this could be an indication that there are serious control problems*].

[*While in-house documentation describing the information security responsibilities of external auditors is generally not prepared, it is nonetheless useful to clarify their roles and responsibilities. These are often stated in an engagement contract or proposal defining the work to be done by external auditors. Beyond the roles and responsibilities mentioned immediately above, external auditing* firms (as well as many other consulting firms) also provide specialized information security related "management advisory services" or MAS consulting. These MAS consulting services can be used to provide specialized technical support, including information security support, when this support is not readily available within your organization. Separately, often in-house workers have exaggerated expectations about the tasks that an External Auditing Firm performs. For example, the Firm is not responsible for detecting fraud, although it may discover fraud in the course of doing financial auditing work. An External Auditing Firm or an outside information security consulting firm can also separately be engaged to evaluate the effectiveness of an in-house information security effort.]

RECORDS MANAGEMENT DEPARTMENT

[*Mission Statement Relevant to Information Security*]

The Records Management Department is charged with establishing and operating a system for the designation and management of archival Company X records. To achieve this goal, the Department trains workers about the need to designate and maintain archival records. It also establishes and maintains administrative systems used to access, protect, and keep track of these same archival records. The Department is additionally responsible for providing technical advice to the entire organization on backup systems that effectively ensure that these critical and/or archival records continue to be available in the event of a disaster, theft, or some other serious problem.

INFORMATION TECHNOLOGY DEPARTMENT

[*Mission Statement Relevant to Information Security*]

The Information Technology Department is charged with planning; specifying, designing, developing, modifying, testing, and operating shared information systems and related communications networks needed to accomplish Company X business goals. These information systems and networks are intended be available on a continuous, predictable, and secure basis so that Company X's reputation for reliable products and services can be enhanced. The Department is also responsible for providing technical and operational management support for a wide variety of information systems projects and activities, including user database development, outsourcing firm processing, and connection to external information resources such as the Internet.

HELP DESK UNIT

[*Mission Statement Relevant to Information Security*]

The Help Desk Unit provides immediate telephone assistance to users who are experiencing problems with any Company X information systems or networks. This 24×7×365 technical support is intended to facilitate users' efforts to promptly perform critical business tasks in a manner that is fully consistent with existing Company X information systems requirements including policies, standards, and procedures [*these, of course, include security*]. The Unit provides ad-hoc training as well as a variety of solutions to problems that users encounter [*such as forgetting a password*]. The Unit is furthermore responsible for notifying the Computer Emergency Response Team (CERT) if a serious information security event has taken place [*as would be the case with a virus infection*].

NETWORK OPERATIONS UNIT

[*Mission Statement Relevant to Information Security*]

The Network Operations Unit is charged with operating internal networks such as wide area networks (WANs) and local area networks (LANs) so that all communications links necessary for business activities remain available, so that user response time stays within acceptable limits, and so that only authorized users utilize Company X networked resources. Operation, in this instance, includes monitoring network management systems, running diagnostic software when problems occur, notifying information security personnel if suspicious activity is detected, and dynamically reconfiguring the network to minimize cost and maximize throughput.

COMPUTER OPERATIONS UNIT

[*Mission Statement Relevant to Information Security*]

The Computer Operations Unit is charged with operating multi-user computer systems so that all critical business activities are performed on schedule, so that user response time stays within acceptable limits, and so that the security of these multi-user systems is not jeopardized. Operation, in this instance, includes monitoring the activities of users and applications, loading and unloading information storage media as necessary, handling backup storage media, distributing printed management reports, and initializing software systems such as nightly batch jobs.

SYSTEMS ADMINISTRATION UNIT

[*Mission Statement Relevant to Information Security*]

The Systems Administration Unit is charged with configuring and updating workstations, servers, networks, firewalls, and other information systems equipment used in support of Company X business activities. The Unit is additionally responsible for configuring and updating systems software on these same information systems so that all applications critical to the business are supported, so that response time is within tolerable limits, and so that security vulnerabili- ties are minimized [*this includes monitoring and applying patches and fixes for systems software*]. The Unit is furthermore in charge of establishing and maintaining user access control systems for those multi-user information systems that are not handled by the Information Security Department. [*Access Control System Administrators within the Information Security Department may handle some of these duties; see Chapter 12, "Job Descriptions" for further details.*]

DATABASE ADMINISTRATION UNIT

[*Mission Statement Relevant to Information Security*]

The Database Administration Unit is charged with designing, configuring, organizing, and maintaining Company X computer-resident databases so that the information contained therein is accurate and up-to-date. The Unit is also responsible for maintaining the database privileges of both users and systems, so that these privileges are allocated only when justified by business needs and approved by designated managers. [*Each working day, specialists known as Database Administrators, or DBAs, help to ensure that systems are consistent with the policies and other requirements issued by the Information Security Department.*]

DATA ADMINISTRATION UNIT

[Mission Statement Relevant to Information Security]

The Data Administration Unit is charged with creating metadata databases, information inventories, as well as information models and architectures that unify and standardize information and information flows throughout Company X. These new tools and systems are intended to facilitate the development of new applications, new management reports, new products and services, and new relationships with third parties. In the process of centralizing and normalizing information throughout Company X, the Data Administration Unit is also charged with fostering standardization efforts that maintain or enhance the accuracy, currency, relevance, usefulness, and security of the information involved.

INSURANCE AND RISK MANAGEMENT DEPARTMENT

[Mission Statement Relevant to Information Security]

The Insurance & Risk Management Department is charged with identifying and analyzing the strategic business risks faced by Company X. These include mergers and acquisitions, new product introductions, product liability lawsuits, and changes in macroeconomic conditions within Company X markets. The Department is responsible for ranking the risks on a cross-organizational basis, as well as suggesting strategies and other high-level approaches for dealing with these risks. For identified risks, the Department is charged with presenting management with the pros and cons regarding risk retention (do nothing), risk reduction (add controls), or risk transfer (buy insurance). *[This Department is an important strategic ally of the Information Security Department, and both departments should work together to identify the types of insurance that Company X needs (the options include records reconstruction insurance, computer crime insurance, business interruption insurance, professional errors and omissions insurance, directors and officers liability insurance, fidelity insurance, credit card fraud insurance, property (theft) insurance, etc.).]*

CONTINGENCY PLANNING UNIT

[Mission Statement Relevant to Information Security]

The Contingency Planning Unit is charged with developing, testing, and maintaining practical and cost-effective processes and systems that will allow critical Company X business activities to continue even though an emergency or a disaster has taken place. The Unit is responsible for identifying the nature of the business interruption threats facing Company X, analyzing the options for preventing or mitigating losses from these threats, and organizing internal staff so that they can expediently deal with these threats if they do occur. *[This mission statement is written broadly to include business contingency planning and systems contingency planning, but some organizations break these activities into separate units. If the two are separated, the business contingency planning unit may report to the Insurance & Risk Management Department, while the systems contingency planning unit may report to the Information Security Department. See Chapter 13, "Reporting Relationships" for further details on reporting relationships (including the six diagrams showing different options).]*

COMPUTER EMERGENCY RESPONSE TEAM

[A CERT is sometimes called a Computer Security Incident Response Team or a CSIRT.]

[Mission Statement Relevant to Information Security]

The Computer Emergency Response Team (CERT) is a group of Company X employees who respond immediately to a variety of information systems emergencies such as virus infections, hacker intrusions, and denial of service attacks. Immediately stopping their normal work activities, the CERT members devote their efforts to quickly reestablishing a secure, reliable, and stable information systems environment. CERT members also act as the primary technical liaisons with consultants, contractors, and others who are needed to reestablish this trusted information systems environment. The CERT additionally develops and/or deploys tools, procedures, and other mechanisms so that financial losses, business interruptions, and damage to Company X's reputation associated with such incidents are all minimized. The CERT is also responsible for documenting all actions taken to restore a trusted information systems environment so that insurance, legal proceedings, and disciplinary actions can be fully supported.

LEGAL DEPARTMENT

[Mission Statement Relevant to Information Security]

The Legal Department is charged with providing the expert legal advice necessary for management to conduct Company X business activities in a manner fully in keeping with existing laws and regulations *[software copyright laws are a good example relevant to information security]*. The Legal Department is also responsible for providing expert advice on the ways that laws, regulations, and contractual relationships can be used to further Company X business interests, including negotiating business deals, drawing-up contracts, resolving disputes, investigating crimes against Company X, and defending against legal actions such as lawsuits *[obtaining agreements not to compete from business partners is an information security example]*. The Legal Department is additionally charged with providing management with advice about the ways to appropriately protect Company X assets, resources, and staff against a variety of legal risks *[management's exposure to lawsuits for not adequately protecting computer resident information is an information security example]*.

HUMAN RESOURCES DEPARTMENT

[Mission Statement Relevant to Information Security]

The Human Resources Department provides guidance to all workers in the interpretation of legal and policy requirements that relate to employment, performance evaluation, career paths, pay scales, and related staffing matters *[Human Resources may thus have something to say about separation of duties, backup personnel for critical information systems positions, etc.]*. The Human Resources Department additionally provides administrative support to keep the records needed to be in compliance with all human resources related laws, regulations, and internal policies *[these records are an important resource for information security activities such as system access control decisions. These records are also often the subject of privacy laws and policies, and thus the Human Resources Department often gets involved in discussions about the controls over these records]*. The Department furthermore coordinates the retention of, work with, and termination of consultants, contractors, and temporaries by department managers using standard procedures, contracts, and other tools.

INFORMATION SECURITY MANAGEMENT COMMITTEE

[Mission Statement Relevant to Information Security]

The Information Security Management Committee provides management direction and a sounding board for the internal Company X information security efforts to ensure that these efforts are appropriately prioritized, appropriately supported by the involved organizational units, appropriately funded, and realistic given Company X's business needs. The Committee is also charged with instructing the Information Security Department in those cases where a compromise between competing information systems objectives needs to be struck. These objectives include cost, response time, ease of use, ease of maintenance, flexibility, scalability, and time-to-market with a new product or service. The Committee is also responsible for designating specific individuals as responsible for various aspects of information security, approving proposals for organization-wide information security initiatives (such as awareness training), and coordinating the work of various departments so that information security goals can be achieved.

INFORMATION TECHNOLOGY STEERING COMMITTEE

[Mission Statement Relevant to Information Security]

The Information Technology Steering Committee is made up of representatives from senior management, major user departments, as well as the Internal Audit Department, the Information Security Department, and the Information Technology Department. The Committee is charged with developing a strategic vision for the deployment and evolution of information technology at Company X. The Committee is also responsible for establishing priorities, arranging necessary resources, and approving major capital expenditures related to the realization of the strategic information technology vision. The Committee furthermore reviews and issues final approval for all policies, standards, and guidelines that relate to information technology at Company X. *[The Committee would, for example, approve information security policies, although policies should also have the personal signature of the Chief Executive Officer. The emphasis of this committee is strategic, while the emphasis of the Information Security Management Committee is more technical and more narrowly-defined.]*

BOARD OF DIRECTORS – AUDIT COMMITTEE

[Mission Statement Relevant to Information Security]

The Audit Committee is a subcommittee of the Board of Directors composed of directors who are independent of the management of Company X, and who are free of any relationship that, in the opinion of the Board of Directors, would interfere with their exercise of independent judgement. The Audit Committee manages the work of external financial auditors, internal auditors, external security consultants, and others who are concerned with internal controls at Company X. The Audit Committee is charged with ensuring that management has established and is diligently maintaining adequate internal controls *[which, of course, include information security measures]*. The Audit Committee is also responsible for monitoring and analyzing the results of examinations that review the extent to which Company X is in compliance with laws and regulations. The Audit Committee is furthermore charged with monitoring the adequacy of management's responses to examinations and audits, the performance of internal auditors, the adequacy of insurance coverage, and compliance with Company X legal obligations. The Audit Committee thus helps to maintain free and open communications between the directors, the independent auditors, and the management of Company X.

INTERNAL CONTROL COMMITTEE

[*Mission Statement Relevant to Information Security*]

The Internal Control Committee is charged with bringing Company X in its entirety into a state of internal control. Chaired by a member of the top management team, and drawing on middle management from critical departments such as Human Resources, Internal Auditing, Physical Security, Information Security, and Accounting, the Committee coordinates, fosters the adaptation of, and follows-up with internal managers to convert Company X into an organization with an internal control mindset. The Committee also coordinates internal control relationships with outside parties such as external auditors, regulators, and others. The Committee stimulates and promotes synergy, which is intended to lead to compliance with internal requirements, both high performance and correct operation of internal business systems, and continued security of business transactions. [*An Internal Control Committee generally works closely with the Board of Directors – Audit Committee, but its work is more hands-on and detailed than the Board of Directors – Audit Committee.*]

FACILITIES MANAGEMENT OUTSOURCING FIRM

[*Mission Statement Relevant to Information Security*]

The Facilities Management Outsourcing Firm is charged with operating Company X information systems, and providing other services that may from time to time be requested by Company X management, in a manner fully consistent with Company X policies, procedures, and other documented requirements [*and these include information security requirements*]. The Firm acknowledges that all policy, procedure, and system design decisions regarding the security or privacy of Company X information or information systems will be made solely by authorized Company X management. The Facilities Management Firm is also responsible for processing, storing, and safeguarding the information assets of Company X in accordance with generally accepted information systems management practices [*which should include security*].

[*The responsibilities of an outsourcing firm are not generally written-up in internal organizational design documents, but are instead often found in an outsourcing firm contract. Their responsibilities were included in this chapter as an indication that outsourcing firms have an important role to play in the information security area. Chapter 16, "Product Vendors" and Chapter 17, "Outsourcing Firms" discuss outsourcing firm responsibilities in further detail.*]

Chapter 12 JOB DESCRIPTIONS

To save you time, this chapter provides specific words that can be copied and internally published when preparing first draft job descriptions. The chapter includes full job descriptions for all those positions that are ordinarily found within a centralized Information Security Department. Examples include Information Security Department Manager, Internal Information Security Consultant, Access Control System Administrator, and Information Systems Contingency Planner. This chapter anticipates that, for these people, you will be writing job descriptions from scratch. These job descriptions come first in the chapter and are easy to spot because the second line of text in the relevant description indicates that the position is found in the Information Security Department.

This chapter also contains specific job description words dealing with information security for those individuals who are a part of the information security team, but who are not customarily part of a centralized Information Security Department. Examples of these positions include Distributed Information Security Coordinator, Systems Administrator, Network Administrator, and Database Administrator. This chapter anticipates that, for these people, you will be adding information security responsibilities to existing job descriptions. These partial job descriptions come later in the chapter. The second line of text in the relevant description indicates that the position is part of a department other than the Information Security Department.

The material in this chapter does not cover certain things that may be included in job descriptions at your organization. For example, the ideal psychological profile and the professional qualifications needed for the positions are not covered. These are covered in Appendix B, "Personal Qualifications" and Appendix D, "Professional Certifications." Likewise, this chapter does not cover educational requirements, experience requirements, language skill requirements, mathematics and reasoning ability requirements, prior supervisory experience requirements, or physical movement requirements. These unmentioned requirements are a function of the business that your organization performs, as well as relevant local laws and regulations, in addition to prevailing expectations in the local labor market. In most organizations with over fifty employees, these additional requirements have already been developed by an in-house Human Resources Depart-

ment, and therefore can be quickly added to a job description once you have come up with a version of the material found in this chapter.

Although common reporting relationships are mentioned in the following job descriptions, these designated relationships are certainly not the only effective way to structure an information security team. For a discussion about the best ways to structure reporting relationships including conflicts of interest, separation of duties, cross training, and personnel backup, you should consult Chapter 13, "Reporting Relationships." Chapter 13 also contains a number of diagrams that show suggested reporting relationships for the positions described in this chapter.

Often the first piece of information on a job description is the job title, also known as a position title. People working in the information security field go by a lot of different titles such as "Information Security Evangelist" as well as more traditional titles such as "Systems Analyst." These general titles are undesirable because they don't really describe what these people do. Rather than something cute or obscure, it is better to have titles that genuinely describe the tasks performed. Instead of Information Security Evangelist, it would be better to use the title Information Security Training & Awareness Coordinator, and in place of Systems Analyst it would be better to use the title Information Security Technical Consultant. The more descriptive the title, the more people will understand from a cursory review of the employer's internal telephone directory, and from a quick glance at the individual's business card.

Some organizations have a philosophy about job descriptions that essentially says that workers should fit into broad and vague categories such as "Technical Staff Member." Job descriptions are then written, on an individual-by-individual basis, for these broad and vague positions. These organizations rely on the individual's immediate manager to define the specific work that each individual performs. This approach is acceptable as long as the immediate manager has documented the roles and responsibilities of each of his or her direct reports. If this doesn't happen, then the individuals involved will have very little reference material to direct their efforts, and their managers will have scant reference material for fair and accurate performance evaluations. If you are in a position where you can suggest an approach for the preparation of job descriptions, this two-tier approach is generally not recommended. The two-tier approach can be confusing for outsiders and others who have not seen the local manager's specific roles and responsibilities. The two-tier approach to job descriptions is additionally not recommended because two documents will be needed when traditionally only one was required. This chapter provides low-level job descriptions, and can be generalized to compile high-level job descriptions, if such an approach has already been adopted at your organization.

Separately, this chapter discusses who interacts with whom to achieve what information security results, who does what information security activities, and who passes what information to other people in support of information security. All of these roles and responsibilities are permanent and ongoing in nature. While all organizational structures will need to be adjusted periodically, the following job descriptions are meant to help organizations establish information security as an activity that has been integrated into the existing organizational structure, and is recognized as an on-going business function. In far too many organizations, information security continues to be seen as a project or a temporary effort (see Chapter 5, "Modification" for further discussion). On a related note, there will be temporary efforts, such as a task force to upgrade information security so that your organization can do business with another firm that has higher security standards, but these temporary efforts should not be reflected in the job descriptions.

Even after you have prepared job descriptions and other documents reflecting roles and responsibilities, you may wish to use the CD-ROM version of this chapter as a reference. One common ad-hoc reference usage of this material would be to determine who should be responsible for certain information security activities. This information could be employed after a major information security event. For example, suppose a customer sued your organization for privacy violation. You could search the CD-ROM version of this book to quickly identify the job titles that have some responsibility for "privacy." This information could then be used in a post-mortem memo describing the ways to prevent privacy problems in the future.

Given the great demand for experienced workers in the information security field, it is not surprising that management at many organizations seeks to lower costs by delegating information security tasks to less experienced and/or less busy workers. While this makes sense for certain narrowly-scoped routine tasks, such as assigning user-IDs and issuing default (temporary) passwords, it is dangerous for more complex non-routine technical tasks. Thus staff in the Human Resources Department may appropriately be called upon to set-up user-IDs and passwords for new workers, but the investigation of suspected break-ins is something best left to the Information Security Manager. While all of the tasks mentioned in the following job descriptions are conceivably potential candidates for delegation, great care should be taken when delegating information security tasks. Delegated tasks should be clearly documented in procedures, and the involved individuals should be adequately trained to competently perform the work in question. In addition, the delegation must not create a conflict of interest or otherwise put the organization at unnecessary risk (this topic is discussed at greater length in Chapter 18, "Smaller Organizations").

INFORMATION SECURITY DEPARTMENT MANAGER

Job Title: Information Security Department Manager [*also known as Information Security Manager, Chief Information Security Officer (CISO), or in high-tech firms, simply Chief Security Officer (CSO)*]
Department: Information Security
Reports To: Chief Information Officer (CIO)
Dotted Line: Board of Directors Audit Committee

Summary:

The Information Security Department Manager directs, coordinates, plans, and organizes information security activities throughout Company X. He or she acts as the focal point for all communications related to information security, both with internal staff and third parties. The Manager works with a wide variety of people from different internal organizational units, bringing them together to manifest controls that reflect workable compromises as well as proactive responses to current and future information security risks.

Responsibilities and Duties:

The Information Security Department Manager is responsible for envisioning and taking steps to implement the controls needed to protect both Company X information as well as information that has been entrusted to Company X by third parties. The position involves overall Company X responsibility for information security regardless of the form that the information takes (paper, blueprint, floppy disk, audio tape, embedded in products or processes, etc.), the information handling technology employed (mainframes, microcomputers, fax machines, telephones, local area networks, file cabinets, etc.), or the people involved (contractors, consultants, employees, vendors, outsourcing firms, etc.).

Threats to information and information systems addressed by the Information Security Department Manager and his or her staff include, but are not limited to: information unavailability, information corruption, unauthorized information destruction, unauthorized information modification, unauthorized information usage, and unauthorized information disclosure. These threats to information and information systems include consideration of physical security matters only if a certain level of physical security is necessary to achieve a certain level of information security (for example, as is necessary to prevent theft of portable computers).

- Acts as the central point of contact within Company X when it comes to all communications dealing with information security problems, issues, and concerns

- Establishes and maintains strong working relationships with the Company X groups involved with information security matters (Legal, Internal Audit, Physical Security, Information Security Management Committee, etc.)

- Establishes, manages, and maintains organizational structures and communications channels with those responsible for information security; these responsible parties include individuals within Company X departments (such as Local Information Security Coordinators) as well as Company X business partners (outsourcing firms, consulting firms, etc.)

- Assists with the clarification of individual information security responsibility and accountability so that necessary information security activities are performed as needed, according to pre-established polices and standards

- Coordinates the information security efforts of all internal groups that have one or more information security-related responsibilities, to ensure that organization-wide information security efforts are consistent across the organization, and that duplication of effort is avoided [*this is a shared responsibility with the Physical Security Department Manager*]

- Coordinates all multi-application or multi-system information security improvement projects at Company X [*a good example would be converting all operating system access control systems to a standard minimum password length*]

- Represents Company X and its information security related interests at industry standards committee meetings, technical conferences, and the like [*smaller or less visible organizations will generally dispense with this duty*]

- Investigates the ways that information security related technologies, requirements statements, internal processes, and organizational structures can be used to achieve the goals found in the Company X strategic plan [*this effort should include consideration of the long range information systems plan, which in turn should be an intermediate link between the business strategic plan and the information security plan*]

- Creates a strategic information security plan with a vision for the future of information security at Company X (utilizing evolving information security technology, this vision meets a variety of objectives such as management's fiduciary and legal responsibilities, customer expectations for secure modern business practices, and the competitive requirements of the marketplace)

- Understands the fundamental business activities performed by Company X, and based on this understanding, suggests appropriate information security solutions that uniquely protect these activities

- Develops action plans, schedules, budgets, status reports and other top management communications intended to improve the status of information security at Company X

- Obtains top management approval and on-going support for all major information security initiatives at Company X (or supervises others in their efforts with these proceedings)

- Brings pressing information security vulnerabilities to top management's attention so that immediate remedial action can be taken

- Performs and/or oversees the performance of periodic Company X risk assessments that identify current and future security vulnerabilities, determines what level of risk is acceptable to management, and identifies the best ways to reduce information security risks to this acceptable level [*in a general sense, the Information Security Department Manager performs information security risk management or else establishes a management structure that has others (such as line managers) perform this function*]

- Examines information security from a cross-organizational viewpoint including Company X's participation in extranets, electronic data interchange (EDI) trading networks, ad-hoc Internet commerce relationships, and other new business structures, and makes related recommendations to protect Company X information and information systems [*the prior paragraph discussing risk assessments deals with internal information systems, while this paragraph is advisable whenever new multi-organizational networks are contemplated or deployed*]

- Directs the development of, or originates self-assessment questionnaires and other tools that assist user department managers and other members of the management team in their efforts to determine the degree of compliance with information security requirements within their respective organizational units

- Periodically initiates quality measurement studies to determine whether the information security function at Company X operates in a manner consistent with standard industry practices (these include customer satisfaction surveys, benchmarking studies, peer comparison efforts, and internal tests)

- Coordinates and directs the development, management approval, implementation, and promulgation of objectives, goals, policies, standards, guidelines, and other requirements needed to support information security throughout Company X as well as within Company X business networks (such as extranets)

- Provides managerial guidance on the development of local, system-specific, and application-specific information security policies, guidelines, standards, and procedures

- Assists with the establishment and refinement of procedures for the identification of Company X information assets as well as the classification of these information assets with respect to criticality, sensitivity, and value [*the availability of this asset information allows appropriate controls to then be chosen by management; see Chapter 15, "Ownership" for further details*]

- Coordinates internal staff in their efforts to determine Company X information security obligations according to external requirements (contractual, regulatory, legal, ethical, etc.)

- Closely monitors changes in society's information security related ethics, values, morals, and attitudes with an eye toward changes that Company X should make in response to these developments

- Designs and manages business processes for the detection, investigation, correction, disciplinary action, and/or prosecution related to information security breaches, violations, and incidents [*these efforts would include an intrusion detection system, also known as an IDS*]

- Manages internal Company X activities pertaining to the investigation, correction, prosecution, and disciplinary action needed for the resolution of information security breaches, violations, and incidents (whether actual or alleged)

- Prepares post mortem analyses of information security breaches, violations, and incidents to illuminate what happened and how this type of problem can be prevented in the future

- Directs the preparation of information systems contingency plans and manages worker groups (such as Computer Emergency Response Teams or CERTs) that respond to information security relevant events (hacker intrusions, virus infections, denial of service attacks, etc.)

- Works with public relations and top management to develop suitable public responses to information security incidents, violations, and problems

- Acts as an external representative for Company X in the event of a hacker break-in or some other information security relevant event [*this may involve news media interviews, discussions with concerned customers, etc.*]

- Acts as an expert witness in information security related legal proceedings involving Company X

- Initiates and manages special projects related to information security that may be needed to appropriately respond to ad-hoc or unexpected information security events

- Provides technical support consulting services on matters related to information security such as the criteria to use when selecting information security products

- Performs management and personnel administration functions associated with Company X's Information Security Department (coaches employees, hires and fires employees, disciplines employees, reviews employee performance, recommends salary increases and promotions, counsels employees, establishes employee task lists and schedules, trains staff, etc.)

- Acts as the primary liaison and decision-maker regarding the work of information security consultants, contractors, temporaries, and outsourcing firms

- Provides technical information security consulting assistance for Company X staff disciplinary measures, civil suits, and criminal prosecutions

- Stays informed about the latest developments in the information security field, including new products and services, through on-line news services, technical magazines, professional association memberships, industry conferences, special training seminars, and other methods

ACCESS CONTROL SYSTEM ADMINISTRATOR

Job Title: Access Control System Administrator
Department: Information Security
Reports To: Information Security Department Manager

Summary:

An Access Control System Administrator manages the user access control privileges associated with shared computer systems and networks that are managed by the Information Technology Department. The Administrator is responsible for maintaining accurate and up-to-date computer resident records that reflect user contact information, current user privileges, and management authorization for these same user privileges. The Administrator is additionally responsible for immediately terminating user privileges when workers change jobs or leave Company X. In a general sense, the Administrator is responsible for promptly updating access control records so that workers have only the access to Company X computers and networks needed to perform their jobs.

Responsibilities and Duties:

- Processes requests to grant computer and/or network access privileges that have been approved by designated members of management [*often this will include approval by information owners; see Chapter 15, "Ownership" for further details*]

- Regularly obtains reauthorization from management that the granted privileges on Company X computer and networks are still appropriate for the workers involved [*often this will include approval by information owners; see Chapter 15 for further details*]

- Modifies the privileges of users in response to employment status notices sent by Department Managers and the Human Resources Department Manager [*for example, if an employee was terminated due to fraud, the system privileges for that individual would need to be immediately turned-off*]

- Establishes and refines procedures and other business processes to promptly update the computer-resident privileges used by computer and network access control systems (these privileges are sometimes called access control lists or ACLs)

- Establishes and refines procedures and other business processes to detect errors and inconsistencies in the computer-resident privileges used by computer and network access control systems [*a procedure to detect user-IDs that have not been used in 90 days, sometimes called dormant user-IDs, would be an example*]

- Monitors logs kept by computer and network access control systems to detect attempts at unauthorized use, and notifies the Computer Emergency Response Team (CERT) as necessary

- Develops or supports the development of automated mechanisms that analyze the security violations found in access control logs to discover patterns and evidence of problems [*this work may involve writing scripts to catch certain abusive activity, or it may involve refinement of the rules used to initiate the alarms triggered by an Intrusion Detection System, also known as an IDS*]

- Provides technical assistance to Systems Administrators, Network Administrators, Commerce Site Administrators, Web Site Administrators, and Database Administrators in their efforts to monitor computer and networks under their control so that unauthorized use will be immediately detected and acted upon

- Integrates the Human Resources Database with computer-resident records of user privileges so that privileges will increasingly be changed exactly at the time when a worker's status with Company X changes

- Maintains and updates computer-resident records that support encryption related processes (such as line encryption devices, virtual public networks (VPNs), digital signatures, and digital certificates and components of a public key infrastructure or PKI) so that Company X business operations can be securely automated

- Assists users in their efforts to use Company X information systems including handling password resets, smart card deactivations, private encryption key revocations, and the like

- Preserves all records indicating changes made to access control lists to facilitate investigations, disciplinary actions, and prosecutions

- Provides filing, typing, word processing, database entry, and related support needed to process requests for changes in user access privileges

- Performs other support activities in support of the Information Security Department

- Attends occasional conferences or training seminars to remain familiar with the latest tools and techniques in the information systems access control area

INTERNAL INFORMATION SECURITY CONSULTANT

Job Title: Internal Information Security Consultant [*also known as Senior Information Security Advisor*]
Department: Information Security
Reports To: Information Security Department Manager

Summary:

An Internal Information Security Consultant provides business and technical advice on a wide variety of information security issues, concerns, and problems. A Consultant makes sure that all business applications developed in-house or developed by outsiders on behalf of Company X include adequate control measures. Working on committees and task forces throughout Company X, an Internal Information Security Consultant is an in-house subject matter expert who diligently assists with the improvement of security on information systems at Company X. A visible internal spokesperson of the Information Security Department, such a Consultant is charged with gaining widespread support of and compliance with information security requirements. [*Larger organizations may have several Internal Information Security Consultants, each with a specialization in a certain area, such as Internet commerce, desktop machines, telecommuting and mobile computing, or secure systems development. If this position is split into several different jobs, the tasks should likewise be split. The hands-on technical implementation work is generally done by an Information Security Engineer.*]

Responsibilities and Duties:

- Provides in-depth technical advice for investigations of information security incidents including internal frauds, hacker break-ins, and system outages

- Assists with the documentation of information security incidents as well as the analysis of the circumstances enabling or permitting these same incidents to take place

- Participates on a computer emergency response team (CERT) that responds to various security incidents such as denial of service attacks, virus infestations, and internal frauds

- Analyzes selected commercially-available information security products and services to determine which of these should be adopted by or tested by Company X

- Provides users and management with technical support on matters related to information security such as the criteria to use when selecting information security products (answers a wide variety of questions about information security)

- Acts as a technical information security reviewer of requirements statements, feasibility analyses, operating procedure manuals, and other documents produced during the systems development process

- Reviews proposals to significantly enhance or modify the configuration or functionality of intranets, firewalls, servers, applications, databases, and other important parts of the Company X information systems infrastructure

- Provides special technical guidance to the Information Technology Department staff about the risks and control measures associated with new and emerging information systems technologies

- Acts as a technical resource to users, user department management, and others within Company X who are seeking more information about information security

- Participates in, and acts as a technical leader in, periodic information systems risk assessments including those associated with the development of new or significantly enhanced business applications

- Reviews the cost-effectiveness and practicality of existing information security procedures and systems, and makes suggestions for the improvement of these same procedures and systems

- Develops detailed proposals and plans for new information security systems that would augment the capabilities of, or enable new capabilities for Company X networks or shared information systems [*for example, develop a proposal for implementing digital certificates within Company X*]

- Prepares and periodically updates draft information security policies, architectures, standards, and/or other technical requirement documents needed to advance information security at Company X

- Interprets information security policies, standards, and other requirements in light of specific internal information systems, and assists with the implementation of these and other information security requirements

- Assists with the selection, installation, and adoption of automated tools that enforce or monitor the compliance with information security policies, procedures, standards, and similar information security requirements [*compliance checking should be the responsibility of the Internal Audit Department, but an Internal Information Security Consultant should provide technical advice on the selection, operation, and implementation of these systems*]

- Conceives of and proposes new approaches that will allow greater standardization and more effective management of information security measures [*integrating a stand-alone intrusion detection system with a 24×7×365 network management system would be an example*]

- Provides technical advice to those who install, administer, and update computer-based access control systems [*the most common example is fixed passwords and user-IDs*]

- Guides developers, users, and other internal staff in their efforts to establish and maintain adequate audit trails so that sufficient evidence of computerized business activities exists to reconcile accounts, to detect frauds, to quickly resolve problems, and to otherwise maintain secure and reliable information systems within Company X

- Assists with internal efforts to inventory and control intellectual property (including restricting unauthorized copying of software)

- Develops and periodically refines a data classification system that allows workers to make quick decisions about the procedures they should use to protect information that has been marked with the designations described by this system

- Designs, develops, delivers, or oversees the delivery of classroom training and/or other information security awareness programs (videos, memos, computer-based training, etc.) delivered to users, technical staff, and management [*a special training program for Distributed Information Security Coordinators is recommended*]

- Working in conjunction with the In-House Trainer, periodically determines the effectiveness of information security awareness programs, and quantifies this effectiveness [*the Internal Information Security Consultant should not be the only one checking the effectiveness of his or her own work; that's one reason why an In-House Trainer is involved*]

- Monitors current and proposed laws, regulations, industry standards, and ethical requirements related to information security and privacy, so that Company X is warned in advance and is ready to be fully compliant with these requirements

- Stays informed about the latest developments in the information security field, including new products and services, through on-line news services, technical magazines, professional associations, industry conferences, training seminars, and other information sources

- Participates as a technical advisor for a variety of ad-hoc information security projects that will be dictated by current business and technological developments

- As needed, acts as an expert witness in information security-related legal proceedings involving Company X

INFORMATION SECURITY ENGINEER

Job Title: Information Security Engineer
Department: Information Security
Reports To: Information Security Department Manager

Summary:

An Information Security Engineer provides technical assistance with the design, installation, operation, service and maintenance of a variety of multi-user information security systems such as virtual private networks (VPNs). A hands-on technical specialist, an Engineer handles the complex and detailed technical work necessary to establish security systems such as firewalls and encryption-based digital signatures. An Engineer configures and sets-up information security systems such as firewalls, or else trains Access Control System Administrators, Systems Administrators, Network Administrators, and/or Database Administrators to do these tasks themselves.

Responsibilities and Duties:

- Provides hands-on technical consulting services to teams of technical specialists working on either integrating centralized or networked systems that will offer enhanced levels of information security [*examples include an active data dictionary, a data warehouse, or a data mart*]

- Provides technical assistance with the initial set-up and secure deployment of systems that support information security including virus detection systems, firewall content filtering systems, and software license management systems

- Offers technical information security consulting services to distributed personnel who are responsible for one or more information security systems; these people include Network Administrators, Systems Administrators, and Database Administrators

- Evaluates information system bug reports, security exploit reports, and other information security notices issued by information system vendors, government agencies, universities, professional associations, and other organizations, and as needed, makes recommendations to internal management to take precautionary steps [*an example of these notices is the periodic reports issued by the CERT at Carnegie-Mellon University*]

- Runs or works with others that periodically run vulnerability identification software packages and related tools to immediately highlight errors in systems configuration, the need for the application of fixes and patches, and other security related changes [*to leave this task solely to Systems Administrators introduces a conflict of interest because the results of such software will often indicate that Systems Administrators need to perform additional work*]

- With management authorization, collects, securely stores, and utilizes software that is able to decrypt encrypted files, automatically guess user passwords, copy software that has been copy-protected, or otherwise circumvent information security measures

- Maintains and, as necessary, documents a collection of software that is able to trace the source of and otherwise investigate attacks on Company X systems

- Conducts selected tests of information security measures in accordance with specific instructions provided by the Information Security Department Manager [*this effort usually includes penetration attacks*]

- Interprets information security policies, standards, and other requirements as they relate to a specific internal information system, and assists with the implementation of these and other information security requirements

- Redesigns and reengineers internal information handling processes so that information is appropriately protected from a wide variety of problems including unauthorized disclosure, unauthorized use, inappropriate modification, premature deletion, and unavailability

- Regularly attends conferences, professional association meetings, and technical symposia to remain aware of the latest information security technological developments

INFORMATION SECURITY DOCUMENTATION SPECIALIST

Job Title: Information Security Documentation Specialist [*sometimes called an Information Security Department Administrative Assistant or Information Security Department Administrative Coordinator*]

Department: Information Security

Reports To: Information Security Department Manager

Summary:

The Information Security Documentation Specialist is an administrative coordinator of information security documents. Somewhat akin to a librarian, the Specialist updates and maintains policies, procedures, standards, architectures, forms, and other documents that facilitate information security activities. He or she organizes this material on an intranet site, and otherwise helps to ensure that the most up-to-date version of these documents is distributed to and used by those who have need for the documents. The Specialist does not act as the leader in the identification of new or evolving information security requirements, but instead performs specialized research that assists the Information Security Department Manager and others with such decisions. [*This position does not update or modify the information systems contingency plan.*]

Responsibilities and Duties:

- Maintains an inventory of all information security documents, with the exception of informal memos, that have been issued by Company X (this inventory should include selected documents issued by other departments such as the Information Technology Department) [*documents can take any form such as paper, fax, html, etc.*]

- Maintains the master copies of, and updates and maintains policies, guidelines, standards, procedures, and other requirements documents in line with new business activities, new business relationships, and new technologies [*the Administrator would not generally initiate the request for technical changes, only handle the documentation reflecting these ideas*]

- Maintains a collection of information security awareness and training materials used by Company X including films, pamphlets, manuals, and computer-based training software

- Distributes information security documents so that those who need such documents have copies or can readily locate the documents via an intranet site

- Maintains an intranet site that reflects the current version of all information security requirements such as policies, standards, and procedures, etc.

- Assists various workers throughout Company X with the interpretation and use of information security documents [*the Information Security Documentation Specialist would not generally provide technical assistance, only administrative assistance*]

- Securely manages the paper files of the Information Security Department so that only authorized workers can gain access to these files (including past risk assessment projects, analyses of information security products, etc.), and so that all critical files are stored at a secure off-site records storage facility

- Researches the continued usefulness, relevance, and currency of information security documents used at Company X and makes recommendations to the Information Security Department Manager that are intended to improve information security documents

- Works with the Internal Intellectual Property Attorney to determine what information security matters should be documented and makes suggestions to the Information Security Department Manager about additional projects

- Maintains an up-to-date log reflecting those in possession of sensitive information, the movement of this information from person to person, and the copying and destruction of such information consistent with data classification system requirements [*the types of "sensitive information" subject to this procedure should be defined in a data classification policy*]

- Acts as a coordinator of meetings and events that involve the Information Security Department so that the right people are brought together to create specific results defined by the Information Security Department Manager

- Manages the software escrow related interactions with software vendors in those cases where Company X has determined that escrow is required [*software escrow involves the storage of source code and other proprietary development documentation with a third party in case the software developer goes out of business or otherwise fails to meet its obligations to Company X*]

- Establishes and maintains organized files containing invoices, contracts, and other agreements with information security vendors, such as those that offer virus detection software, software license management software, single sign-on software, and paper document destruction services

- Coordinates the development, issuance, and decision-making activities relevant to requests for proposals (RFPs), vendor bid solicitations, consulting contracts, and other documents describing products or services provided by third-party information security vendors

- Coordinates the shipping, receipt, inventory, and fixed assets control associated with information systems equipment and office equipment used in the Information Security Department

- Maintains a library of information security technical publications used by the Information Security Department [*these materials are published by government agencies, consulting firms, and additional organizations other than Company X*]

- Maintains a sufficient inventory of paper, pencils, staples, fax paper, copier paper, and other office equipment and supplies such that members of the Information Security Department can get their jobs done efficiently and effectively

- Acts as the primary administrative contact for the Information Security Department with the Human Resources Department, the Accounting Department, and other staff departments within Company X [*typically this would involve distribution of certain handbooks, forms, etc.*]

- Documents Information Security Department internal procedures so that new members of the Department can be quickly and expeditiously trained and so that essential tasks can be performed even if critical staff are unavailable

- Makes suggestions to the Information Security Department Manager about the ways that administrative activities within the department can be improved

INFORMATION SYSTEMS CONTINGENCY PLANNER

Job Title: Information Systems Contingency Planner
Department: Information Security
Reports To: Information Security Department Manager

Summary:

The Information Systems Contingency Planner acts as the primary focal point for all efforts to design, develop, and test information systems contingency plans at Company X. Providing technical expertise to a wide variety of people throughout Company X, the Planner is a subject matter expert who brings best practices found in the industry and in the high-technology field to bear on the contingency planning challenges faced by Company X. The Planner also coordinates efforts to integrate information systems contingency plans with business contingency plans. The planner does the necessary groundwork so that critical business transactions can continue to be processed by Company X information systems, even if an interruption or problem of some sort has occurred.

Responsibilities and Duties:

- For shared multi-departmental information systems and networks, such as firewalls, develops and maintains up-to-date and practical contingency plans that assist Company X in quickly restoring operations after an emergency or a disaster

- Makes arrangements with a wide variety of vendors needed to support a recovery effort in the event that multi-departmental information systems and networks are unavailable, unexpectedly too slow, or seriously malfunctioning

- Evaluates contingency planning tools, such as those that run on a desktop computer, and makes recommendations about the packages that would best support Company X information systems contingency planning efforts

- Participates in information security risk assessments to determine the impact of various threat events including sabotage, industrial espionage, fraud and embezzlement, errors and omissions, natural disasters, and privacy violations

- Performs periodic business impact analyses (BIAs) which examine the potential problems that would be caused by major outages or other serious problems associated with critical information systems at Company X

- Prepares budgets, cost/benefit analyses, and other financial evaluations of the currently available contingency planning options

- Develops and applies procedures that prioritize applications, systems, and networks within Company X so that limited resources can be devoted to the most critical information systems resources [*these procedures may, for example, include a framework for information owners to rank production business applications by criticality; see Chapter 15, "Ownership" for details*]

- Participates in a computer emergency response team (CERT) that responds to various security incidents such as denial of service attacks, virus infestations, and internal frauds

- Develops, implements, and refines management decision-making processes that facilitate a rapid and appropriate response to information systems emergencies and disasters

- Develops customized damage assessment and reporting methods to be used after an information systems emergency or disaster, and periodically performs "post mortems" to determine the degree to which these methods are accurate and useful

- Assists with information systems related insurance claim investigations that are necessary in order for Company X to receive the proceeds from insurance policies

- Periodically performs analyses that seek to establish the rough value of information owned by or in the possession of Company X [*this valuation is important to make sure that contingency planning measures, and for that matter other information security control measures, are cost-effective*]

- Develops or assists in the design of information system asset inventories that will assist with information systems recovery efforts (these include data dictionaries, computer equipment inventories, and the like)

- Assists with the development and refinement of conceptual and organizational structures which help ensure that Company X is prepared for various information systems related threat events [*an example would be a departmental contingency planning testing process that requires each department to develop their own local contingency plans*]

- Develops methodologies and instructional material that assist Company X workers with the preparation of their own contingency plans to deal with decentralized or single department information systems such as a departmental server

- Provides expert technical assistance related to contingency planning to departments throughout Company X who are preparing, testing, and updating their own information systems contingency plans

- Trains Information Technology Department staff in the proper use of contingency planning documentation relevant to multi-departmental information systems and networks

- Plans, executes, and reports to management on the success of tests to information systems contingency plans

- Reviews the contingency plans developed by departments and other organizational units to ensure that they meet Company X standards, and also to ensure that they have integrated all applicable Company X contingency planning practices [*these contingency plans include emergency response and disaster recovery procedures*]

- Works with computer and network performance and capacity analysts to ensure that adequate excess capacity and bandwidth exists to realistically support information systems contingency plans

- Researches and stays abreast of all major threats that could adversely impact Company X's information systems including virus infestations, denial of service attacks, hacker intrusions, fires in computer centers, hurricanes, tornadoes, and earthquakes

- Attends several conferences or training seminars per year to become acquainted with the latest tools and techniques for information systems contingency planning

- Coordinates information systems contingency planning efforts with the Business Contingency Planner's activities

LOCAL INFORMATION SECURITY COORDINATOR

Job Title: Local Information Security Coordinator [*also known as Regional Information Security Coordinator, Departmental Information Security Coordinator, or Divisional Information Security Coordinator*]

Department: [*insert a user department name*]

Reports To: Manager of [*insert user department name*]

Dotted Line: Information Security Department Manager

Summary:

A Local Information Security Coordinator is familiar with local business conditions including prevailing laws, organizational culture, and management style. A Coordinator uses these local conditions to interpret and implement the information security requirements issued by the Information Security Department. A Coordinator serves as a liaison between the Information Security Department and the users and management in his or her own local organizational unit. Not a full-time information security specialist, the Coordinator is ordinarily responsible for other information systems activities such as systems administration.

Responsibilities and Duties in Information Security:

- Introduces new information security issues and requirements to management within the department [*or another more appropriate organizational unit*]

- Represents the needs and wishes of the department [*or some other organizational unit*] at Company X information security meetings [*these meetings typically take place every few months, and give the Coordinators a chance to meet and talk with each other as well as with members of the Information Security Department*]

- Interprets information security policies, standards, procedures, and other requirements in light of local needs, and assists user department staff in the implementation of these and other information security requirements [*these include data classification systems, application criticality ranking systems, and other models for coming to terms with information security needs*]

- Provides information security advice and perspective to users and management within the department, and when questions or issues cannot be resolved locally, acts as a liaison with the Information Security Department Manager [*rather than a department, the coordinator could be responsible for a division, all operations within a country, or some other organizational unit*]

- Coordinates the activities of users, local Systems Administrators, and local Network Administrators to help ensure that all documented information security requirements have been met

- Provides a first level information security review of feasibility studies, upgrade proposals, implementation plans, conversion plans, outsourcing plans, and related information systems change documents

- Brings local department information security issues, vulnerabilities, violations, and compliance problems that have not been adequately addressed to the attention of the Information Security Department Manager

CHIEF INFORMATION OFFICER

Job Title: Chief Information Officer (CIO)
Department: Information Technology
Reports To: Chief Executive Officer

Responsibilities and Duties in Information Security:

- Assigns information ownership duties to departmental managers who are most likely to benefit from the information in question [*see Chapter 15, "Ownership" for details*]

- Allocates sufficient resources and manages Information Technology Department staff so that internal information systems are designed, built, and operated in a manner that is secure, reliable, and consistent with Company X business objectives

- Takes steps to ensure that all workers in the Information Technology Department are conducting their daily activities in a manner that is in compliance with established policies, standards, procedures and other management directives

- Educates top management about the need for reliable, well managed, and well maintained information systems [*the CIO will be the conduit for information security information if and only if the CIO has the Information Security Department Manager reporting to him or her; see Chapter 13, "Reporting Relationships" for further discussion*]

- Conceives of new information systems architectures and strategies that could advance Company X's business objectives [*these architectures and strategies may include the use of information security tools such as digital signatures*]

INFORMATION SYSTEMS ANALYST/BUSINESS ANALYST

Job Title: Information Systems Analyst/Business Analyst
Department: Information Technology
Reports To: Manager of Systems Development

Responsibilities and Duties in Information Security:

- Utilizes Company X systems development processes to ensure that all necessary steps have been performed prior to bringing up an application in a production operating environment [*these steps include consideration of security at several phases such as in the generalized systems design phase*]

- Evaluates user department security and privacy needs (in conjunction with the Information Security Department Manager) and includes suitable controls in all proposed information systems solutions

- Documents and teaches user department to employ clear decision-making criteria so that management can appropriately choose between conflicting objectives such as information integrity, information availability, information timeliness, and information security

- Provides technical support consulting services to users and user department managers so as to allow them to achieve business goals while at the same time ensuring that the envisioned system is adequately secure, reliable, and supportable

- Offers training and/or assists with the development of training materials to user departments for those systems that the Analyst helped to design [*training in many instances should include security*]

SYSTEMS PROGRAMMER

Job Title: Systems Programmer
Department: Information Technology
Reports To: Manager of Systems Development

Responsibilities and Duties in Information Security:

- Installs and maintains security-related systems software, such as fixed password access control systems, smart card systems, and user activity logging systems

- Provides technical support consulting services to the Computer Operations Manager, Business Application Programmers, and Information Systems Analysts to help them understand the systems software issues associated with achieving certain performance, reliability, and security goals

- Documents all systems software that has been developed in-house, according to existing documentation standards, to facilitate future maintenance and enhancements, as well as to quickly diagnose problems

BUSINESS APPLICATIONS PROGRAMMER

Job Title: Business Applications Programmer
Department: Information Technology
Reports To: Manager of Systems Development

Responsibilities and Duties in Information Security:

- Employs the risk assessment methodology issued by the Information Security Department to determine specifically which controls are needed for business application software being developed, significantly enhanced, or externally provided (outsourced)

- Builds appropriate controls into business application software so that the resulting business activity will be both secure and reliable

- Follows the systems development process conventions published by the Information Technology Department to ensure that all important steps in the development process have been adequately performed

- Performs alpha tests of his or her own application software to ensure that it operates according to functional specifications before releasing it to the Quality Assurance Department for further testing

- Diligently documents all application systems developed in-house to facilitate future maintenance and enhancements

- Helps the In-House Trainer to develop user-training materials which assist workers in properly operating the business application software that he or she developed

- Notifies management about potential problems associated with the application systems that they have been working on, which are not adequately addressed by control mechanisms [*these problems include potential privacy violations*]

COMPUTER OPERATIONS MANAGER

Job Title: Computer Operations Manager
Department: Information Technology
Reports To: Chief Information Officer

Responsibilities and Duties in Information Security:

- Manages electrical power, telephone, air conditioning, humidity control, fire detection and suppression, and other environmental systems that are necessary for the smooth and continuous operation of computer-center-based information systems resources such as servers, hubs, routers, and firewalls [*perhaps most importantly among these systems is an Uninterruptible Power System or UPS*]

- Establishes and refines operating procedures for computer center staff to follow to ensure that all production applications are completed on time, in a manner that is secure and reliable

- Manages the work of Computer Operators, Network Operators, Computer Performance Analysts, and others who tend the operations of the information systems and networks managed by the Information Systems Department, so that reliable, secure, and cost-effective service is provided to internal users

- Supervises the change control process for equipment, facilities, and software such that only changes authorized by management are made (exceptions will be made in the case of emergencies, although all emergency changes must be followed-up by a justification memo)

- Plans and supervises hardware and software conversions for those information systems managed by the Information Technology Department so that information system reliability, availability, and security are maintained

- Prepares budgets, project plans, and other proposals that would enhance the reliability, cost-effectiveness, and security of the information systems managed by the Information Technology Department

- Maintains an up-to-date inventory of shared information systems equipment including routers, hubs, servers, firewalls, and monitors [*if an organization doesn't know what equipment and systems it has, securing them will be very difficult if not impossible*]

- Performs in-house technical consulting to assist Business Application Developers and users with their efforts to best utilize the equipment and computer center environmental systems managed by the Information Technology Department

- Performs analyses of the capacity and performance of the equipment, facilities, and software located in the computer center [*these analyses may highlight unusual conditions which could indicate that a security problem exists*]

- Keeps checks, customer statement stationery, and other forms in a secured location and grants access only to those who have a genuine business need

- Establishes and supervises a system of printed output distribution such that sensitive reports, negotiable materials (such as paychecks), and other output is seen by and received by only authorized parties

- Designs and regularly refines workflow and foot traffic movement patterns so that only authorized personnel are permitted to enter the data center

- Supervises the work of information system vendor personnel when they are in the computer center

COMPUTER OPERATOR

Job Title: Computer Operator
Department: Information Technology
Reports To: Computer Operations Manager

Responsibilities and Duties in Information Security:

- Monitors the status of multi-user computers including system load, available disk space, and response time to ensure that all activities are in keeping with management intentions [*this monitoring is often the first line of defense for noticing hacker intrusions and other inappropriate activity*]

- Monitors daily computer operations with an eye toward unusual events, and notifies the Computer Emergency Response Team (CERT) immediately of any suspected intrusions, virus infestations, or other abuses that may continue, and notifies the Information Security Department Manager of all other suspicious activities (suspected fraud, sabotage, etc.)

- Maintains and reviews logs, audit trails, and other shared information systems records indicating the activity that took place [*these logs can be essential for break-in investigations and problem resolution efforts*]

- Adjusts the applications running, users logged-in, system configuration, data media loaded, and other aspects of multi-user computers so that business activity on shared information systems proceeds in an efficient, recoverable, and reliable manner [*these adjustments sometimes involve terminating the session of a hacker and revoking all privileges associated with the involved user-ID; these adjustments also involve loading tapes and other data media needed for backup processes*]

- Assists with and monitors the movement of new software into the production environment to ensure that only duly authorized software is used to process production information

- Restricts physical access to the licensed application program library and back-up tape library to authorized personnel

- Manages the secure handling of backup tapes, diskettes, cartridges, CDs, and other data recording media such that only authorized people are permitted to have possession of these media

- Follows documented instructions for the production operation of application systems software, including comparison of batch control totals, digital signatures, and other audit and security parameters

- Maintains the physical security of all information systems equipment contained in computer centers, permitting only authorized personnel into the facility, and as necessary supervising the activities of outsiders such as vendor maintenance staff

INFORMATION SYSTEMS QUALITY ASSURANCE ANALYST

Job Title: Information Systems Quality Assurance Analyst
Department: Information Technology
Reports To: Manager of Systems Development

Responsibilities and Duties in Information Security:

- Researches the latest testing techniques that will cost-effectively determine whether hardware and/or software will perform in a manner consistent with specifications [*it is at least ten times more expensive to fix security problems after an application has moved into production than if this fixing process was performed before an application went into production, so security mechanisms need to be properly tested before conversion to production takes place*]

- Compiles and documents clear-cut and specific testing criteria to determine whether a particular hardware and/or software system performs in a manner that matches its documented specifications [*this testing includes testing of security mechanisms built into hardware and/or software systems, although people working in this position do not generally perform penetration attacks or other highly-specialized information security tests (those could be performed by an Information Security Engineer or by an external consultant)*]

- Manages and documents selected tests of business application software, systems software, and other information system components, so that, if need be, lawsuits, personnel actions, and other significant events based on system performance can be justified [*the source of these components is deliberately not specified here, so the quality assurance process should therefore be applied to software developed by outside parties*]

- Evaluates externally developed software packages as well as packages developed in-house to ensure that they perform in accord with specifications and that they will have, so far as can be readily determined, no damaging or disruptive impact on the computing environment into which they will be placed

- Performs post-implementation quality testing to determine whether the new system is operating in a manner consistent with requirements and related documents [*based on this type of testing, security lapses may be discovered and reported to the Information Security Department Manager*]

- Where cost-effective, utilizes testing software such as simulators to automate and formalize the testing process

- Periodically reviews staff use of the production application change control system and the systems development methodology to determine whether they are being followed according to management instructions, and reports findings and recommendations to project managers and the Internal Audit Department Manager, as necessary [*a change control system is essential to the whole quality assurance process, and if it is compromised, then there is little point in having a quality assurance process*]

- Notifies management about potential problems associated with the systems that they have been testing [*these problems include inadequate documentation, insufficient user training, overly optimistic deployment schedules, and insufficient user access controls*]

HELP DESK ASSOCIATE

Job Title: Help Desk Associate
Department: Information Technology
Reports To: Computer Operations Manager

Responsibilities and Duties in Information Security:

- Promptly documents and creates trouble tickets for all reports of information systems problems including system unavailability, unacceptable response time, unauthorized access, missing files, and virus infection [*proper documentation could be very important for prompt problem resolution, training of new staff, prosecution and disciplinary action, as well as insurance claims*]

- Immediately notifies Computer Emergency Response Team (CERT) members if an information security incident meets the criteria established by the team

- Remains familiar with the current Company X organizational structure and the information systems related activities performed by other organizational units, so that users can be quickly referred to the appropriate organizational unit

- Remains familiar with the current version of information security policies and procedures so that quick answers to users with simple questions can be provided [*more complex questions would be referred to the Information Security Department*]

- Notifies information security staff of chronic information security difficulties and other indicators that information security problems may exist

- Resets fixed passwords, resynchronizes smart cards, or otherwise reinitializes user access control mechanisms, after the involved user has adequately authenticated his or her identity [*this task may alternatively be performed by Systems Administrators, Network Administrators, Database Administrators, and/or Access Control System Administrators*]

- Attends classes, reads manuals, and otherwise becomes familiar with the user perspective needed to operate computers, networks, and other information systems equipment utilized at Company X [*provides the technical background that could enable a Help Desk Associate to identify information security problems*]

ARCHIVES MANAGER/RECORDS MANAGER

Job Title: Archives Manager/Records Manager
Department: Information Technology
Reports To: Chief Information Officer

Responsibilities and Duties in Information Security:

- Develops, applies, and occasionally enhances a policy that clearly designates certain types of Company X information as an archival record

- Maintains a concise but complete listing of all document types that need to be retained as archival records [*web site pages are an important example of archive information that many organizations often don't retain*], and displays this on the Company X intranet

- Defines a data retention schedule for archival records by periodically working in conjunction with the Internal Intellectual Property Attorney

- Assists information owners in the process of determining whether information under their control should be designated as an archival record, determining what period of time different types of information should be retained, and determining who should be allowed to access these types of information [*see Chapter 15 for more information on owners*]

- Receives, categorizes, and otherwise prepares information submitted from people throughout Company X for insertion into the Company X archival records

- Assists workers throughout Company X with efforts to retrieve and reconstruct archival records in support of various business objectives

- Trains Systems Administrators, Network Administrators, Database Administrators and other workers who operate information backup systems about the need for and procedures associated with archival records

- Periodically disposes of (or destroys) archival information in accordance with existing policies and procedures [*the most important of these policies and procedures would be a data retention schedule; this destruction process would be particularly important if there is a threat that archival electronic mail could be used in discovery proceedings by an opposing attorney*]

- Periodically checks archival information storage media (such as magnetic tape) to make sure that the information stored thereon is readily retrievable

- Transfers information from existing archival storage media to new and more permanent archival media if and when the information contained thereon is in jeopardy

- Maintains an inventory of tape drives, floppy disk drives, zip drives, and related data storage and data retrieval equipment needed to access archival records

- Maintains an up-to-date inventory of all critical documents and computer-readable media that allows the archived information to be readily retrieved

- As needed, maintains a history of the movement and current location of sensitive, valuable, or critical information that is at the same time an archival record

- Establishes, maintains, and enhances environmental systems (humidity control, air conditioning, etc.) so as to keep archival records from prematurely deteriorating

- Manages the activities of vendors who are in possession of or who otherwise handle Company X archival records

- Ensures that physical access controls over all archival records is sufficient to prevent unauthorized access and damage to the information stored therein

- Establishes and maintains authorization and documentation systems so that only authorized personnel can access and/or remove information contained in the archival records

- Researches the latest research and products for indexing, cataloging, organizing, storing, and protecting archival records, and makes recommendations to the Chief Information Officer as warranted

TELECOMMUNICATIONS MANAGER

Job Title: Telecommunications Manager
Department: Information Technology
Reports To: Chief Information Officer

Responsibilities and Duties in Information Security:

- Periodically reviews commercially-available technology to determine whether it is cost-effective for Company X to upgrade its internal network to improve reliability, improve quality of service, or reduce cost

- Works with the Information Security Department Manager to ensure that voicemail, fax, intranet, and other communications systems that employ computers have adequate access control measures, contingency plans, and other controls

- Acts as a liaison with voice and data network providers, such as Internet Security Providers (ISPs), including negotiating and administering contracts so that Company X business objectives are met [*security and privacy would be topics covered by these contracts*]

- Manages contractual relationships with telecommunications vendors including long distance vendors, Internet Service Providers, and others so that economical and continuously available high-quality service is provided to Company X

- Plans and extrapolates network usage and requirements so that appropriate contracts with voice and data network providers can be arranged in advance

- Monitors performance statistics about network traffic and usage so that Company X networks are available to meet business needs

- Performs troubleshooting services to isolate, diagnose, and fix problems dealing with shared servers and connected equipment [*the Telecommunications Manager may be a member of the CERT*]

- Participates in the recovery of voice and/or data network services in the event of a disaster or an emergency

- Performs periodic inventories to determine the technological nature, the locations, and the connections of current communications networks used by Company X [*if users are able to independently establish their own data lines to their desks, they may be able to thwart access controls via dial-up lines*]

- Establishes, maintains, and periodically validates the accuracy of a database of telephone circuits including location, number, and jack type [*important for contingency planning purposes*]

- Assists with the establishment of usage policies for internal networks [*such as the use of message broadcasting facilities on a public address system or the transmission of chain letters via electronic mail systems*]

SYSTEMS ADMINISTRATOR/NETWORK ADMINISTRATOR

Job Title: Systems Administrator/Network Administrator
Department: Information Technology
Reports To: Computer Operations Manager
Dotted Line: Access Control System Administrator

Responsibilities and Duties in Information Security:

- Configures, installs, and connects hardware so that users will be able to perform business activities in accordance with management's intentions [*the work of an Administrator includes setting-up printers, routers, hubs, local area network servers, and the like*]

- Reconfigures and reinstalls operating systems and other security systems according to established policies and procedures whenever there is clear evidence that the security of a system has been compromised

- Periodically runs software that inventories the hardware and software resident on Company X networks, in part to determine whether software is properly licensed and whether hardware is still connected to the network

- Installs and configures software that has been legally purchased by Company X, or that is in the public domain but validated as reliable by a trusted third party

- Periodically runs and administers auto discovery software license management systems that, in a user-transparent fashion, determine whether software resident on various machines is properly licensed

- Disables and erases all licensed software (except legal demo copies) that has not been legally purchased by Company X

- Runs automatic software distribution systems to periodically transmit and install the latest software updates on involved computers

- Promptly posts all vendor-supplied patches and fixes to operating systems and other systems software to ensure the security and reliability of such systems

- Upgrades systems software as needed to ensure secure, reliable, and stable operation of servers and related equipment (including migration to other operating system platforms, other network protocols, etc.)

- Maintains in a safe place an inventory of the original installation disks, CDs, and other data storage media for licensed software used on the systems that the Administrator attends to

- Issues user-IDs and fixed passwords, or other access control mechanisms (such as identity tokens), and otherwise assists users in the secure usage of systems (including handling password resets)

- Establishes and maintains access control systems so that only one individual has access to each user-ID, so that individuals who have left Company X no longer have any system privileges, so that the privileges of dormant user-IDs are automatically revoked, and so that individuals who have switched jobs have only the privileges required to perform their new jobs [*an Administrator does this work for distributed systems, whereas an Access Control Administrator does this work for centralized systems*]

- Configures and maintains access control systems so that users can access only those machines, software, and information that are needed to perform their jobs [*this may include routers, hubs, firewalls, servers, and other equipment*]

- Promptly updates user access control privileges in response to management instructions, communicating to the requesting party when there will be a delay in posting a requested change

- Periodically revalidates the continued business need for users to have the privileges that they have been authorized to receive [*this is often simply a memo sent to the relevant manager requesting confirmation that existing privileges are in fact still needed*]

- Disables user-IDs and/or privileges immediately in those events where an employee is found guilty of a major crime, has seriously violated internal policy, or has left the organization (especially in duress terminations)

- Faithfully follows established procedures for all changes to access control systems and documents all such changes so that problems may be quickly resolved

- Securely preserves all records indicating changes made to access control lists to facilitate investigations, disciplinary actions, and prosecutions

- Establishes and maintains network directories, router tables, and other information systems collections that are used to interconnect Company X networks and computers [*for example, Lightweight Directory Access Protocol (LDAP) is a directory-based approach to providing network access control services, and the Administrator should manage this system*]

- Periodically utilizes freeware and shareware vulnerability identification tools to determine whether systems are correctly designed and configured, and whether all necessary software patches and fixes have been applied [*ideally this task would be expanded to include tools that your organization licenses, but at the very least, the Administrator should run free tools*]

- Monitors computer and network activity including system load, response time, available disk space, and user activities to ensure that all activities are in keeping with management intentions

- Monitors electronic mail and other data communications sent over Company X's network to determine that these communications are fully consistent with Company X policies [*this item may be deleted if the company doesn't perform such monitoring*]

- Periodically reviews access control system logs and reports to ensure that the system is working properly and that no unauthorized activity is taking place

- Notifies management about potential problems associated with the systems that they have been working on [*these problems include inadequate disk space, untested contingency plans, etc.*]

- Participates in a computer emergency response team (CERT) that responds to various security incidents such as denial of service attacks, virus infestations, and internal frauds

- Notifies the Information Security Department Manager of all intrusions or other suspected information security problems

- Configures and monitors an Intrusion Detection System (IDS) to ensure that only authorized personnel have access to Company X systems and networks

- Establishes and administers software and information backup systems, including the procedures and transmission paths used to securely move software and information to a secure remote location

- Develops, tests, and maintains information systems contingency plans that allow the systems and networks under his or her control to be quickly regenerated and used for business purposes at a remote site [*this work should include both emergency response and also disaster recovery*]

- Performs troubleshooting services to isolate, diagnose, and fix problems dealing with servers and other equipment under the Administrator's control

- Responds promptly to user requests for assistance in efforts to get information systems under the Administrator's control to operate in a manner that supports the achievement of user-specified business goals [*these requests for assistance could be caused by a virus infection or other security related problems*]

- Works with the Information Security Department Manager or his or her delegate to ensure that all information security requirements have been met on the systems under the Administrator's control

- Closely monitors, and where possible, personally escorts, all third-party computer service personnel including representatives from hardware vendors, computer supplies vendors, outsourcing firms, and other outside organizations if these personnel are working on information systems equipment that is physically located on Company X premises, and for which the Administrator is responsible

- Monitors developments in the information security field to be able to make suggestions for the improvement of systems/network security and reliability; these activities include periodically reviewing notices about new vulnerabilities relevant to the systems for which the Administrator is responsible

WEB SITE ADMINISTRATOR/COMMERCE SITE ADMINISTRATOR

Job Title: Web Site Administrator/Commerce Site Administrator
Department: Information Technology
Reports To: Computer Operations Manager
Dotted Line: Access Control System Administrator

[*This job description could be easily modified so that it's appropriate for an Intranet Site Administrator as well. A Web Site Administrator may also be called a Web Master.*]

Responsibilities and Duties in Information Security:

- Installs, connects, configures, and inventories firewalls, routers, servers, and other network equipment associated with web/commerce systems in a manner consistent with the Company X information security policies as well as Information Technology Department policies

- Reconfigures and reinstalls operating systems and other Internet related security systems according to established policies and procedures whenever there is clear evidence that the security of a system has been compromised

- Upgrades systems software as needed to ensure secure, reliable, and stable operation of servers and related equipment

- Maintains in a safe place an inventory of the original installation disks, CDs, and other data storage media for licensed software used in the Administrator's web site and commerce site related activities

- Installs, maintains, and operates filtering software that screens inbound information flows for viruses, Trojan horses, and other unauthorized software, and screens outbound web traffic such that this traffic only connects to sites that are consistent with authorized business purposes

- Generates and distributes outbound Internet web browsing activity reports, including attempted but denied connections, for management review and remedial action

- Installs, maintains, and operates change detection software that immediately flags any changes to critical software or files on Internet connected systems

- Installs, configures, tests, and as necessary trains users on applications and systems software that runs on Company X's web/commerce systems in a manner consistent with Company X information security policies as well as Information Technology Department policies

- Monitors and projects current and future traffic loads, response time, and related capacity planning statistics on firewalls and other Internet network equipment and makes recommendations to upgrade or fine-tune this equipment as needed [*this may also be called capacity planning*]

- Installs and fine tunes load balancing software that allocates traffic to various machines on the web/commerce systems [*this software can help deal with mail bombs and denial of service attacks*]

- Makes changes to the web/commerce site only after approval by the appropriate management representatives has been obtained (exceptions will be made in emergencies) [*in many organizations, approval comes from a web/commerce site committee*]

- Immediately removes all unauthorized content or programs that have been placed on the web/commerce site to limit Company X liability and to thwart intruders [*if the site has a "zombie computer" (a remotely-controlled machine that is a participant in an attack), your organization may be held liable for damages that the zombie computer causes; likewise, if the site is a temporary waystation for the transmission of stolen credit card numbers, the organization may also be held responsible*]

- Establishes and securely maintains a permanent archive of all pages posted on the web/commerce site, including dates when the pages were used

- Establishes and administers web/commerce site software and hardware needed for back-up systems, including the definition of transmission paths used to securely move software and information to a secure remote location [*the latter is also called electronic vaulting*]

- Establishes procedures and then follows these same procedures for the regular backup of files stored on Internet web servers and commerce servers [*these procedures should include off-site secure storage of backups*]

- Participates on a computer emergency response team (CERT) that responds to various security incidents such as denial of service attacks, virus infestations, and credit card frauds

- Configures and monitors an Intrusion Detection System (IDS) to ensure that only authorized personnel have access to Company X systems and networks

- Performs troubleshooting services to isolate, diagnose, and fix problems dealing with shared servers and connected equipment (this work typically involves interactions with ISPs, ASPs, credit card processing bureaus, and other third parties)

- Notifies management about potential problems associated with the systems that the Administrator has been working on [*these problems include inadequate disk space, untested contingency plans, etc.*]

- Develops, tests, and maintains web/commerce site contingency plans that allow the systems and networks under the Administrator's control to be quickly regenerated and used for business purposes at a remote site [*this work should include both emergency response and also disaster recovery*]

- Periodically utilizes freeware and shareware vulnerability identification tools to determine whether the site is correctly designed and configured, and whether all necessary patches have been applied [*ideally this would be expanded to include tools that your organization licenses, but at the very least, the Administrator should run free tools*]

- Assigns and distributes user-IDs and initial expired passwords to authorized users according to established procedures [*alternatively, an organization can use more sophisticated technologies such as one-time password smart cards*]

- Maintains access control systems on the web/commerce sites so that only one individual has access to each user-ID, so that individuals who have left Company X no longer have any system privileges, so that users have only those privileges needed to perform their jobs, and so that individuals who have switched jobs have only the privileges of their new jobs

- Promptly updates user access control privileges in response to instructions from top management or members of the Information Security Department

- Disables user-IDs and/or privileges immediately in those events where an employee is found guilty of a major crime, has seriously violated internal policy, or has left the organization (especially important for duress terminations)

- Periodically revalidates the continued business need for users to have the privileges that they currently possess [*this typically involves the issuance of a memo to management, asking them to confirm the continued need for the currently enabled user privileges*]

- Securely preserves all records indicating changes made to access control lists to facilitate investigations, disciplinary actions, and prosecutions

- Periodically reviews access control system logs and reports to ensure that the web/commerce site is working properly and that no unauthorized activity is taking place

- Establishes and monitors automated time synchronization systems so that all web/commerce system logs reflect accurate time/date stamps

- Faithfully follows established procedures for all changes to web/commerce site access control systems (as well as content changes), and documents all such changes so that problems may be quickly resolved

- Assists with domain name registrations, server digital certificates, search engine registrations, and other Internet directory listing efforts

- Serves as Company X's first level of contact with Internet web/commerce vendors, suppliers, and outsourcing firms, and to these parties communicates Company X's technological needs [*this communication should include mentioning Company X's security requirements*]

- Closely monitors, and where possible, personally escorts, all computer service personnel from hardware vendors, computer supplies vendors, outsourcing firms, and similar third-party organizations if these personnel are working on equipment that is physically located on Company X premises

- Monitors developments in the Internet security and privacy field to be able to make suggestions for the improvement of systems/network security and reliability; these activities include periodically reviewing notices about new vulnerabilities relevant to the equipment for which the Administrator is responsible

DATABASE ADMINISTRATOR

Job Title: Database Administrator (DBA)
Department: Information Technology
Reports To: Computer Operations Manager
Dotted Line: Access Control System Administrator

Responsibilities and Duties in Information Security:

- Assigns and distributes database user-IDs and initial expired passwords to authorized users according to established procedures [*a more sophisticated user authentication technology could alternatively be specified here, for example, smart cards that generate one-time passwords*]

- Resets fixed passwords or otherwise reinitializes user access control mechanisms associated with specific database applications after authorized users have failed to authenticate their identities to the system [*again, a more sophisticated user authentication technology than fixed passwords could be used here*]

- Promptly updates user access control privileges at the database level in response to management instructions, communicating to the requesting party whenever there will be a delay in posting a requested change

- Identifies and proposes database management system access control mechanisms that Company X could use to control who gains access to shared production databases, and what they do once they have gained such access [*these mechanisms include schemas or views, which allow users to see only the information they are authorized to access*]

- Follows information security policies, guidelines, procedures, and other requirements when assigning and updating the privileges of users in shared databases

- Securely preserves all records indicating changes made to access control privileges to facilitate investigations, disciplinary actions, and prosecutions

- Generates and analyzes reports indicating database activity to highlight potential performance problems, security violations, and other problems needing attention

- Installs and monitors the performance of mechanisms to maintain and enhance the integrity and availability of the data contained in shared production databases [*an example of such a technology is data replication*]

- Designs, maintains, and controls access to a production application data dictionary [*Business Application Programmers would design application data dictionaries, but Database Administrators would maintain and control such application data dictionaries if Company X uses them*]

- Researches and explains to management the privacy, security, decision-making, and other implications of combining databases via database matching and database consolidation (as, for example, in a data warehouse, data repository, or data mart) [*the bringing together of previously separate types of information, through the Internet or other means, remains one of the greatest privacy risks of the modern age*]

- Notifies the Information Security Department Manager about risks that may be encountered when shared production databases are used in new and different ways [*for example, if a new distributed database system is being contemplated, the Administrator can bring distributed data integrity issues to the attention of the Information Security Department Manager*]

- Maintains in a safe place an inventory of the original installation disks, CDs, and other data storage media for licensed software used in the Administrator's database related activities

- Monitors developments in the database technology and management areas so as to be able to make suggestions for the improvement of database activities

DATA ADMINISTRATION MANAGER

Job Title: Data Administration Manager
Department: Information Technology
Reports To: Chief Information Officer (CIO)

Responsibilities and Duties in Information Security:

- Develops a corporate data dictionary that reflects the critical information used throughout the organization [*this data dictionary could reflect data classification, data location, and access control restrictions; the data dictionary will also be important for contingency planning efforts*]

- Develops a secure and reliable data warehouse that brings together current information from disparate Company X systems, and normalizes this data so that structured queries can be run against this data, and regular management reports can be prepared [*access control to the data warehouse is a major headache and many new issues are introduced by the process of building a data warehouse (such as mosaic theory problems); a data warehouse may also be called a data repository or a data mart*]

- Leads and/or collaborates in efforts to develop and refine an information management architecture for Company X [*this information architecture could define conventions and ways of organizing, collecting, and dispensing information that will assist in bringing both order and security to the information systems management process*]

- Works with the Information Security Department Manager on the refinement of information ownership policies and procedures to ensure that all Company X critical information has an identified owner, and that these owners are performing their assigned duties [*see Chapter 15, "Ownership" for more details*]

PHYSICAL SECURITY DEPARTMENT MANAGER

Job Title: Physical Security Department Manager
Department: Physical Security
Reports To: Legal Department Manager

Responsibilities and Duties in Information Security:

- Acts as liaison with all internal groups that have one or more security-related responsibilities to ensure that organization-wide security efforts are coordinated and that duplication of effort is avoided [*this is a shared responsibility with the Information Security Department Manager*]

- Acts as a permanent member of the Company X computer emergency response team (CERT), which quickly responds to a variety of events such as hacker break-ins, virus infestations, and insider computer fraud

- Establishes and refines a crisis management system that can assist top management in the decision-making process, assist the Public Relations Department with the words to say, and assist internal staff in quickly resolving the crisis [*this system could be pressed into action with particularly severe information security problems such as a denial of service attack against an Internet merchant*]

- Acts as liaison with law enforcement personnel including the local police force, the state police force, and the Federal Bureau of Investigation (FBI) on all criminal investigation matters pertaining to Company X

- Investigates all alleged criminal activities that involved Company X resources, which took place on Company X premises or were committed by people in the course of working for Company X [*some organizations include alleged violations of organizational policy, but these could alternately be handled either by the involved organizational unit manager or the Human Resources Department Manager*]

- Investigates and immediately stops leaks and inadvertent disclosures of confidential information [*the Information Security Department Manager will often assist with this activity*]

- Establishes and maintains physical access control systems which help to ensure that all people who are present within Company X offices or facilities are authorized to be within these same areas, that the entrances and exits of these people through a secure perimeter is logged, and that all attempts to breach this perimeter are recorded for subsequent investigation

- Supervises the installation, maintenance, and operation of security systems including CCTV surveillance systems, burglar alarm systems, and time and attendance systems [*these systems help to determine who was in what location at what time, and can therefore provide important information for investigations as well as serve as a deterrent*]

- Periodically commissions bug sweeps to ensure that Company X senior management offices, the Board Room, and other locations where sensitive information is discussed do not contain eavesdropping devices

- Establishes and supervises a force of Guards that maintains the safety of Company X employees as well as protects Company X physical property [*Guards help to keep unauthorized people out of offices that might contain sensitive information*]

- Trains the force of Guards in appropriate responses to a variety of circumstances including burglary alarms, violence in the workplace, and theft of Company X property [*property as used here includes portable computers*]

- Establishes and manages a team of personnel who collect sensitive information stored in locked containers and who then shred, burn, or otherwise destroy this sensitive information according to Company X policy [*local shredders may also be necessary for telecommuters*]

- Writes and periodically updates policies and procedures for facility management, facility access control, facility security surveillance, facility environmental controls, facility layout and design, facility fixed asset inventory, facility maintenance, facility alarm responses, as well as personnel health and safety when in Company X facilities

- Develops and refines awareness material for all workers that deals with physical security and personal safety, and then provides this material to the In-House Trainer [*personal protection ideas can also prevent theft of Company X property such as portable computers*]

- Provides consulting and technical assistance in the establishment and operation of secure inventory control systems to monitor and control valuable Company X property and negotiable instruments (examples include portable computers, blank check stock, and company credit cards)

- Offers advice and counsel about the ways that Company X should best protect itself against a variety of physical security risks including fire, wind storm, flood, earthquake, burglary, kidnapping, assault, battery, vandalism, and industrial accidents [*these physical security recommendations will often help with the protection of both information systems and information itself*]

- Organizes and periodically updates a background checking system to verify the representations of job candidates to ensure that stated qualifications, work experience, academic degrees, and references meet Company X standards

- Acts as a coordinator of the physical security for special events such as stockholders meetings and Board of Directors meetings [*these meetings may involve disclosure of significant sensitive information*]

PHYSICAL ASSET PROTECTION SPECIALIST

Job Title: Physical Asset Protection Specialist
Department: Physical Security
Reports To: Physical Security Department Manager

Responsibilities and Duties in Information Security:

- Periodically performs physical security reviews to determine whether existing or proposed Company X facilities are adequately protected against burglary, vandalism, bomb explosion, fire, flood, earthquake, wind storm, and other threats

- Designs and supervises the installation and operation of CCTV and other systems that monitor the physical security of Company X offices and facilities [*including the data center and areas where sensitive information is stored*]

- Designs and supervises the installation and operation of environmental control systems for offices and other Company X buildings (air conditioning, heating, ventilation, drainage, electrical shock prevention, burglary prevention, etc.)

- Evaluates proposed changes to offices and facilities to ensure that adequate physical security measures have been included in the design of these offices and buildings [*good physical security is a prerequisite to good information security, and if people can simply walk away with a server's hard drive, it doesn't matter whether users employed strong passwords*]

- Issues, updates, and revokes badges that control access to Company X buildings and facilities in line with current worker duties and relationships [*perhaps physical keys are used, in which case the wording here would be changed*]

- Provides direction and advice to the Property Administrators so that they can periodically take inventory and also take steps to prevent damage to, or loss of, property within their departments [*Property Administrators keep track of portable computers, office furniture, overhead projectors and other equipment, some of which contains Company X information*]

- Manages an inventory of hardware that is intended to assist workers in the protection of Company X information (shredders, locking file cabinets, etc.)

- Manages physical keys that protect Company X information and property such as those that control access to file cabinets, office doors, and closets (this includes issuing keys to authorized personnel, maintaining records reflecting key copies made and the people in possession of keys, ensuring that related locks are properly maintained, and rekeying locks as necessary)

- Maintains the secure working status of all safes, gun cabinets, door locks, company car locks, and other physical mechanisms used to protect both Company X physical property and sensitive information

- Manages and supervises the maintenance of fire detection and suppression devices and systems [*including those within the computer data center*]

- Maintains an ongoing history of security incidents including computer break-ins, theft of portable computers, vandalized cars, traffic accidents, and the like (including estimated dollar losses, time lost and business consequences) [*this is also called a loss history*]

- Conducts investigations of alleged abusive acts, criminal acts, or violations of Company X policy, as instructed by the Physical Security Department Manager [*these acts include hacker break-ins, information systems equipment theft, and other information security loss events*]

- Monitors Company X's compliance with Department of Defense classified document handling procedures, and makes recommendations for changes where appropriate [*use this only if Company X handles national defense information*]

- Oversees efforts to dispose of Company X property including gifts to charity, scrap recovery, or refurbishment and reissue [*computers that go through these processes must be purged of all Company X information*]

- Monitors the disposal of sensitive paper records through shredding, burning, or other authorized measures [*confidential information in paper form can be easily and often legally scavenged from trash bins and needs to be properly destroyed prior to disposal*]

- Researches the latest developments in physical security and executive protection, and recommends specific products and services if these same products and services would be likely to benefit Company X or its staff

BUILDING AND FACILITIES GUARD

Job Title: Building and Facilities Guard
Department: Physical Security
Reports To: Physical Security Department Manager

[*A Receptionist is generally used to greet visitors in low security environments while Building and Facilities Guards are generally used for this purpose in high security environments; Receptionists can also be used to establish and maintain physically protected areas (like an executive suite) inside the perimeter maintained by Building and Facilities Guards.*]

Responsibilities and Duties in Information Security:

- Signs for packages in the lobby and otherwise keeps delivery personnel and other third parties out of Company X offices unless they are escorted by an authorized Company X worker

- Politely greets all people who are not authorized Company X workers (employees, contractors, consultants, temporaries, etc.) and who seek to enter Company X offices, and then asks them to wait in the lobby until an escort takes them into a restricted access area

- Checks identification of all parties wishing to gain access to Company X buildings and facilities without an escort, and if proper identification is not provided, prevents these parties from gaining such access [*most often proper identification is by picture badge, and badges may be read by automated readers, and these readers may then be monitored by Guards*]

- Monitors and/or maintains logs of people gaining access to Company X buildings and facilities including visitors, those seeking employment, consultants, contractors, temporaries, and regular employees

- Monitors the materials that people remove from Company X premises to ensure that all equipment is accompanied by an authorized property pass [*although rare, in some instances, Guards may also monitor the removal of paper documents, floppy disks, and other computer media*]

- Monitors the status of remote closed circuit TV cameras, environmental sensors (such as fire detection systems), and other building and facilities control gear [*these systems will generally be integrated into a front desk console in larger organizations, and may be accompanied by video taping gear*]

- Tours Company X offices and facilities after hours to ensure that door locks remain secured, that security lighting remains turned on, and that environmental control systems (such as fire detection systems) remain functional

- Notifies local police, local ambulance services, and local fire department as needed according to procedures defined by the Physical Security Department Manager [*computer crimes should be reported to criminal justice authorities only after the approval of the Internal Intellectual Property Attorney and the Information Security Department Manager have been obtained*]

- Immediately notifies the Physical Security Department Manager and other designated members of the Company X management team of any activity that could be reasonably expected to lead to a major loss for Company X (a leaky roof, loitering by suspicious people in a parking lot, etc.)

- Provides after-hours telephone operator services and otherwise assists authorized workers with their performance of authorized business activities [*it is desirable to have somebody who can act as a centralized contact point in case of after-hours emergency or disaster*]

OFFICE MAINTENANCE WORKER

Job Title: Office Maintenance Worker
Department: Physical Security
Reports To: Physical Security Department Manager

Responsibilities and Duties in Information Security:

- Maintains a sequence of trusted custody for confidential information in paper and other forms according to Company X policies and procedures [*in other words, no unauthorized parties have had possession prior to destruction of the information*]

- Destroys confidential information in paper and other forms according to Company X policies and procedures (employing shredders, burning, etc.)

- Disposes of general office trash via locked containers and other systems that prevent unauthorized persons from gaining access

- Alerts the Physical Security Department Manager when and if there appears to be sensitive information in the general office trash [*this is an indication that better worker training is needed*]

- Notifies the Information Security Department Manager if there appears to be sensitive information left out in the open during non-working hours [*this policy is consistent with a clean desk policy that requires workers to lock-up all sensitive information when the information is not in use*]

INTERNAL AUDIT DEPARTMENT MANAGER

Job Title: Internal Audit Department Manager
Department: Internal Audit
Reports To: Chief Executive Officer

Responsibilities and Duties in Information Security:

- Develops audit plans which rank the overall risks that Company X faces and allocates internal audit resources in a manner consistent with these risks facing the organization [*in the last few years, this risk ranking approach to the development of audit plans has meant that information security receives a lot of attention*]

- Appraises, evaluates, and reports to top management on the existence of, effectiveness of, and need for changes in internal controls such as computer password systems

- Acts as the eyes and ears of top management, performing internal audits that determine whether workers are carrying out their duties in accordance with top management intentions (including confrontation of unethical, illegal, and questionable practices)

- Documents and follows up on all reported ethical problems, legal problems, policy violations, criminal behavior, and other matters anonymously reported in the Company X hotline's voicemail box

- Evaluates the degree to which Company X operations are in compliance with external requirements including contractual agreements, societal ethical expectations, laws, and regulations

- Serves as a liaison with both top management and the Board of Directors' Audit Committee, providing specialized advice and counsel about the need for changes in internal controls [*these internal controls would include information security measures*]

- Arranges for independent specialized third parties to periodically inspect, test, and provide suggestions for the improvement of internal control measures such as computer access controls [*this would, for example, include periodic third-party penetration attacks*]

- Orchestrates use of the risk acceptance process whereby departmental managers and others jointly agree to temporarily approve and support a situation that is out of compliance with existing Company X policies or standards

EDP AUDITOR

Job Title: Electronic Data Processing (EDP) Auditor
Department: Internal Audit
Reports To: Internal Audit Department Manager

Responsibilities and Duties in Information Security:

- Researches and writes audit reports indicating the existence of, effectiveness of, and need for changes in internal controls such as computer password access control systems

- Determines whether in-house information systems are in compliance with existing policies, standards, architectures, procedures and other requirements [*these include information security requirements*]

- Determines whether in-house information systems policies, standards, architectures, procedures, organizational structures and other management tools are consistent with good practices found elsewhere in the industry [*also known as determining whether Company X is consistent with a baseline set of controls or a standard of due care*]

- Determines whether information systems are designed, specified, configured, tested, operated, and managed in a manner that is efficient, reliable, secure, and consistent with organizational objectives [*as part of this activity, an EDP auditor performs risk assessments although they are often called EDP audits*]

- Acts as the eyes and ears of top management, performing internal audits that determine whether workers are carrying out their information systems related duties in accordance with top management intentions (including confrontation of unethical, illegal, and questionable practices) [*this includes evaluating the Information Security Department Manager's effectiveness and efficiency*]

- Determines whether workers have been assigned specific responsibility and accountability for information systems related controls, and as needed, makes specific recommendations for clarifying and assigning both responsibility and accountability

- Gathers statistically valid samples of the records at Company X, and analyzes these records to determine whether internal controls are operating effectively

- Periodically reviews compliance with information systems related contractual terms and conditions to ensure that both vendors and Company X remain in compliance with these same terms and conditions (software licenses, hardware leases, outsourcing contracts, etc.)

- Reviews proposals for outsourcing business activities to determine whether the benefits that the vendor alleges are likely to be achieved, whether the vendor is in a position to adequately handle Company X business, and whether controls would be compromised in the course of outsourcing the proposed activities

INTERNAL INTELLECTUAL PROPERTY ATTORNEY

Job Title: Internal Intellectual Property Attorney
Department: Legal
Reports To: Legal Department Manager

Responsibilities and Duties in Information Security:

- Monitors and evaluates new legislation, new regulations, and new case law in the jurisdictions where Company X does business, and provides management with recommendations dealing with appropriate responses [*these include information security and privacy issues such as the trans-border data flow laws in Europe*]

- Periodically reviews the liability of Company X management for a wide variety of threats including negligence, breach of fiduciary duty, and violation of various statutes, and provides recommendations as needed [*these reviews can uncover the need for additional internal controls to protect information assets, violation of privacy statutes, etc.*]

- Acquaints management with its legal responsibilities as well as its exposure to liability allegations under prevailing laws and regulations (Foreign Corrupt Practices Act, Fair Credit Reporting Act, etc.)

- Makes legal recommendations to prevent Company X from taking on undue risks as a result of its use of new technologies such as Internet commerce

- Informs appropriate Company X staff about the legal data retention requirements for various types of information as well as other requirements that apply to Company X

- Works with the Information Security Department Manager in the creation and enhancement of a data classification system and related controls that protect sensitive information owned by or in the custody of Company X

- Drafts and reviews legal documents related to the handling of intellectual property including confidentiality (non-disclosure) agreements, agreements not to compete, software licensing contracts, and outsourcing agreements

- Identifies and specifies ways that management can preserve and protect Company X intellectual property rights (copyrights, patents, trade secrets, trademarks, etc.)

- Supervises a staff member or outside service that monitors the information available on the Internet and through other public sources to ensure that no unauthorized use of Company X intellectual property is taking place [*defense of intellectual property rights assumes that violations are discovered*]

- Provide advice and guidance regarding periodic inventories of Company X intellectual property assets

- Assists with the legal aspects of negotiations that deal with either third-party intellectual property entrusted to Company X, or Company X intellectual property entrusted to third parties

- Represents Company X in all legal and regulatory proceedings related to intellectual property including court appearances, preparation of court documents, and applications to government agencies

- Acts as a liaison with district attorneys and other members of the criminal justice system when Company X is engaged in prosecutions and other legal actions

- Provides legal advice to investigations of alleged violations involving organizational policies as well as laws and regulations

- Provides strategic and tactical advice on civil and criminal proceedings, as well as internal disciplinary actions, associated with breaches of Company X policies as well as violations of various laws and regulations

- Provides internal management guidance on legal actions related to employee terminations, disciplinary actions, background checks, and related human resources matters

- Establishes and maintains a compliance program to ensure that the organization is in compliance with relevant laws and regulations, and that it can readily demonstrate this compliance [*in some industries, particularly those that are highly regulated, this is sometimes a separate organizational unit*]

HUMAN RESOURCES DEPARTMENT MANAGER

Job Title: Human Resources Department Manager
Department: Human Resources
Reports To: Operations Vice President

Responsibilities and Duties in Information Security:

- Working in conjunction with other members of the top management team, defines and periodically revises a code of conduct for all workers [*this code often addresses a number of information security issues such as use of Company X information for personal purposes, right to know certain information (such as workplace hazards), and freedom of speech*]

- Establishes, documents, and supervises the equitable application of a disciplinary process that has progressively more severe penalties for those who are not in compliance with internal policies, standards, and other requirements [*this can and should be used for information security policies, standards, and other requirements*]

- Establishes and supervises the use of a process for screening prospective workers to make sure that they are suitable employees prior to actually extending an offer of employment (or signing a consulting or contracting agreement) [*contingent offers of employment can be extended, if the offer may be withdrawn due to the discovery of previously undisclosed negative information*]

- Provides top management with observations about and suggestions for the evolution of organizational culture [*this area is sometimes called corporate culture rather than organizational culture; this task includes some information security issues such as the openness with which information flows between individuals*]

HUMAN RESOURCES CONSULTANT

Job Title: Human Resources Consultant
Department: Human Resources
Reports To: Human Resources Department Manager

Responsibilities and Duties in Information Security:

- Periodically reviews organizational culture and the ways that this culture supports or damages the accomplishment of business goals and objectives [*this culture review may uncover a problem with existing incentive systems, such that information security is compromised in favor of competing objectives*]

- Maintains the human resources database so that it accurately reflects the current status of all workers including full- and part-time employees, consultants, contractors, temporaries, and outsourcing firm personnel [*this database is increasingly being used as the source of input for computer access control systems*]

- Communicates all departures from Company X immediately to the Physical Security Department Manager, Access Control System Administrators, Systems/Network Administrators, Web/Commerce Site Administrators, Receptionists, Guards, and others with a need to know [*this will allow privileges to be revoked before fired or laid-off employees engage in vengeful acts*]

- Performs exit interviews for all employee departures, and during those interviews—or immediately afterwards—recovers Company X property in the possession of departing workers [*these include portable computers, palmtop computers, pagers, cellular phones, and company credit cards*]

- Checks the employment history, academic credentials, references, and other personal details associated with prospective workers (employees, contractors, and consultants) so that only appropriate people are working at Company X

- Performs special in-depth background checks prior to employment for those applicants seeking positions that entail access to sensitive Company X information, and/or provide powerful information systems privileges that could be used to disrupt or otherwise damage Company X business operations

- In conjunction with the Internal Intellectual Property Attorney, interprets privacy laws and regulations and submits suggested changes in internal systems and procedures to the Human Resources Department Manager as well as the Information Security Department Manager

- Prepares government reports indicating compliance with human resources laws and regulations such as affirmative action, trans-border data flows (privacy), and employee access privileges to their own records

- Administers worker counseling programs, short-term loan programs, and other employee benefits [*these will help prevent or alleviate problems that may, if not handled, later show up as computer crimes*]

RECEPTIONIST

Job Title: Receptionist
Department: Human Resources
Reports To: Human Resources Department Manager

[*A Receptionist is generally used to greet visitors in low security environments while Building and Facilities Guards are generally used for this purpose in high security environments; Receptionists can also be used to establish and maintain physically protected areas (like an executive suite) inside the outside perimeter maintained by Building and Facilities Guards.*]

Responsibilities and Duties in Information Security:

- Politely greets all people who are not authorized Company X workers (employees, contractors, consultants, temporaries, etc.), who seek to enter Company X offices, and then asks them to wait in the lobby until an escort takes them into a restricted access area [*if outsiders are permitted to have physical access to information and information systems, security will be noticeably degraded*]

- Signs for packages in the lobby and otherwise keeps delivery personnel and other third parties out of Company X offices unless they are escorted by an authorized Company X worker

- Recognizes all parties wishing to gain access to Company X buildings and facilities, and if the person is unknown, asks this person to provide proper identification before he or she is permitted access to restricted access areas [*this low security approach is for smaller offices that do not require picture ID badges to be worn at all times*]

- Notifies local police, local ambulance services, and local fire department as needed according to procedures defined by the Physical Security Department Manager [*computer crimes should be reported to criminal justice authorities only after the approval of the Internal Intellectual Property Attorney and the Information Security Department Manager have been obtained*]

- Immediately notifies the Physical Security Department Manager and other designated members of the Company X management team of any activity or condition that could reasonably be expected to lead to a loss for Company X (for example, smoking in areas where combustible materials are stored)

- Provides telephone operator services to connect callers with authorized Company X workers in a manner that is consistent with information security policies (without disclosing private or confidential information, such as the home telephone numbers of employees)

OUTSOURCING CONTRACT ADMINISTRATOR

Job Title: Outsourcing Contract Administrator
Department: Human Resources
Reports To: Human Resources Department Manager

Responsibilities and Duties in Information Security:

- Maintains an organized collection of all contracts with outsourcing firms, facilities management firms, and other third parties retained by Company X to perform services on an ongoing basis [*security requirements should be written into these contracts; see Chapter 17, "Outsourcing Firms" for further details*]

- Monitors the performance of outsourcing firms, facilities management firms, and other third parties to ensure that they meet the terms and conditions stipulated in the relevant contracts [*this includes receiving reports about the status of security and any incidents that took place*]

- Schedules periodic audits of outsourcing firms, facilities management firms, and other third parties to ensure that these organizations are living up to the terms and conditions specified in the relevant contracts

- Negotiates initial contracts, and renegotiates existing contracts when these contracts expire, with outsourcing firms, facilities management firms, and other third parties, to help ensure that essential Company X requirements are included in all contracts [*this would typically include service level agreements (SLAs), which in part should address security, such as how long will it take before an outsourcing firm will respond to a break-in by a hacker*]

- Establishes and periodically convenes advisory committees (made up of selected Company X employees) that provide advice regarding the use of outsourcing firms, facilities management firms, and other third parties [*the Information Security Department Manager would typically sit on these committees*]

- Performs due diligence investigations of outsourcing firms, facilities management firms, and other third parties that Company X is considering for the performance of critical Company X business activities [*this includes reference checks, review of financial condition, determination whether third-party staff have necessary knowledge and skills; see Chapter 17, "Outsourcing Firms" for an extended list of these efforts*]

- Establishes efficient and effective communications channels with staff at outsourcing firms, facilities management firms, and other third parties working on behalf of Company X [*the Contract Administrator may or may not be a liaison; these communications channels should include a computer emergency response team, also known as a CERT (see "Computer Emergency Response Team" on page 51 for a definition); these communication channels should also include privilege change processes, as well as problem reporting and resolution processes*]

IN-HOUSE TRAINER

Job Title: In-House Trainer
Department: Human Resources
Reports To: Human Resources Department Manager

Responsibilities and Duties in Information Security:

- In conjunction with the Information Security Department Manager, designs, develops, and measures the effectiveness of information security training and awareness material provided to new hires, employees, contractors, consultants, and others who have access to sensitive information or information systems

- Conducts orientation classes to familiarize newly-hired workers with the various departments within Company X, the roles and responsibilities of each department, and the organizational culture [*this class should let new hires know whom to contact in case there is an information security problem, how top management perceives information security (assuming they are serious), etc.*]

- Working with the Information Technology Department, provides ongoing information systems training so that workers can best utilize the available tools and technologies [*this activity is often outsourced to a training company, but nonetheless, users who know the technology will be able to spot problems such as virus infections and take appropriate action*]

- Researches new tools and methods for delivering training to Company X employees and makes suggestions for use of these new tools and methods as appropriate (these methods include computer based training or CBT)

- Periodically conducts needs analyses to determine what types of training workers need to accomplish organizational objectives [*in many cases, this activity will include a determination that workers need more information security training and awareness material*]

INSURANCE AND RISK MANAGEMENT DEPARTMENT MANAGER

Job Title: Insurance and Risk Management Department Manager
Department: Insurance and Risk Management
Reports To: Operations Vice President

Responsibilities and Duties in Information Security:

- Fosters an integrated risk management approach that prepares periodic reports showing the nature of Company X's exposure across departments such as Finance, Information Technology, Physical Security, Legal, and Human Resources

- Coordinates business contingency planning and information systems contingency planning efforts so that an integrated contingency planning effort addresses all areas critical to Company X's business

- Remains familiar with the latest mechanisms to transfer risk away from Company X and engages top management in a discussion about the suitability of these mechanisms where appropriate [*one example is insurance against Internet commerce credit card fraud*]

- Acts as a liaison with insurance companies for the determination of the adequacy of coverage, the acquisition of various types of insurance, as well as processing of claims [*insurance against information security problems such as credit card fraud would be handled by this manager*]

INSURANCE AND RISK MANAGEMENT ANALYST

Job Title: Insurance and Risk Management Analyst
Department: Insurance and Risk Management
Reports To: Insurance and Risk Management Department Manager

Responsibilities and Duties in Information Security:

- Based on risk assessments or EDP audit reports, determines the nature and extent of the perils faced by Company X in the information systems area including fraud facilitated by information systems and interruption of business activities due to information systems unavailability

- In conjunction with the Physical Security and Information Security Department Managers, monitors loss experience in the information systems area, including privacy violations, credit card fraud, and equipment theft

- Periodically reviews insurance coverage to determine whether Company X is adequately insured against information systems risks such as errors and omissions, business interruption, credit card fraud, identity theft, industrial espionage, equipment theft, and information systems sabotage

BUSINESS CONTINGENCY PLANNER

Job Title: Business Contingency Planner
Department: Insurance and Risk Management
Reports To: Insurance and Risk Management Department Manager

Responsibilities and Duties in Information Security:

- Researches and stays abreast of all major threats that could impact Company X's business activities including mergers/acquisitions, earthquakes, and changes in economic conditions [*this activity may also be performed by a strategic planner, and this research is important input to a risk assessment*]

- Assists with the development and refinement of conceptual and organizational structures (such as a business application criticality ranking criteria and a management escalation procedure) which ensure that Company X is prepared for various threat events

- Develops and maintains up-to-date and practical contingency plans which assist Company X in quickly restoring operations after an emergency or a disaster that affects centralized multi-departmental business resources, such as office buildings

- Develops methodologies and instructional material that assist Company X workers in preparing their own business contingency plans to deal with decentralized or single department business resources, such as a remote sales office

- Provides expert technical assistance related to contingency planning to departments throughout Company X who are preparing, testing, and updating their own contingency plans for decentralized or single department business resources

- Plans, executes, and reports to management on the success of a variety of tests to business contingency plans

- Coordinates business contingency planning efforts with the Information Systems Contingency Planner's activities

PUBLIC RELATIONS MANAGER

Job Title: Public Relations Manager
Department: Public Relations
Reports To: Marketing Vice President

Responsibilities and Duties in Information Security:

- Acts as a spokesperson or relay person for all news media communications including those occasioned by disasters, lawsuits, and interruptions in the provision of Company X products or services [*this would include hacker break-ins, information systems outages, and other information security problems*]

- Coaches and trains internal management staff so that they may appropriately represent Company X in professional society conferences, television shows, newspaper story interviews, and the like [*it is important that management not inadvertently disclose sensitive information, unwittingly make the organization look bad, or otherwise appear to be unprofessional*]

- Acts as the manager of the Internet Web Site Committee, and in this capacity leads others in the establishment of checks and balances to ensure that all postings to the Company X Internet web site are professionally presented and consistent with existing presentation standards

CHIEF FINANCIAL OFFICER

Job Title: Chief Financial Officer
Department: Accounting & Finance
Reports To: Chief Executive Officer

Responsibilities and Duties in Information Security:

- Establishes and maintains a system of internal controls that accurately keeps track of transactions and fairly represents the financial status of Company X [*these internal controls include information security*]

- Arranges the annual engagement of external auditors who examine the financial records of Company X [*the external auditors may provide a management letter that includes information security suggestions*]

- Establishes internal financial accounting systems that provide incentives for, and information about, the attainment of Company X goals and objectives [*a chargeback system for information systems usage would be one such system, but information security consulting and related services should not be charged back to user departments because this would discourage usage; in this respect the CFO is in charge of changing incentive systems, such as bonus structures, to encourage the achievement of an appropriate level of information security; see Appendix C, "Performance Criteria" for further discussion*]

PURCHASING AGENT

Job Title: Purchasing Agent
Department: Accounting & Finance
Reports To: Chief Financial Officer

Responsibilities and Duties in Information Security:

- Negotiates volume purchase agreements (VPAs) and other discount arrangements with software vendors, information content vendors, and other third parties in a manner that is practical from an operational standpoint, fully in keeping with applicable laws and regulations, and fully in compliance with the vendor's terms and conditions [*the Purchasing Agent can assist with software licensing and related information security matters*]

- Screens all major information, software, hardware, and telecommunications equipment purchases to ensure that these are in compliance with established internal standards (such as the Desktop Configuration Standard issued by the Information Technology Department) and to block those purchases that are not consistent with standards unless a waiver has been granted by the Purchasing Department Manager [*this will only be practical if local departments do not have the authority to independently purchase their own information systems hardware and software*]

- Makes sure that all necessary paperwork for major acquisitions has been prepared prior to generating a purchase order or otherwise making any commitment to a vendor [*this paperwork, for information systems acquisitions, could include a risk assessment as part of the systems development process*]

- Ensures that contracts with outsourcing firms, consultants, and contractors and other third parties include confidentiality agreements and other security requirements [*agreements not to compete may also be covered*]

CHIEF EXECUTIVE OFFICER

Job Title: Chief Executive Officer
Department: Executive Management
Reports To: Board of Directors

Responsibilities and Duties in Information Security:

- Establishes new organizational units and alters the functions performed by existing organizational units so that Company X can best respond to current and anticipated business needs [*this includes setting up an Information Security Department*]

- Directs others to establish and operate control systems that safeguard organizational assets from material loss and ensure that workers are following policies, standards, procedures, and other management directives [*the CEO is ultimately responsible for allocating sufficient resources for information security, as well as giving it the attention it deserves*]

- Directs others to establish and operate a system of accounting-related internal controls that accurately keeps track of transactions and fairly represents the financial status of Company X [*these internal controls include information security*]

- Reviews the decisions made by line managers to ensure that these decisions are consistent with both the business's strategic direction and internal control requirements

- Provides clearly evident support and encouragement for those working on critical business activities [*such as information security initiatives*]

- Sets the moral and ethical tone for Company X operations and as such is expected to operate with the utmost integrity in both business and personal areas

Chapter 13 REPORTING RELATIONSHIPS

This chapter covers the generally-accepted and frequently-encountered reporting relationships for an Information Security Department. The pros and cons of twelve options are explored and six reporting relationships are recommended. Because there are many places in the organizational hierarchy where an Information Security Department could be situated, you should review the list of pros and cons for each option, thinking about what is most important in your organization. I suggest that while you go through this chapter, you use a highlighter, pen, or pencil to indicate relevant objectives for the reporting relationship. You should then summarize these considerations in a memo, and after this memo is prepared, you will most likely be leaning in the direction of one of these reporting relationships. At that point in time, a clear and well-justified proposal for an Information Security Department reporting relationship can be formulated.

A good place to start a discussion about reporting relationships is to find a common characteristic of nearly every successful Information Security Department's organizational structure. In successful organizational structures, the Department reports high-up in the management hierarchy. Reporting directly to top management is advisable for the Information Security Department Manager because it fosters objectivity and the ability to perceive what's truly in the best interest of the organization as a whole, rather than what's in the best interest of a particular department (such as the Information Technology Department). A highly-placed executive in charge of information security will also be more readily able to gain management's attention, and this in turn will increase the likelihood that the Information Security Department will obtain the necessary budget and staffing resources. An Information Security Department that reports high up on the management ladder will also be more readily able to force compliance with certain requirements such as a standard specifying consistent implementation of certain encryption technology.

In a few progressive organizations, being located high on the management ladder means that the Information Security Department Manager is a Senior Vice President who reports directly to the Chief Executive Officer (CEO). This is, for example, the organizational structure now found at a well-known credit card company. Having an Information Security Manager who reports directly to the CEO may also be appropriate for a short while until major improvements in the information security area have been made. This temporary reporting structure clearly communicates that information security is important and worthy of top management's attention.

Nonetheless, for a medium to large-scale organization, the most common reporting structure involves one or two levels of management between the Information Security Department Manager and the CEO. In general, the smaller the number of intermediate levels of management, the greater the strategic importance of the information security function. It is important that the distance between the CEO and the Information Security Manager be minimized. As famous management theorist Peter F. Drucker has observed, every time you insert another level of management in an organization's hierarchy, the noise is doubled and the message is cut in half. An information security function already has a difficult time delivering its new and different message to top management, and having a long line of intermediate managers will only make this worse.

Just who the middle managers between the Information Security Department Manager and the CEO should be is the topic of a great many squabbles. One perspective on this troublesome question is opportunistic, looking to see who these individuals are, rather than what their assigned duties happen to be. With this perspective, you would choose sympathetic executives who understand the need for information security and are willing to fight for the necessary funds when departmental budgets are prepared. If you are establishing an information security function for the first time, or if a major reorganization is underway, you should seriously think about which middle managers would best serve as the conduit for messages sent to the CEO. Other desirable attributes are:

- openness to new ideas

- clout with top management

- respect in the eyes of a wide variety of employees

- comfort and familiarity with basic information systems concepts

- willingness to take a stand for those things that are genuinely in the long-term best interest of the organization

The ideal middle level manager should report directly to the CEO, or as high up on the organizational hierarchy as possible. The manager's organizational unit will also need a credible day-to-day relationship with, or a strategic tie-in with, the information security function. For example, a Risk and Insurance Management Department would have such a tie-in, but an Assembly Line Operations Department most often would not. The candidates are many, but some common choices are the Executive Vice President Administrative Services, the Legal Department Manager (Chief Legal Officer), and the Chief Information Officer (CIO).

This chapter makes reference to six diagrams labeled Option 1 through 6. These six reporting relationships are explored in that sequence. After that, six other options, which are not as frequently encountered, are discussed. The six diagrams are illustrative of real-world organizations and are not in any way meant to be hypothetical or normative. Throughout this book, I have attempted to be descriptive rather than to propose a new paradigm, and in that respect, because these options are based on real-world experience, you can be assured that any one of these six initial options could be effective within your organization. The diagrams are also meant to convey an indication of good practice on which you can rely.

Option 1: Information Technology

In the Option 1 diagram, you will note that in this organizational structure the Information Security Department reports to the Information Technology Department (the latter may also be called the Data Processing Department, the Information Services Department, or the Management Information Systems Department). Here the Information Security Department Manager reports directly to the Chief Information Officer (CIO), or the Vice President of Information Systems. In this option, you will find the most common organizational structure. Various statistical studies show that over 50% of organizations use this reporting relationship. This option is desirable because the manager to whom the Information Security Department Manager reports generally has clout with top management, and understands (in broad and general terms) the information systems technological issues. This option is also advantageous because it involves only one manager between the Information Security Department Manager

and the Chief Executive Officer (CEO). The option is additionally advisable because the Information Security Department staff, on a day-to-day basis, must spend a good deal of time with the Information Technology Department staff. In that respect, this option is convenient. Nonetheless, this option is flawed because it includes an inherent conflict of interest. When confronted with resource allocation issues, or when required to strike a tradeoff, the CIO is likely to discriminate against the information security function. Other objectives such as cost minimization, user friendliness, or time-to-market with a new product or service will likely take precedence over information security. Another drawback of this option involves the implied conclusion that information security is strictly a technological issue, which clearly it is not. Although common, this organizational structure is not as desirable as several of the other options, and for that reason is not particularly recommended.

Note that the Option 1 diagram does not have information security reporting to a Computer Operations Manager, the Management Information Systems Manager, the Information Resources Manager, or some other manager who in turn reports to the CIO or the Vice President of Information Systems. This one additional level of middle management can make a world of difference for the Information Security Department. The CIO is dealing with the business uses of information systems, for example, using these systems to achieve strategic advantage. At the same time, the Computer Operations Manager is dealing with the bits and bytes of everyday computer operations and related technical matters. The CIO is more removed from the technology and is therefore better able to make appropriate trade-offs between security and competing objectives like response time. But, because that's what he or she knows and is measured by, the Computer Operations Manager in many cases will favor response time, ease-of-use, and other technical objectives rather than information security. Having an additional level of management also increases the likelihood that messages sent from the Information Security Department to the CEO will be corrupted in transit (the so-called "whisper down the lane problem"). Other reasons not to pursue this organizational structure are covered in "Option 8: Help Desk" on page 103.

Option 1: Information Security Reports to Information Technology Department

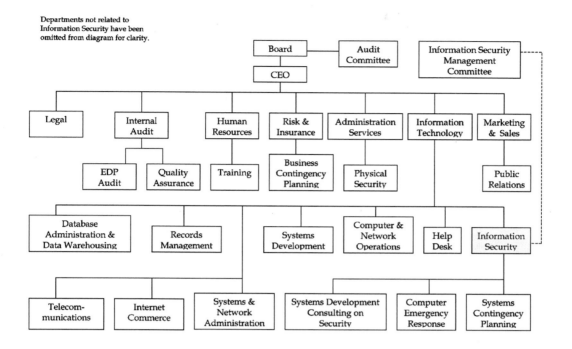

In the Option 1 diagram, you should note that the Information Security Department Manager also has a dotted line reporting relationship with the Information Security Management Committee. Although they are highly recommended, both this dotted line relationship and the Committee can be omitted for smaller organizations. A Committee of this nature is a good idea because it provides a sounding board, a management direction setting body, and a communication path with the rest of the organization. A mission statement for this Committee can be found under "Information Security Management Committee" on page 52. Because this Committee is relevant no matter where the Information Security Department reports, it has been shown on all six diagrams. In fact this Committee is relevant to every one of the options described in this chapter. A drawback of using a committee like this is that it may take longer to get management approval for certain initiatives, but the approval that is obtained is likely to be more lasting and more widely distributed throughout the organization.

Option 2: Security

Another popular option, which again is not necessarily recommended, involves the Information Security Department Reporting to the Security Department. In this case, the information security function is perceived to be primarily protective in nature, and therefore comparable to the Physical Security Department as well as the Personnel Security & Safety Department. Where this organizational design prevails, you may occasionally find the Information Security Department is instead referred to as the Information Protection Department. Shown in Option 2 diagram, this approach is desirable because it facilitates communication with others who have both a security perspective and related security responsibilities. This may help with incident investigations as well as reaching practical solutions to problems like laptop computer theft (which involves a combination of physical and information security). This option is also desirable because it brings a longer-term preventive viewpoint to information security activities, which in turn is likely to lower overall information security costs.

Option 2: Information Security Reports to Broadly Defined Security Department

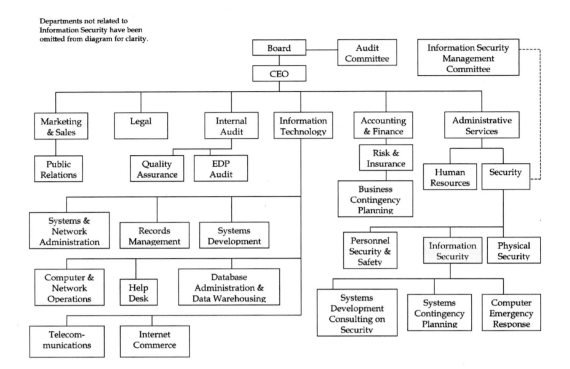

Departments not related to Information Security have been omitted from diagram for clarity.

Nonetheless, there are some problems with this structure. Although the information security and physical security functions may at first seem to be philosophically aligned, there is a significant cultural difference between the two. For example, information security staff see themselves as high-tech workers, while physical security staff see themselves as participants in the criminal justice system. These cultural differences may cause some information security specialists to feel that it's not appropriate to be managed by a specialist in physical security, which will most often be the background of the Security Department Manager. This option is moreover undesirable because, at most firms, the budget for physical security has not increased much over the last few years, but the budget for information security has rapidly escalated; by combining these two departments under the Security Department umbrella, top management may underestimate the resources that the information security function will need. Option 2 is furthermore undesirable because the Security Department Manager will often lack an appreciation of information systems technology, and so may be a poor communicator with top management. This option is furthermore ill-advised because it involves two middle managers in the communication path between the Information Security Department Manager and the

CEO. To make it still less appealing, this option is likely to indirectly communicate that the Information Security Department is a new type of police; this perspective will make it more difficult for the Information Security Department to establish consultative relationships with other departments. On balance, this organizational structure is acceptable, but not as desirable as some of the other diagrams described.

Option 3: Administrative Services

Another way to do things, which is a significant improvement over both Option 1 and 2, is shown in the Option 3 diagram. Here the Information Security Department reports to the Administrative Services Department (which may also be called Administrative Support). In this case, the Information Security Department Manager reports to the Administrative Services Department Manager or the Vice President of Administration. This approach assumes that the Information Security Department is advisory in nature (also called a *staff function*), and performs services for workers throughout the organization, much like the Human Resources Department. This option is desirable because there is only one middle manager between the Information Security Department Manager and the CEO. The approach is also advisable because it acknowledges that information and information systems are found everywhere throughout the organization, and that workers throughout the organization are expected to work with the Information Security Department. This option is also attractive because it supports efforts to secure information no matter what form it takes (on paper, verbal, etc.), rather than viewing the information security function as strictly a computer and network oriented activity.

In many cases, depending on who fills the Administrative Services Vice President position, this option suffers because the Vice President doesn't know much about information systems technology, and this in turn may hamper his or her efforts to communicate with the CEO about information security. This option may also be ill-advised for those organizations that could severely suffer, or even go out of business, if major information security problems were encountered. An Internet merchant (a so-called "dot-com" firm) fits this billing. For these firms, this option doesn't give information security the prominence it deserves, nor does it give it the strategic and long-term focus that information security requires. Thus, with this option, the Information Security Department may be subject to more cost-cutting pressure from top management than it would with Option 4 or 5. On balance though, for organizations that are not highly information intensive, such as a chain of restaurants, this is a desirable and recommended option.

Option 3: Information Security Reports to Administrative Services Department

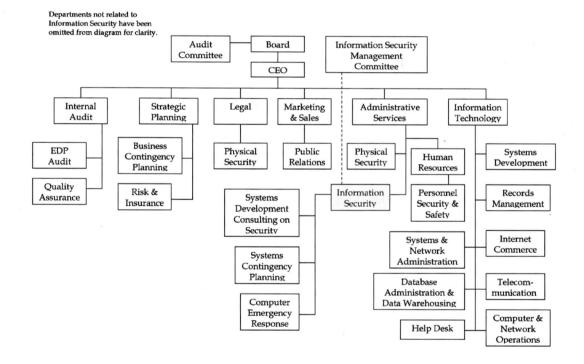

Option 4: Insurance & Risk Management

The Option 4 diagram shows how the Information Security Department can report to the Insurance & Risk Management Department. With this approach, the Information Security Department Manager would typically report to the Chief Risk Manager (CRM) or the Vice President of Risk & Insurance Management. This option is desirable because it fosters what is often called an integrated risk management perspective. With this viewpoint, a centralized perspective prioritizes and compares all risks across the organization. The application of this idea typically involves assessing the extent of potential losses and the likelihood of losses across all functional departments including Information Security, Physical Security, Legal, Internal Audit, Customer Relations, Accounting & Finance, etc. The intention is to see the big picture and be able to allocate resources to those departments and risk management efforts that most need these resources. You are strongly urged to foster the integrated risk management viewpoint, even if the current or proposed organizational structure doesn't reflect it, because information security will often be shown to be a serious and largely unaddressed problem area deserving greater organizational resources and greater management attention. Beyond integrated risk management, this option is desirable because it involves only one middle manager between the Information Security Department Manager and the CEO.

The CRM is also likely to be prevention oriented, adopt a longer-term viewpoint, and is able to engage the CEO in intelligent discussions about *risk acceptance* (doing nothing), *risk mitigation* (adding controls), and *risk transfer* (buying insurance). A CRM is also likely to be comfortable thinking about the future and generating scenarios reflecting a number of different possibilities, including information security scenarios such as a denial of service (DOS) attack. The CRM, however, is often not familiar with information systems technology, and so may need some special coaching or extra background research from the Information Security Department Manager to make important points with the CEO. Another problem with this approach is that its focus is strategic, and the operational and administrative aspects of information security (such as changing privileges when people change jobs) may not get the attention that they deserve from the CRM. Nonetheless, on balance this is a desirable option and is recommended for organizations that are information intensive such as banks, stock brokerages, telephone companies, and research institutes.

Option 4: Information Security Reports to Insurance & Risk Management Department

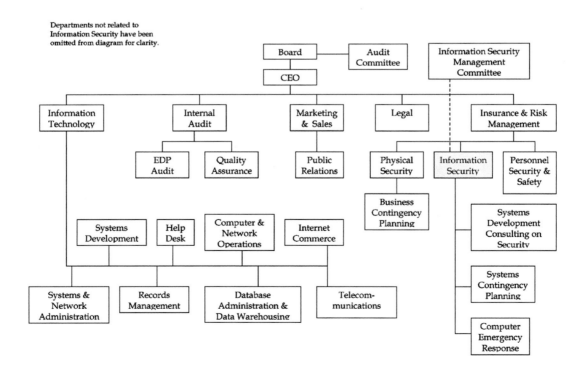

Option 5: Strategy & Planning

In the Option 5 diagram, you will find still another possible organizational structure found in the real world. Here the Information Security Department reports to the Strategy & Planning Department. In this case, the Information Security Department Manager reports directly to the Vice President of Strategy & Planning. This option views the information security function as critical to the success of the organization. This option would be appropriate for an Internet merchant (a so-called "dot-com" enterprise) or a credit card company, both of which are critically dependent on the success of the information security function. This option is desirable because it involves only one middle manager between the Information Security Department Manager and the CEO. It is thus just one step down from the option mentioned at the beginning of this chapter, where the Senior Vice President of Information Security reports directly to the CEO.

Option 5 is desirable because it underscores the need for documented information security requirements (policies, standards, procedures, etc.) that apply to the entire organization. Like Options 3 and 4, this reporting structure also acknowledges the multi-departmental and multi-disciplinary nature of information security tasks

such as risk analysis and incident investigations. This option is also advisable because the Information Security Department works with others that share a scenario-oriented view of the world (they often ask "what if…" questions). Another desirable aspect of this approach is that it implicitly communicates that information security is very importantly a management and people issue, not just a technological issue.

This same advantage can be a disadvantage if workers in the Information Technology Department consider the staff in the Information Security Department to be management-oriented, and out of touch when it comes to the technology (of course, the work of the Information Security Department can clearly communicate that this is a misperception). One problem with this approach is that the focus is strategic, and the operational and administrative aspects of information security (such as changing privileges when people change jobs) may not get the attention that they deserve from the Vice President of Strategy & Planning. On balance though, this is an advisable reporting relationship for the information security function, and should be something that the Information Department Manager is considering for the long-run even if he or she is not proposing it today.

Option 5: Information Security Reports to Strategy & Planning Department

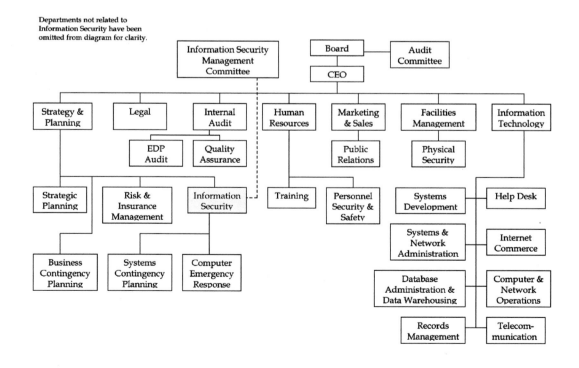

Option 6: Legal

The Option 6 diagram shows an unusual but nonetheless viable and recommended organizational structure. In this case the Information Security Department reports to the Legal Department. This option correctly emphasizes that information is the asset of primary concern, not information systems. This option thus places great emphasis on copyrights, patents, trademarks, and related intellectual property protection mechanisms. As they should, contracts—such as non-disclosure agreements (NDAs) and outsourcing agreements—will also get great attention with this organizational structure. With this option there is also great emphasis on compliance with laws, regulations, and ethical standards (like privacy). Information security is increasingly mandated by law, regulated, and affected by ethical standards, so Option 6 is really an organizational structure for the future. If your organization happens to be in a highly regulated industry, such as credit bureaus or defense contractors, then this organizational structure could be appropriate today. This option is desirable because access to top management is provided through only one middle manager—the Legal Department Manager, sometimes called the Chief Legal Officer (CLO). This manager is often quite articulate and credible and often a desirable carrier of Information Security Department messages to the CEO. This reporting structure is also advisable because the members of the Legal Department are comfortable with, and spend a lot of time developing, documentation such as policies and procedures; and documentation showing that the organization is in compliance with the information security standard of due care is increasingly important.

On the downside of Option 6 is the potential overemphasis on compliance, with the potential consequential under emphasis on other aspects of information security, such as access control administration. This organizational structure might also inadvertently lead to the Information Security Department doing compliance checking work, which presents a clear conflict of interest (as explained in "Option 7: Internal Audit"). Compliance checking should be performed by an Internal Auditing Department, not the Information Security Department. On balance though this organizational structure has much to recommend it, and will probably be encountered in an increasing number of organizations in the years ahead.

Option 6: Information Security Reports to Legal Department

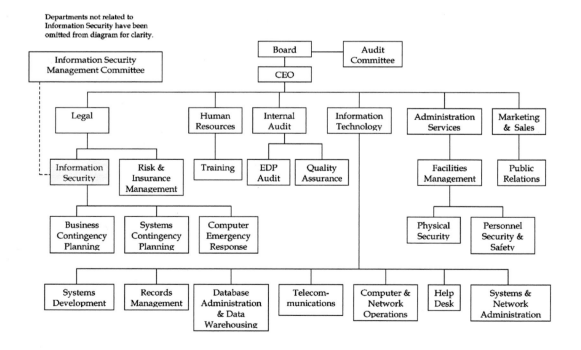

Option 7: Internal Audit

Although I have seen it in the real world, the Information Security Department should definitely not report to the Internal Audit Department. This is why you will not find a diagram for this option. In this case, the Information Security Department Manager reports to the Internal Auditing Department Manager. An examination of the mission statement for the Internal Audit Department (see "Internal Audit Department" on page 47 for details) reveals that Internal Audit is charged with reviewing the work done by other units, including the Information Security Department. If the Information Security Department were to report to the Internal Audit Department, a conflict of interest would exist. Internal Audit would be tempted to exaggerate the good work of the Information Security Department so that the Internal Audit Department as a whole would look good. A controls-oriented Chief Internal Auditor may also be tempted to allocate more resources to an Information Security Department than are realistically warranted, and this in turn could create an undue security burden for the rest of the organization as well as a backlash that could take years to overcome. Reporting to the Internal Audit Department may also be contra-indicated because Internal Audit often has adversarial relationships with other departments, and the perspectives that go along with those relationships could be unwittingly transferred to relationships between the Information Security Department and other departments. To foster smooth working relationships, an Information Security Department should instead be considered advisory in nature, and not a new type of auditor. The Internal Audit Department Manager may also lack sufficient technical expertise to understand what the Information Security Department is doing, and this may make it hard to convey messages from the Information Security Department Manager to the CEO. On the other hand, one advantage of reporting to the Internal Audit Department is that the Internal Audit Department Manager has a controls perspective and will at least in theory support what an Information Security Department is trying to do. Another reason in favor of reporting to Internal Audit reflects the tremendous clout that this group has with top management and the Board of Directors. Nothing in this paragraph is meant to discourage the Information Security Department from establishing a close and mutually-beneficial working relationship with an Internal Audit Department, and such a good working relationship is characteristic of firms with successful information security efforts.

Just because there is no direct reporting relationship to EDP Audit (or Internal Audit for that matter), doesn't mean it isn't a good idea to have a dotted line reporting relationship to the Audit Committee on the Board of Directors. This dotted line relationship is intended to be a periodic reporting relationship as well as a safety valve. Information Security can provide quarterly reports about the status of information security to the Audit Committee. If the Committee doesn't like what they are hearing, they can then redirect the efforts of top managers. Likewise, if top management is relatively unreceptive to the Information Security Department's point of view, Information Security can take its concerns to the Audit Committee. This dotted line reporting relationship doesn't currently exist in many organizations, but there are many efforts now underway to establish this type of relationship. Because it's unusual, this dotted line relationship has been deliberately omitted from the six diagrams that go along with this chapter.

Option 8: Help Desk

Another option involves having the Information Security Department report to the Help Desk Department. In this case, the Information Security Department Manager reports to the Help Desk Department Manager. As is the case with reporting into the Internal Audit Department, this option was not presented in a diagram because it is not advised. A Help Desk Department is a lower level technical group that does not get much top management attention or respect. Likewise, the Help Desk Department generally does not command many resources, and this scarcity of resources may be carried over into the Information Security Department. If the Information Security Department reported to the Help Desk Department, there would be at least two levels of middle management between the Information Security Department Manager and the CEO, and this could further hinder the acquisition of adequate resources. Another reason not to establish an organizational structure like this involves the Help Desk Department's customer-focus and service-orientation. While this may at first be perceived to be a desirable characteristic, it may also force the Information Security Department to opt for quick response, ease of use, and other objectives besides a high level of security. It could, nonetheless, be advantageous to report to the Help Desk Department in terms of mobilization after a break-in, for example, when it comes time to get a computer emergency response team (CERT) into action. This is because a Help Desk Department is on the front lines, and is often first to hear about a problem. This reporting structure could also be beneficial because the Help Desk

Department's trouble ticket system could be directly tied into logs of information security problems. Analysis of these logs could provide the Information Security Department with important insight into problems as they are occurring. On balance though, this reporting relationship, like reporting relationships to other lower level departments, is strongly discouraged. Similar remarks could be offered for organizational designs involving the reporting of an Information Security Department into other subgroups within the Information Technology Department. Examples include the Computer Operations Department, the Systems Development Department, and the Records Management Department.

Option 9: Accounting & Finance through I.T.

Another option involves the Information Security Department reporting to the Accounting & Finance Department through the Information Technology Department. This option is not recommended and is therefore not shown in a diagram. This very traditional organizational structure is a reflection of the early days of information systems where, at least in the commercial world, the computer was applied largely to accounting and finance tasks. The uses of computers and networks have expanded dramatically over the last few decades, and so the Information Technology Department should report higher in the organizational ladder, not through the Accounting & Finance Department. This option is undesirable for the reasons mentioned under "Option 1: Information Technology" (notably trade-offs with competing objectives). This option is furthermore undesirable because the Information Security Department would be buried deep in the organizational hierarchy, and would be therefore unlikely to get the resources and top management attention that it needs. While the Information Security Department is a staff (advisory service) department like the Accounting & Finance Department, it is growing much more rapidly than the Accounting & Finance Department. Integration with the Accounting & Finance Department may thus conceal this rapid growth rate from top management, which in turn could lead to under-funded information security efforts. Reporting to the Accounting & Finance Department may also cause the needs of the Information Security Department to be lost within, and overshadowed by, the needs of the Accounting & Finance Department. If the Information Security Department is combined with other activities in the Accounting & Finance Department, top management is likely to see the information security function as a back-office operation, and not a strategic issue worthy of

top management attention. Reporting through the Accounting & Finance Department appears to some people to be advisable because the Accounting & Finance Department Manager is controls-oriented, but this in many cases does not compensate for the other deficiencies. In fact, reporting to the Accounting & Finance Department may put additional pressure on an Information Security Department to cut costs, a move that would pay-off in the short-run but that could spell serious problems in the long-run.

Option 10: Human Resources

Still another possibility for the Information Security Department is reporting to the Human Resources Department. Because this option is not recommended, it has not been shown in a diagram. This relatively rare organizational structure places emphasis primarily on the people side of information security, and down plays the technological side of information security. There is a certain synergy that could be achieved when the Information Security Department is part of the Human Resources Department; this comes from both groups developing policies that must be followed by workers throughout the organization. For example, the Human Resources disciplinary process is used to deal with those who are not in compliance with information security policies. If the Human Resources Department also handles the staff training function, this synergy can be magnified. Nonetheless, this is generally considered an ill-advised organizational position for the Information Security Department because the Human Resources Department Manager often knows very little about information systems, and is therefore most often not a credible conduit for communications to top management. Another reason not to have the Information Security Department report to the Human Resources Department is that little of the day-to-day work of information security involves the people working in Human Resources. With this option, there is therefore much less of an opportunity for cross-pollination between groups than if the Information Security Department is part of the Information Technology Department. Reporting to the Human Resources Department is furthermore not advised because the strategic importance of the information security function is likely to be lost amidst the clerical, legal, and regulatory work that the Human Resources Department performs. This option is furthermore discouraged because it leads the rank-and-file staff to consider the information security function as something administrative rather than strategic in nature.

Option 11: Facilities Management

Yet another option for the Information Security Department involves reporting to the Facilities Management Department (sometimes called Buildings & Grounds). Since this option is not recommended, no diagram has been provided. This is a rare but occasionally encountered organizational structure that views the information security function as something similar to the building guards who help prevent burglary. With this organizational structure, the Information Security Department is seen by top management as an asset protection function much like the Physical Security Department. This option thus implies no strategic importance whatsoever for the information security function. This option implies that the information security function is basically a low-level administrative activity, which it has been in days gone past, but which it is no longer in progressive organizations. This option is not a good idea because it typically involves an extra layer of management between the Information Security Department and top management (Option 3, where the Information Security Department reports to the Administrative Services Department, is preferable). This option is furthermore ill-advised because the Manager of the Facilities Management Department is often unfamiliar with information systems technology, and thus may not be a credible conduit of messages to top management. This option is furthermore discouraged because it encourages rank-and-file staff to view the information security function as another type of police, and this may interfere with efforts to establish consultative relationships within your organization.

Option 12: Operations

The last option to be discussed involves reporting to the Operations Department. Under this approach, the Information Security Department Manager reports to the Chief Operating Officer (COO). This approach assumes that information security is a line management responsibility, and a topic that all department managers must consider in their day-to-day activities. While it is desirable to emphasize management's responsibilities, it is also true that information security is a staff function, a function that provides advice and guidance to other departments. This organizational structure says nothing about the important staff nature of information security work, and as a result, I do not recommend it. Separately, information security is a strategic information handling function, not a production-oriented function (as is the case with assembly line manufacturing). The information security staff thus has little in common with workers who are in operating divisions of the organiza-

tion. Information security specialists are often highly-paid technical professionals, while operations personnel typically earn less and are often not technical. The people in an Operations Department are typically focused on getting the work done, and anything that might impair their production objectives is likely to suffer. Thus this organizational structure is likely to result in information security objectives that have been compromised in the interests of operating objectives like low cost, time-to-market with a new product, and meeting customer commitments. Although this organizational structure has only one manager between the CEO and the Information Security Department Manager, the COO in many cases will be physically-oriented rather than information-oriented. As a result, he or she may not be a credible or articulate conduit to carry messages from the Information Security Department to the CEO.

Summary

The Information Security Department at many organizations has been an unwelcome stepchild, handed back and forth between various groups, none of which felt as though they were its proper home. Consider what happened to the information security function at a major commercial bank. The function originated in the Internal Audit Department. Over the course of twenty years it migrated to the Information Technology Department, primarily because the Internal Audit Department lacked in-depth technical expertise. Because security objectives were in conflict with other Information Technology Department objectives like ease-of-use and low costs, the information security function was then moved to the Insurance & Risk Management Department. While there were some synergies in the contingency planning area, the financial mindset of the Insurance & Risk Management Department was decidedly different from the technical and operational mindset of the Information Security Department. As a result, the Information Security Department was moved again to the Physical (Industrial) Security Department, where it remains to this day. At this bank, the Physical Security Department was considered to be a good home for the Information Security Department because the asset protection objectives are similar, and because top management acknowledges that Physical Security is a necessary business activity like Accounting and Marketing. This example shows that the Information Security Department often moves around the organization, and that today's reporting relationship may be quite different from tomorrow's. This story should also encourage you to suggest reporting relationship changes that would further the evolution of the information security effort at your organization. While these organizational realignments are unquestionably disruptive, they are often very much worth the effort.

Smaller organizations will want to have a part-time Information Security Coordinator or Information Security Manager (see Chapter 18, "Smaller Organizations" for more details). Small to medium sized organizations will often require at least one full-time person, and medium to large organizations will often require several full-time information security staff (see Appendix A, "Staffing Levels" for specific staffing ranges by organizational size). Since so few people are involved, in smaller organizations, the formal designation of a separate department will be considered to be unwarranted. But for all other organizations, no matter where the information security function happens to report, it is desirable to designate a separate department that has been formally recognized by top management. Words such as "Committee," "Project," and "Team" are discouraged because they don't convey a sense of permanency. Certainly the word "Department" is not essential—you could use whatever word the organization's staff is accustomed to, such as "Division," "Unit," "Group," "Section," or "Regiment." To designate a separate department is advisable because it is in keeping with general business practice whereby special needs are recognized with unique departments. For example, credit card processing companies typically have a Fraud Department that is separate and distinct from both the Information Security Department and the Physical Security Department. This is because credit card fraud is a serious problem that requires the use of different tools, techniques, and perspectives. To have a separate department for the information security function is to subtly communicate that this area is expected to grow, that this area deserves special consideration, and that this area is different. All these messages can be helpful to an information security effort.

While this chapter has examined the placement of an Information Security Department in the traditional notion of a hierarchical organizational structure, there are certainly other ways to do things. One common alternative is called a *matrix* or *networked organizational structure*, where individual workers have more than one immediate manager. In this case, the Information Security Department Manager reports to two or more managers. If you work with an organizational structure like this, you can combine the considerations mentioned above to come up with an appropriate spot for the Information Security Department.

Having more than one conceptual structure to clearly define roles and responsibilities is also advisable. This is different than the networked organizational structure. Here a traditional hierarchical organizational structure can be combined with other models like the owner, custodian, user (O/C/U) approach. The latter approach involves the placement of all workers into at least one of these three categories, and then defines the information security roles and responsibilities of each. For those organizations that are relatively sophisticated in the information security area, the use of more than one conceptual model is advisable. This is because it helps to create checks and balances that will ensure that critical information security tasks are getting done. More than one conceptual model is additionally desirable because it helps to foster a widespread appreciation that each worker who comes in contact with information or information systems has specific information security duties. The O/C/U model is discussed at length in Chapter 15, "Ownership."

Chapter 14 CUSTOMIZATION FACTORS

Although this book attempts to make it as easy as possible for you to prepare roles and responsibilities documentation, it is not possible to provide a single set of documents that will be uniformly applicable to all organizations. You will need to make adjustments to these templates so that the result is responsive to the needs of your organization. In an attempt to sensitize you to the changes that will need to be made, this chapter provides a list of customization factors. For each of these factors, I have provided at least one specific action step that you can take to best learn how this factor affects the organization's information security roles and responsibilities documentation. The factors listed are shown in rough order from most to least important.

Local Laws and Regulations

Certain countries have laws and regulations that dictate management activities with respect to information security. For example, western European nations generally take the privacy of citizens very seriously. Organizations in Western Europe must register all databases containing personal information with a government agency. In other countries, such as the United States, organizations are bound by no such laws or regulations. Where these and other legal and regulatory requirements exist, you will need to add the appropriate words to the job descriptions of the Information Security Manager and Intellectual Property Legal Counsel. Separately, if your organization has operations in more than one country, you will need to consider the laws of each of these countries. For example, trans-border data flow (TBDF) laws affect the types of data that can be legally transmitted from one country to another. Likewise, various country-specific statutes affect the exportability of encryption software and hardware. The best way to learn about information security laws and regulations is to discuss these matters with the Intellectual Property Legal Counsel at your organization.

Industry Category

Certain industries have unique information security requirements. For example, in the commercial banking industry in the United States there is a requirement that contingency plans be documented and periodically audited by government officials. As another example, the existing standard of due care in the United States dictates a higher level of privacy protection at consumer credit bureaus than it does at mailing houses that distribute junk mail, even though both organizations handle much the same information. In some industries, such as with commercial banks, the overall reputation of an organization will be highly dependent on customer confidence—and this confidence could be seriously damaged by publicly-known information security incidents. In other industries, such as high-tech firms, the impact may not be so serious. If you do not already know about them, the best way to learn about these industry differences is to talk to both the Director of Marketing and the Director of Strategic Planning at your organization. This type of information may also be available from industry associations such as the American Bankers Association.

Criticality to the Business

If information security is critical to a business, then the roles and responsibilities documentation should incorporate supplementary organization-specific job description duties. One example of a supplementary duty could involve the Information Security Department Manager periodically meeting with the Strategic Planning Department Manager. If top management at a particular firm didn't think that information security function was all that critical, a periodic discussion with the Strategic Planning Manager would not appear in the Information Security Department Manager's job description. Separately, three attitudes are reasonably good indicators that top management thinks information security is critical. First, top management may see the information security as an essential function, something necessary for continued organizational survival. Second, top management may see the information security function as a competitive necessity, as something they must do to keep up with the competition. Third, top management may see the information security function as a strategy for achieving competitive advantage, as a way to distinguish themselves from the competition. If any of these three attitudes prevail at your organization, then information security will receive considerably more top management attention, and the job descriptions may warrant additional duties. The best way for you to learn about management's perspective is to interview a few executives. This attitude information can be obtained from top management at the same time that you are conducting initial interviews for an information security roles and responsibilities project.

Chapter 7, "Review and Approval," provides a list of questions that can be asked when conducting these interviews with top management.

Line or Staff

This customization factor takes the notion of "criticality to the business" one step further by examining the way that management sees the information security function relative to other business activities. In most organizations, an Information Security Department will perform a *staff function*. In other words, the Information Security Department provides administrative support and expert advice that may be accepted or rejected by top management. As a staff group, the Information Security Department does not have the power to impose its perspective on the rest of the organization. This role is distinctly different when the Information Security Department is viewed as a *line function*. Line functions are concerned with the basic objectives of the organization, and line functions have decision-making power. In the vast majority of organizations, the information security function is still a staff function, but this is slowly changing. Organizations such as an Internet electronic bill payment service would probably be well advised to define the information security function as a line function. This is because the business is critically dependent on information security; if the level of information security is inadequate, then the whole business can quickly disappear. If an Information Security Department performs as a staff function, then it typically will be lower on the management hierarchy than it would be if it were recognized as a line function. Likewise, if it's a staff function, the Information Security Department will generally not be directly involved with decision-making processes such as application change control. However, if it's a line function, it may be directly involved and may be able to force certain actions if the result would be improved security. As you might expect, the roles and responsibilities documentation for a staff function will generally be less detailed than it would be for a line function.

Organizational Culture

Organizational culture may be influenced by religious, spiritual, ethical, or other regional cultural norms. Organizational culture, in turn, will affect how roles and responsibilities will be documented. For example, certain organizations have recently adopted the notion of "open book management" as a fundamental way to run their business. Open book management suggests that all information, including financial data previously reserved for top management, should be available to all workers (of course, certain exceptions are made for information protected by law, such as staff medical treatment expense claims). This radically open approach to information security places a very different slant on the roles and responsibilities of an information security unit. Relative to other organizations, an organization with an open book management approach will have an information security unit that spends considerably more time on information integrity and availability, and considerably less time on information confidentiality. The best place to find information about organizational culture is to read the organization's code of conduct, its mission statement, its in-house newspaper, its recent press releases, and its annual reports. If a new hire orientation course has recently been compiled, this too could contain some information about organizational culture. You could also consult with the Director of Human Resources and the Director of Strategic Planning to get a better sense for the organizational culture relevant to information security.

Scope of Information Security Function

Certain organizations have a very narrowly defined information security function, while others have a broadly defined function. (In an effort to make life easier for you, this book contains a broadly defined function because deleting functionality is always easier than adding it.) Exemplifying the difference in scope, in some organizations you will find an information security unit responsible for contingency planning whereas in other organizations the unit will not have this responsibility. In some organizations, compliance checking is the information security function's responsibility, whereas in others it is not (for conflict of interest reasons, I advocate performance of this work by the EDP Audit Department). You need to clearly understand which functions management expects information security to perform before you write up roles and responsibilities documentation. The best way to learn about these scope matters is to consult with the Managers in charge of related Departments including EDP Audit, Physical Security, Quality Assurance, Legal, Human Resources, and Information Systems. In these interviews, you can go down the list of activities described in Chapter 11, "Mission Statements."

Information Security Effort Sophistication

Certain organizations are just starting to get their information security efforts underway, while others have had an information security function in place for a decade or more. The extent of an organization's information security experience (which often correlates directly with the degree of sophistication) will affect the activities performed by an information security unit. For example, newly-minted information security units may not have the power and clout to prevent a new application system from being moved into production processing mode, even if this application system has inadequate controls. On the other hand, a well-established and well-respected information security function may have the power and clout to act in this way. Some of the words in the templates provided in this book may need to be diluted for a new information security function. For example, instead of "dictate virus screening standards" the documentation that you prepare might say "provide advice on virus screening standards." The best way for you to learn about the power and clout that the information security organization previously had and currently has is to examine all prior internal documentation dealing with information security roles and responsibilities. The level of sophistication is also discussed in Chapter 10, "Current Documents," which deals with the different documents where roles and responsibilities could be mentioned.

Size of Organization

Large organizations generally will have need for considerably more roles and responsibilities documentation than smaller organizations. This is simply a matter of complexity, since the larger organizations have so many more people and activities to coordinate than smaller organizations. This complexity can be seen, for example, in the computer hardware and software procurement process. In a large organization, the purchase of a computer may be subjected to several screening processes (internal network interface standards, information security standards, etc.). In smaller organizations, these screens are typically absent or abbreviated. The best way for you to learn about the role and responsibility implications associated with various processes is to trace the processes through to conclusion. Time constraints often don't normally allow you to do this, so a discussion with various participants may suffice. Each participant should be asked what they do and what other participants are a part of the process. A set of questions that may help in this regard is provided in Chapter 7, "Review and Approval." Another approach, which is not recommended, is to circulate the draft templates in this book without any significant background investigation. In this case, you are simply saying to the recipients, "Alter this to suit our needs." The reason why this is not recommended is that the recipients will resent doing the work that should be done by you, and the level of participation will vary widely from person to person. Some investigation will then be needed anyway to fill the gaps

in the material received as well as to compensate for the internal politics that will have been provoked by the material distributed for comment.

Outsourcing

The complexity of information security roles and responsibilities documentation will be expanded whenever an organization has automated systems that are linked with other organizations (extranets, electronic data interchange networks, third-party credit card processing firms, third-party data entry firms, facilities management firms, outsourcing firms, etc.). The greater the number of business functions that are performed by these third parties, the more the need to formalize the information security roles and responsibilities, usually in the form of legal contracts. The greater the number of different third parties, the more the interactions between each of them will need to be documented. If any of these organizations are located in different countries or significantly different legal jurisdictions, then still more attention will be needed to precisely define the third-party roles and responsibilities involved. This topic is taken up in greater detail in Chapter 11, "Mission Statements," and in Chapter 17, "Outsourcing Firms." The best way for you to gather information about outsourcing is to review existing legal agreements. You may also wish to speak with the legal counsel involved in drafting these agreements as well as the Chief Information Officer.

Intended Audience

The intended audience for your information security roles and responsibility documentation should also be considered before writing gets underway. If only managers will see the documentation, then a number of lower-level and detailed considerations may in certain circumstances be eliminated. If the audience is familiar with high-technology terms, then certain definitions and explanations will not be necessary. If the audience is made up of immigrants or doesn't speak English well (or if it's not familiar with the language used to publish roles and responsibilities statements), then the material may need to be considerably simplified. There are certainly many other audience-related adjustments that need to be made; these observations were offered only as examples of how the materials found in this book will need to be adjusted. You probably already know a good deal about the audience at your organization, but if you want to know more, the In-House Trainer (who often reports to the Human Resources Department Manager) is a good reference point.

Separation of Duties

The organizational structure described in Chapter 11, Chapter 12, and Chapter 13 has been designed so that it already includes separation of duties. In other words, checks and balances have been incorporated into these job descriptions. For example, the access control systems established by an Access Control System Administrator should be periodically reviewed by an Internal Auditor. If you delete a number of the suggested positions, or delete a number of the duties for the suggested positions, you must take special care so as not to create a potential lapse of internal control. The best way to ensure that problems are not created with a streamlined organizational structure is to clearly define the essential areas that must have separation of duties. These include, but are not limited to, development vs. testing of new application systems, management authorization vs. systems administration of access control systems, and design of encryption systems vs. administration of the keys for encryption systems. After these essential areas are clarified, you can go back and make sure that the streamlined organizational structure has not inadvertently created a potential lapse of internal control.

Cross-Training and Backup

Another factor to consider when streamlining the recommended organizational structure defined in Chapter 11, Chapter 12, and Chapter 13 is the need to have at least two trained and immediately-available information security experts. Suppose that the primary internal expert was to take a job with a competitor on one week's notice—would your organization have a difficult time replacing him or her? In this case, what would happen if a hacker broke in just after this person left the organization? The best ways to ensure adequate backup staffing is to do ample cross-training in the information security area, and to accurately document the day-to-day procedures of people working in the information security area. The cross-training and documentation will also enable immediate response to security problems even though one of the staff members is away on vacation, taking sick leave, or attending an off-site conference. In terms of the organizational structure suggested in Chapter 11, Chapter 12, and Chapter 13, having adequate backup does not imply changes to the suggested roles and responsibilities. What is affected is the number of people who hold certain job titles such as Systems Administrator.

Formatting

Of course, you will also need to make various editorial changes to the templates provided in this book. Generic organizational names (like "Company X") will need to be replaced with the actual organizational unit names. Company logos and graphics will need to be added. Type fonts and margins will need to be changed. You will likewise also need to reformat and repackage the material to suit the organization's internal documentation standards. For example, if a management approval date appears at the bottom of each job description found within your organization, a similar date should be applied to the material extracted from this book.

Chapter 15 OWNERSHIP

Just as the old-fashioned concept of "computer security" erroneously focused on the technology when the real issue was the information itself, so too have many businesses erroneously assumed that information security was solely the responsibility of the Information Systems Department. More and more responsibility for information security day-to-day decisions is now being passed to the user community—where it should have been all along. One of the most popular ways of clearly specifying the responsibility for user department managers, end-users, and those who have the day-to-day possession of information is through the roles of owners, custodians, and users. This chapter describes these roles and responsibilities as well as how best to implement a related organizational structure. These roles and responsibilities are often documented in an information security policy manual (a description of information security documents, including a policies manual, can be found in Chapter 10, "Current Documents"). You are additionally directed to Chapter 11 and Chapter 12, which contain mission statements and job descriptions for those working in the information security area.

Owners

Owners (sometimes called sponsors or stewards) are employees who have been assigned responsibility for the proper management and handling of a particular type of information on behalf of Company X. An Owner's responsibilities may not be delegated to external service providers. Owners do not legally own the information in question; they instead make decisions on behalf of Company X, which legally owns the information.

Owners must understand how the information they are charged with overseeing is used inside and outside of the organization. They must also understand the potential problems associated with this type of information. These include unauthorized disclosure, unauthorized modification, as well as unauthorized deletion, plus the consequences that might take place when these and other problems occur. For this reason, Owners are most often managers in charge of departments that use or otherwise manage the information in question.

If an owner has not been officially assigned, the creator of the information (if this person is a Company X employee) must act as an interim Owner. Thus an employee working at his workstation becomes an

interim Owner if he compiles a new type of information that will be used for production information systems at Company X. Production information systems are systems that are repeatedly used in the normal course of business, such as an information system that evaluates the credit of potential customers.

Often a new information type is created when existing information types are combined. If any of the existing information types were previously in the possession of Company X, the Owners of these existing information types should determine who the Owner of the new type of information should be. If the sources of the new information are entirely external to Company X, or if the internal sources had no previously designated Owner, then the Chief Information Officer must promptly designate an Owner for the new type of information.

Owners are responsible for classifying Company X information based on its sensitivity and criticality. Generally there will be a scale for sensitivity, and in an increasing number of organizations, a scale for criticality as well. Typical positions on a sensitivity scale are *confidential* and *secret*. Typical positions on a criticality scale are *highly critical* and *deferrable*. Criticality scales can also be defined based on the number of hours, days, or weeks that may elapse before the information or information service must be restored.

The categories that information is placed into, in terms of sensitivity and criticality, will imply certain basic control measures. For example, *secret* information may need to be encrypted when not in use. These requirements should be specified in policies and other information security requirements. Owners do not develop these requirements. The Information Security Department is responsible for developing and revising these requirements. Owners do, however, select an appropriate sensitivity (and perhaps criticality) level for the information that they have been charged with managing.

Beyond the controls automatically implied by certain levels of information sensitivity and criticality, owners are also responsible for selecting supplementary information security measures. These supplementary security measures are often needed because the basic requirements for most Company X information at that same level may not adequately protect the information in question. For example, the information in question may need to be handled in a manner that is in compliance with privacy regulations issued by a government agency. To select supplementary information security measures, Owners may be asked to place a rough value on the information in question.

Owners are responsible for approving all requests for access to the information for which they are the designated owner. This access typically takes the form of privilege levels that are associated with a business application system such as a human resources database system. The Director of the HR Department may be the Owner of human resources information, in which case he or she would decide who should be able to examine, modify, delete, and otherwise use this human resources information. Note that the Owner does not usually handle the administration associated with access controls and privileges. This is instead handled by Systems Administrators or Access Control System Administrators (see Chapter 12, "Job Descriptions" for the specific duties of each).

Owners will most often employ standard forms and standard rules for making these access decisions. The development and refinement of these forms and standard rules are the responsibility of the Information Security Department. For the Owners, this access control decision-making is a relatively straightforward select-from-predefined-categories process, but it is more complicated these days because consultants, contractors, temporaries, outsourcing firm staff, and business partners need to have access.

Owners must be employees, and preferably members of the management team. This is because the decisions are basic asset management and protection decisions that may not be delegated. Management has a fiduciary duty to protect assets, including information, and this duty implies that they must be personally involved in these decisions.

Custodians

Custodians are workers who have been entrusted with the safekeeping and secure processing of information that has been provided by either internal Company X Owners or third parties (such as business partners). Safekeeping can take many forms such as regularly backing-up information. This safekeeping includes the provision of secure processing facilities, traditionally involving the administration of a password-based access control system. To securely process information

entrusted to them, Custodians most often will need to provide general security systems that can be used for multiple data types.

Custodians are responsible for complying with the instructions provided by information Owners. Custodians are also responsible for complying with organization-wide information security requirements that are not specific to certain types of information (a policy regarding the prompt installation of operating system upgrades is an example). Custodians are responsible for the day-to-day handling of information that has been entrusted to them, including help desk assistance, in a manner that observes all of these instructions.

Custodians must provide Owners with periodic reports showing all people who have been granted access to the information in question. Custodians must also provide Owners with technical advice about the ways to best protect the confidentiality, integrity, and availability of the information that they have been charged to safeguard and process. This technical advice is supplemented by the advice provided by the Information Security Department.

Custodians can be employees, contractors, consultants, temporaries or outsourcing firm staff. The job of Custodian is often outsourced to people who act as Systems Administrators, Computer Operators, and Data Control Specialists (the latter may, for example, manage data stored at an off-site location). The distinguishing characteristic of a Custodian is the fact that he or she is in possession of the information and that he or she runs the systems that handle the information.

Users

Users are workers who have been granted access to Company X information and/or information systems to do their jobs. If they do not currently have authorization to access information and/or information systems, they must first request and receive permission from the relevant information Owner. Users are forbidden from using any Company X information for purposes other than those expressly authorized by the information Owner or by their immediate manager. Likewise, Users must not disclose the Company X information to anyone without the prior authorization of the information Owner.

Users must follow the information systems control requirements specified by Custodians and by the Information Security Department. An example of a Custodian-specified control would be the need to change passwords in response to a suspected break-in.

An example of an Information Security Department specified requirement would be the need to construct a fixed password of at least ten characters that is made up of both numeric and alphabetic characters. The most important control requirements issued by the Information Security Department can be found in the information security policies manual.

Users are responsible for the secure handling of information in their immediate possession. For example, users must manage their desktop and portable computers in such a manner that unauthorized access does not take place. This includes keeping both a password-based access control package and a virus detection package enabled on these computers. Users must also securely handle sensitive information in other forms, such as shredding hardcopy reports rather than throwing them in the trash. Users are additionally responsible for safeguarding all storage media containing sensitive information (CD-ROMs, floppy disks, magnetic access cards, etc.).

Users must report all errors and anomalies in the information to which they have been given access to the Owner and/or their immediate manager. Users must also report all suspected information security problems or violations to the Information Security Department.

Users can be full- or part-time workers, so long as they have business need to have access to Company X information. Users can be temporaries, consultants, contractors, or outsourcing staff. Users typically have a wide variety of job titles including Department Manager, Receptionist, and Data Entry Operator. The privileges of users must be turned off when they no longer have a business need for such access (for example when they leave Company X).

Summary

Within this three-way division of responsibilities there is a great deal of scripted already-existent structure. This structure is intended to minimize the possibility that people in any one of these categories would act in a way that would jeopardize security, or make a decision that would jeopardize security. The burden on Users is deliberately light in large measure because there are so many of them. This approach minimizes the costs of and productivity impacts of information security measures. Another reason to have few responsibilities for Users is that the people in this category are often the least interested in information security across all three categories.

Before your organization adopts an Owner/Custodian/ User (O/C/U) assignment of roles and responsibilities, it should have several basic elements of an information security infrastructure in place. These include:

- a data classification system—for sensitivity, and perhaps for criticality as well

- a list of basic information systems controls that go along with each of the categories appearing in the data classification system

- a set of policies that define basic information security requirements for managers, technical staff and users

- already installed computer-based information access control mechanisms

- a documented process for requesting and approving access to information systems

Note that the O/C/U roles and responsibilities are in addition to job descriptions, departmental mission statements, reporting relationship diagrams and other documentation defined in this book (see Chapter 10, "Current Documents" for a list of other documents). While this three-way assignment of responsibility can often simplify discussions and allow projects to proceed in an expedited manner, it should be adopted after these other role and responsibility documents have already been endorsed by management and integrated into the existing organizational structure.

The O/C/U roles and responsibilities are information-oriented whereas job descriptions, departmental mission statements, and reporting relationship diagrams are duties oriented. This means that the two approaches are complimentary and not redundant. Information security is such a new and still embryonic field that every organization needs multiple models for roles and responsibilities to minimize losses to both information and information systems. Table 15-1 on page 114 summarizes the duties for the O/C/U roles.

Table 15-1: Summary of Owner, Custodian, and User Duties

Role	Duties
Owner	• Understand major risks to, and all internal uses of, a type of information • Select information sensitivity and criticality levels for this information • Specify supplementary control measures to protect this information • Approve user access requests to the information • Review user access control lists to determine which should lose privileges
Custodian	• Safeguard and maintain physical possession of information • Follow Owner's instructions for information handling and processing • Provide Owner with periodic reports showing all who have access • Make technological and procedural suggestions to Owner • Maintain secure access facilities for the information in question • Enforce controls specified by the Owner
User	• Request access to information and systems from the Owner • Refrain from using information or systems unless authorization is obtained • Employ secure access facilities provided by Custodian • Comply with controls specified by both Company X and the Owner • Report errors and anomalies in the information to the Owner • Report vulnerabilities and violations to Information Security Department

Chapter 16 PRODUCT VENDORS

An important and evolutionary shift of information security responsibility from user organizations to vendor organizations is now underway. The problem is that nobody seems to be talking about it, much less planning for it. This shift impacts Information Security Department mission statements, job descriptions, staffing plans, project plans, outsourcing contracts, systems architectures, and many other aspects of the information security management process. This chapter defines that shift and makes some suggestions about appropriate next steps.

Traditionally, information systems security has been primarily the user organization's responsibility. In this context, reference is made to the entire user organization as separate and distinct from vendors such as systems integrators, systems outsourcing firms, software publishers, and hardware manufacturers. In this context, when the words "user's responsibility" appear, I am not talking about user departments, such as Accounting or Marketing, but instead making reference to the entire user organization. In the past, user organizations were responsible for performing risk assessments, identifying and implementing the controls needed to address their organization's unique risks, as well as administering and maintaining these controls. While these responsibilities will not disappear, in the future user organizations will orchestrate a team made up of both inside staff members and a variety of outside organizations (contractors, consultants, temporaries, outsourcing firm staff, etc.). Beyond these people, these outside team members will include information systems product vendors, software vendors, and information content publishers.

Not only is the law increasingly holding vendors and publishers responsible for incorporating adequate security into their products, but the technology itself is now making it possible for vendors and publishers to provide new and refined security mechanisms as standard functionality. Consider the toll fraud area related to private branch exchanges (PBXs). Carriers are being subjected to an increasing number of lawsuits alleging that they did not provide adequate controls, adequate training, or adequate notice of potential security problems. The recent introduction of new anti-fraud offerings, such as expert systems that examine calling patterns, clearly shows that vendors are feeling pressure from user organizations and responding to it. In addition, vendors like SPRINT are now offering

insurance to help prevent devastating toll fraud losses. Telephone companies are also forming working groups such as the Toll Fraud Prevention Committee to help address this problem.

Another example involves unauthorized software copying. It is, in the long run, totally inappropriate for software publishers to hold user organizations responsible for looking after the publisher's copyrights. A host of new products now allow vendors to control unauthorized copying, executing, forwarding, and printing of software (these vendors include Gradient Technologies and QVtech). Vendors will soon release their software accompanied by anti-copying security mechanisms, including built-in license management systems. This means that the copyright infringement audits performed by the Information Industry Association (formerly the Software Publishers Association and the Business Software Alliance) are a temporary phenomenon. Several years from now, these user organization software license audits will be unnecessary. As a result, user organizations will need to spend much less time educating end-users about software licensing, releasing no-copying policies, performing compliance audits, and the like. In large measure, information systems will be required to take care of their own security.

Yet another example can be found in the information publishing field, specifically involving electronic document viewers. These products allow multimedia documents to be published and viewed without requiring the user organization to be in possession of a copy of the software used to create the documents. Examples include Novell's Envoy and Adobe's Acrobat. These systems increasingly incorporate security measures allowing the publisher to define and enforce the rights it wishes to convey. For example, electronic documents can be made read-only, or users can be permitted to append annotations, or permitted to print the documents. These security features are incorporated into the document itself, and are not a function of the underlying operating system, an access control package, or some other software. Whatever rights publishers choose to convey will be automatically enforced.

Nobody knows more about the complexities of their products and services than vendors and publishers. It only makes sense that they should fundamentally be responsible for the security of their systems and content. Of course, how a user organization installs, manages, maintains, and otherwise utilizes a product is still an important factor. You will not see the elimination of user organization responsibility for security, particularly when contributory negligence is involved. Instead, the field is evolving towards a more balanced situation where responsibility is shared in a manner commensurate with the actions that can be taken by the organizations involved. Vendors and publishers will be responsible for incorporating adequate security mechanisms into their products, for training user organizations in the usage of these mechanisms, and for making changes to maintain adequate security in light of new vulnerabilities. User organizations will continue to be responsible for the way they deploy and use these products.

If your organization is not already using these and other new tools whereby systems manage their own security, an investigation into their applicability should be soon undertaken. These and related products may hold the promise of significantly reducing the need for user training as well as administrative support for information security. For example if unauthorized software copying was prevented technologically, the need to train users not to make copies would be significantly reduced. To ensure the consistent application of security measures throughout an organization, and to reduce reliance on people who may not fully support information security, vendors will continue to automate many security activities that in days gone past were handled by humans. User organization management will also appreciate that it is in their own best interests to automate as many information security tasks as possible, so that reliance on individual users is reduced. When information security tasks are automated, they can readily be turned into packaged products, and then they can be transferred from user organization to both vendors and publishers.

If your organization is relying on end-user goodwill and understanding, to the extent that current technology allows it, an automated solution would be a preferable alternative. If your organization has been feeling like it has an undue burden for security, that vendors have not been shouldering their share, it is high time to enlist the cooperation of vendors so that a more equitable and more sustainable balance can be achieved. For example, when outsourcing contracts are up for annual review, the information security related responsibilities can be more clearly defined and perhaps some can be transferred from a user organization to an outsourcing vendor. (See Chapter 17, "Outsourcing Firms" for further details.) When new arrangements are made with

consultants, contractors, and temporary support firms, information security responsibilities can be clarified and at least partially transferred to these outsiders.

In many cases, when a consultant, contractor or temporary is hired, that individual may sign a confidentiality agreement, but the individual does not typically go through new hire orientation. Likewise, that individual does not usually go through an information security training class. This is inconsistent since both new hire orientation and an information security class are generally required for employees. To have some members of a team receive this training and some not is likely to lead to misunderstandings, and perhaps serious security lapses as well. All members of the information security team need to receive comparable training as well as receive clearly written descriptions of their responsibilities. The cost of providing this training and the cost of clarifying these responsibilities are now inconsequential relative to the risks that a user organization faces if it does not adopt this consistent approach.

A further example of the steps that your organization can take to establish a more equitable distribution of information security responsibilities includes leveraging the organization's buying power. If the user organization has some significant buying power, preference can be given to those vendors who have products that automatically take care of their own security. This preference can manifest as a volume purchase agreement (VPA) or some other sort of long-term commitment. Requests for proposals (RFPs) can likewise be written so that vendors are required to take on a greater portion of the responsibility for information security. Similarly, organizations can complain to their vendors and make formal requests that additional security responsibilities be adopted by these same vendors.

Because they don't represent much potential revenue, smaller organizations will not, generally, be able to engage vendors in a serious discussion about sharing information security responsibility. These organizations will simply be presented with a license agreement or some other contractual document that they will be required to sign, that is if they wish to purchase the vendor's products or services. For these organizations, it will be sufficient to simply understand just what the license agreement or other contractual document says and to take action in light of this understanding. Far too many organizations don't pay attention to these documents. It is these same organizations that may find themselves in trouble with the Information Industry Association, and the targets of a copyright violation audit. It is these same organizations that may find themselves in a stockholders' lawsuit alleging management's failure to adequately protect corporate assets.

This new-shared responsibility could be documented in renegotiated organizational-license contracts, outsourcing firm contracts, and consulting engagement contracts. The job description responsibilities shown in Chapter 12 are a good place to get ideas for responsibilities that could be off-loaded to vendors. Vendors in most instances have greater technical expertise and more extensive business contacts than most user organizations, so on balance the overall level of information security is likely to be improved. For further discussion about the pros and cons of using vendors, see Chapter 17, "Outsourcing Firms."

Chapter 17 OUTSOURCING FIRMS

Chapter 16, "Product Vendors," addressed the ways in which third-party information security roles and responsibilities are evolving. If you have not yet read that chapter, I suggest that you go back and read that chapter before proceeding. This chapter discusses the risks of outsourcing an information security effort and covers the specific information security roles and responsibilities that an outsourcing firm could be called upon to perform. After that, you will find a section on the topics to be covered in a contract with an outsourcing firm and a discussion of the due diligence that should be performed before an outsourcing firm is used to handle information security. All of these ideas can be used as input to the preparation of a contract, an agreement, or a memo of understanding. Throughout the chapter, the term *outsourcing firm* is used generically and includes Internet Service Providers (ISPs), Application Service Providers (ASPs), Internet web site or commerce site hosting firms, facilities management firms, and other similar organizations.

Risks of Outsourcing

The decision to outsource an information security function, in whole or in part, should not be taken lightly. Far too many organizations are dazzled by the potential cost savings, the alleged access to third-party expertise, and the potential to refocus internal operations on activities that they consider to be strategic or critical to the business. While these are important objectives, management at your organization should not rush into an information security outsourcing deal without first having performed a risk assessment pertaining to the outsourcing effort.

Unlike other risk assessments, a risk assessment dealing with an outsourcing effort should not be performed by the Information Security Department. Instead, the work should be performed by an outside consultant (who doesn't work for a potential outsourcing firm) or a member of the Internal Audit Department staff. For this type of a risk assessment, the Information Security Department is likely to have a conflict of interest. Fearing that they may lose their jobs, members of the Information Security Department may paint an unrealistically negative and gloomy picture of the consequences associated with outsourcing information security work.

Although statistical studies, such as those from The Outsourcing Institute, indicate the popularity of outsourcing is unquestionably increasing, there are a number of serious risks associated with this new business arrangement. These risks fall into a number of broad categories including:

- Sensitive information may be disclosed to outsiders who should not have access to such information (this may take place because the outsourcing firm also processes the business transactions of competitors)

- Critical or strategic information may be lost due to an error or omission on the part of outsourcing staff

- Access privileges may be exploited by outsourcing staff to perpetrate fraud, to violate privacy, or to commit other crimes and abuses

- Important customized controls that your organization developed to handle unique business circumstances may be abandoned because the outsourcing firm has a standardized approach that must be used by all of its customers

- Operational control may be lost because the outsourcing firm staff doesn't understand the complexities of internal systems at your organization

- Knowledge about outsourcing staff activities may not flow to your organization and this can in turn lead to a situation where your organization is unduly at risk (for example a high security server may have been improperly configured but this fact may not be revealed until the system has been compromised)

- Mechanisms that allow your organization to control the outsourcing firm staff may be insufficient and/or ineffective, and as a result, your organization may be unable to get the outsourcing firm to provide essential security products or services

- Technical experts at your organization may leave because they think the interesting or important work is now being done by the outsourcing firm

- Technical experts at your organization may leave, in which case the organization would have nobody who can realistically evaluate whether or not the outsourcing firm is doing a good job in the information security area, nobody who can credibly determine whether the information security representations of the outsourcing firm are in fact true, and nobody who can credibly manage the work of the outsourcing firm staff

- In-house technical staff may now have the impression that management doesn't care about them, only the bottom line, and this may lead to new or exacerbated loyalty problems

- Outsourcing may foster an attitude among top managers that information systems are no longer critical to the success of your business, that they are non-strategic, and this may encourage budget cuts, reduced management attention, and related problems

- Outsourcing staff may not be motivated because your organization is just one of many organizations demanding service

- Inflexible outsourcing staff may refuse to take on additional information security tasks that are genuinely needed, but have not been explicitly defined in the outsourcing contract

- A tightly-defined contract and outsourcing arrangement may impose a level of inflexibility that makes it exceedingly difficult for your organization to rapidly respond to new products or services offered by a competitor

- A long-term contract may lock your organization into a relationship that fundamentally doesn't meet the needs of your organization and can't be broken without considerable financial hardship

- Total costs for outsourcing may be higher than necessary because your organization has been too strict in its definition of information security requirements, thereby eliminating or diluting one of the prime motivations for outsourcing (saving money)

- Intruders may exploit unknown information security exposures introduced because your organization did not sufficiently understand what security was needed, and thus the outsourcing contract did not specify adequate security requirements

- Quality of service may erode because the outsourcing firm doesn't use sufficiently competent or technically trained staff to handle information security

- Quality of service may be reduced because the processes involved are rapidly evolving or especially complicated and therefore better handled in-house

- Service from the outsourcing firm may degrade because the involved workers are complacent and don't appreciate how their work impacts your organization

- Communications problems with the outsourcing firm staff may delay appropriate responses to information security problems like hacker intrusions

- Outsourcing firm staff may be unavailable when heroic personal contributions would be forthcoming from in-house staff (for example after a disaster)

- Awkward modifications to internal control processes at your organization may need to be made so that the work can fit into the outsourcing firm's internal processes

- Poor performance on the part of the outsourcing firm may cause financial losses, reputation losses, or business disruptions to be suffered by your organization

- Significant outsourcing staff overtime and additional consulting support may be required because a large number of adjustments are necessary to properly process your organization's transactions

- Outsourcing firm management may have unanticipated disagreements with your organization management due to fundamentally different information security views, goals, policies, and procedures

The performance of such a risk assessment should take place before an outsourcing vendor has been arranged and before a contract has been signed. The risk assessment can help define which tasks are suitably outsourced and which should remain in-house. For example, certain managers at your organization should maintain ultimate decision-making responsibility for all information security requirements. Likewise, while an outsourcing firm or consultant can assist by preparing draft information security policies, an internal manager should be the one who ultimately makes the decision about the content and wording of these same policies.

Similarly, while an outsourcing firm or consultant can propose the specifics of an information security architecture, an internal manager should be the one who ultimately determines which requirements will go into that same architecture.

In the course of clarifying the scope of the services that should be outsourced and those which should remain in-house, you should also define the nature of the relationship between your organization and the outsourcing firm. For instance, you should clarify which decisions will be left to the outsourcing firm, and which will be reserved for your organization. If a hacker breaks into your organization's internal network, should the outsourcing firm initiate the response via a computer emergency response team (CERT), or should your organization do that? If automated systems detect the fact that a specific user has unusual computer usage patterns, should the outsourcing firm revoke that user's privileges or should the revocation be left to your organization? If electrical power is interrupted in the data center, should the outsourcing firm determine when operations get moved to a remote site, or should that decision be reserved for in-house management?

Many outsourcing firms have not paid enough attention to security. Managers at customer organizations often think, "But of course information security duties will be handled, because after all, this outsourcing firm is a professional organization that seems to have its act together." You need to clearly articulate and diplomatically challenge this assumption via the risk assessment process. The risks of making this or a similar assumption need to be clearly articulated, and many questions need to be asked of those who are promoting the outsourcing effort. As a side effect of this questioning, managers involved in this discussion will be reeducated about the many services that an internal Information Technology Department, an Internal Audit Department, and an internal Information Security Department can perform.

There is some merit to the old adage, "If it ain't broken, don't fix it." In many cases management does not fully realize the cost and disruption associated with the movement of the information security function from in-house personnel to an outsourcing firm, or from one outsourcing firm to yet another. This disruption and cost can be prohibitive if the organization is frequently changing outsourcing firms and not seeking to establish a long-term mutually rewarding relationship with an outsourcing firm. Consider the relationships that staff in an internal information security group have developed over the years with others throughout the organization. These relationships are not transferable to an outsourcing firm—the outsourcing firm must start from the beginning with each of the people involved.

In a similar manner, you should challenge management's claims of special access to certain expertise that would come along with an outsourcing contract. The alleged experts may leave the outsourcing firm before the contract is signed, or the experts—even though they remain employed at the outsourcing firm—may never work on the organization's affairs. There are less expensive ways to gain access to expertise that are much less disruptive than outsourcing. These include retaining expert consultants or contractors, or even hiring additional full-time information security staff. Consultants and contractors are often used as a way to obtain specialized technical services such as penetration attacks. Keeping some information security staff as employees at your organization is highly desirable because it helps maintain a continuity of operations that is less likely to be encountered when outsourcing firms are used.

With the exception of legal problems, nothing related to information security seems to get top management attention as much as *reputation risk*. Top management is often very concerned about the organization's image, specifically about the way the organization is perceived by various constituencies such as customers, suppliers, and business partners. The person performing an outsourcing risk assessment should be sure to examine the impact on the organization's reputation as well as the personal reputation of the managers who are promoting the outsourcing effort. Discussions with management likewise should be sure to emphasize the reputation risk associated with an outsourcing effort.

While one or two information security outsourcing firms may be manageable, having more than this may quickly lead to breakdowns in communication. As the number of parties involved in dealing with information security increases linearly, the number of required communications between these same parties increases exponentially. Having many outsourcing firms will also require a greater commitment to training. For these and related reasons, many organizations are considering consolidating their outsourcing vendors with a smaller number of companies. These concerns argue for signing-up with an outsourcing company that handles many information security tasks, perhaps including physical security tasks.

Typical Areas to Outsource

The typical areas where information security activities are outsourced include:

- performing risk assessments such as penetration attacks

- developing information security architectures, policies, and other security requirements

- preparing requests for proposals and reviewing vendor responses

- integrating systems from various vendors into a turn-key system

- training in-house staff

- network intrusion monitoring

- vulnerability identification and notification

- systems security administration.

While management may be excited about the prospect of using an outsourcing firm, it is your responsibility to ensure that your organization has precisely defined all the information security roles and responsibilities that the outsourcing firm is slated to perform. This will be difficult, if not impossible, if your organization has not clarified its own internal information security roles and responsibilities. Accordingly, the prospect of outsourcing some or all of the information security work can, in fact, be a prime motivator for management—forcing them to get into action to specify what information security activities need to be performed. Only after all of these activities are defined can management then definitively determine which of them should be performed with in-house personnel and which should be performed with outsourcing firm personnel.

A spreadsheet or a word processing program table can be used to get the big picture about all of the information security activities that should be performed. The information security roles and responsibilities could, for example, be listed on the rows, and organizations that have one or more information security responsibilities could be listed on the columns. When preparing such a spreadsheet or word processing table, you can think of

the outsourcing firm's relationship to your organization as something comparable to an employee's relationship to a department head. This means that the level of specificity brought to an outsourcing contract or an outsourcing performance measurement system should be comparable to the level of specificity found in a job description. For your convenience, a list of job description related roles and responsibilities can be found in Chapter 12, "Job Descriptions."

In general, activities to protect physical assets (such as nighttime guard patrols) are much more likely to be outsourced than activities to protect information assets (such as computer access control administration). Mission-critical functions such as crisis management and contingency planning should generally be managed by full-time employees, although outside specialists can, and often do, assist with these activities. Those activities which require technical skills that in-house staff do not possess are also good candidates for outsourcing (Internet commerce security reviews, for example). Since employees are generally more loyal, more focused on the long-term needs of their employer, more familiar with the business needs of the employer, and more willing to provide extraordinary assistance in the time of a crisis, an employee should often be preferred over an outsourcing firm.

Just as the outsourcing process is assisted by knowing what information security tasks need to be performed, so the process will be assisted by the prior performance of an organization-wide information security risk assessment (a general risk assessment as opposed to an outsourcing-specific risk assessment). An organization-wide risk assessment identifies the unique risks that the organization faces, and these unique risks in turn indicate tasks that need to be performed. For example, a photo bank that sells pictures over the Internet may have some unique risks associated with plagiarism that could be in part addressed with digital watermarks. It may be a certain person's job to automatically scan Internet web pages to make sure that third-party uses of the organization's photos are all paid for and properly licensed. These unique information security tasks could additionally be specified in a contract or agreement with an outsourcing firm.

Topics to Cover in an Outsourcing Contract

In far too many outsourcing contracts there are few words about the outsourcing firm's information security roles and responsibilities. To foster a more explicit treatment of this area in contracts, this section lists information security topics that should be covered in an outsourcing contract. Further details of these responsibilities can be found in Chapter 11 and Chapter 12.

- Background checks and subsequent client approval of specific outsourcing firm workers who will handle Company X information and systems

- Client approval of access privileges for all workers who gain access to information and systems entrusted to the outsourcing firm

- Client approval for changes in the procedures or other operational details associated with the handling of Company X business applications or sensitive information

- Client approval for changes in interfaces, system configuration, and network connections (for example, who makes decisions about firewall rules)

- Client determination of acceptable responses to bring the outsourcing firm back within the acceptable range on target parameters (often handled via service level agreements or SLAs)

- Who will determine the circumstances when penalties and/or reductions in fees take place due to security-related failings or ongoing vulnerabilities

- Who is to perform monitoring of user access privileges that have been assigned as well as user activity (for instance through a network management system and operating system logs)

- Client specification of the policies and procedures to be used by staff at the outsourcing firm

- Client specification of the physical access controls to be employed at the outsourcing firm's data center and adjoining offices

- Client preparation and update of documentation describing the procedures used to process Company X information (including emergency response plans and contingency plans)

- Client preparation and update of information systems contingency plans

- Client notification of efforts to install or upgrade hardware, software, and telecommunication systems

- Outsourcing firm modifications to application software and operating system software in response to newly reported vulnerabilities

- Client-sponsored audits of outsourcing firm workers to ensure they are in compliance with terms and conditions in the contract

- Who will run software that determines whether security measures are being followed and/or whether they are effective (software license management systems are an example)

- Who will take what response to intrusions, outages, errors, and other security relevant events

- Who will respond to requests for password resets, smart card lock-out condition alleviation, and other help desk security problems

- Who will provide troubleshooting, in addition to documentation of and resolution of service complaints (such as system down)—this may involve a trouble ticket system

- Who will provide expert technical consulting assistance with information security (advice on options, suggests products, etc.)

- How the outsourcing firm will help with the resolution of problems or complaints, including the use of problem or complaint tracking (perhaps through a trouble ticket system)

- What liability and financial responsibility for information security problems the outsourcing firm is willing to assume

- What notification process takes place when the outsourcing firm does any work for competitors to your organization

- When the outsourcing firm will generate and deliver status reports (including security incidents, changes in information security policy, changes in key personnel, changes in system or network configurations, suspected security weaknesses, and results of security testing activities)

- Whether the outsourcing firm will return all information and software assets in its possession when the contract is terminated (including operational information such as OS security logs)

Due Diligence to Perform Before Outsourcing

Before any commitment is made to an outsourcing firm, appropriate *due diligence* should be performed. Besides getting several competing bids, this typically involves talking to existing customers of the best outsourcing firms to determine whether their customers are satisfied with the services they are receiving. Likewise, no matter how large and well-known an outsourcing vendor may be, people from your organization should visit the outsourcing firm's data centers and offices to confirm representations that were made in a proposal. This confirmation process may, for example, involve a check to see that an Uninterruptible Power System (UPS) is indeed installed and operational. Due diligence also means checking the financial stability of the outsourcing firm by reviewing financial statements, examining credit reports, and searching legal records to see whether the outsourcing firm is in trouble with its customers or others. Prospective customers will probably want to confirm the level of training that outsourcing firm personnel receive as well as the qualifications of these same personnel. Additionally, prospective customers should examine outsourcing firm documentation such as information security policies, operational procedures, job descriptions, employee confidentiality agreements, and prospective employee background checking procedures.

Due diligence should be performed after the contract is signed as well. For example, your organization should include words in the contract that allow either internal auditors or external auditors to review the outsourcing firm's operations. Outsourcing firm customer internal auditors are preferred in this context because they are more familiar with the specific business needs of your organization. In some instances, external auditors may perform what is known as a *SAS-70 review* (Statement on Auditing Standards 70, issued by the American Institute of Certified Public Accountants). These SAS-70 reviews may be too general in nature, and may not satisfy management at your organization who are trying to determine whether everything is being handled in a secure and reliable fashion.

It is important to structure a contract with an information security outsourcing firm such that a variety of ways are defined for dealing with problems. These include unilateral or mutually-developed problem correction plans, formal problem resolution processes, formal complaint processes, and restatements of performance levels. Better than dealing with problems that have already taken place are proactive approaches such as monthly reviews of service expectations and service level agreements (SLAs). Ideally the contract should be very specific about specific ways to measure performance, and SLAs are one popular way to do this. For example, an SLA could specify the acceptable time frame for a response to a hacker intrusion. Additional ideas for SLAs can be found in Appendix C, "Performance Criteria."

If your organization has already sent out an outsourcing *request for proposal* (RFP) document, and has established a schedule for the review and decision-making on proposals, it may be appropriate to contact the prospective outsourcing firms now, and let them know that the review and decision-making processes will be extended. This postponement gives the Internal Audit Department additional time to perform appropriate due diligence, to establish a more specific performance measurement system, and to better clarify the specific roles and responsibilities of the outsourcing vendor. This delay can additionally allow your organization to add more requirements to the RFP. Your organization will be in a much stronger position if requirements are written into the contract rather than identified after the contract has been signed.

Chapter 18 SMALLER ORGANIZATIONS

The descriptions of information security organizational structure found in this book will understandably be too expensive and complicated for some smaller organizations. This does not mean that these template materials should be abandoned. You should instead pare down the words found in Chapter 11, Chapter 12, and Chapter 13 in a manner consistent with the customization factors defined in Chapter 14, "Customization Factors." Removal of inappropriate words is much faster and more efficient than compiling these documents from scratch. To assist with this editing process, this chapter offers some tips on an abbreviated and scaled-back approach intended to allow smaller organizations to cover all the essential information security areas. This chapter also includes quantitative reference points for budgets in the hope that this information will assist smaller organizations in their efforts to find the appropriate spending level for information security.

The establishment of a formal Information Security Department is going to be too expensive for some smaller organizations, such as those with fewer than 100 employees. Instead, you should assign a specific individual to be the Coordinator of Information Security across the entire organization. Because information security is multi-disciplinary, multi-departmental, and increasingly multi-organizational, it is essential that one person bring it all together and provide management with the big picture. This person can have many of the duties that an Information Security Manager has (see "Information Security Department Manager" on page 57 for a job description). Rather than having a staff to assist, such a Coordinator of Information Security often works alone and reports to the Chief Information Officer or the Director of Physical Security (see Chapter 13, "Reporting Relationships" for a discussion about reporting relationships). Reasons to have at least one centralized coordinator are presented in Chapter 19, "Organizational Structure."

If you establish a Coordinator of Information Security position, it is desirable that this individual be focused on information security on a full-time basis. A full-time information security specialist is less likely to be caught in conflicts of interest that are present if a full-time worker devotes only part of his or her time to information security. For example, if a Systems Administrator, Database Administrator, or Computer Operator were to be assigned a part-time role as Coordinator of Information Security, he or she would be confused about where

to draw the line on a variety of trade-offs. More specifically, a Database Administrator may compromise access control security so that he or she doesn't need to spend so much time handling user-IDs and passwords. Likewise, a Computer Operator may compromise intrusion detection systems monitoring so that he or she doesn't need to spend so much time attending to the current operational status of systems. Full-time specialists will also be less likely to be "temporarily reassigned" to non-information security tasks when deadlines are fast approaching (the Y2K efforts of the recent past provide a good example).

In some small organizations, even a single full-time person is not going to be acceptable from a budgetary standpoint. These organizations can hire someone who works only part-time, and thereby avoid the conflict of interest problem. These organizations can also use outsourcing firms that increasingly are providing information security services. In many instances outsourcing firms will provide only a portion of the services that the Coordinator of Information Security needs to provide. For example, one outsourcing firm may provide network intrusion detection monitoring services and break-in response team services. Another outsourcing firm may provide risk assessment and security administration services. Accordingly, if you are seeking outsourcing firm support, you may find that several firms are required to meet the needs of the organization. Since employees are generally more loyal, more focused on the long-term needs of their employer, more familiar with the business needs of the employer, and more willing to provide extraordinary assistance in a time of a crisis, in these limited budget situations, an employee is to be preferred over an outsourcing firm. Employees are also more likely to be without time conflicts than consultants; these conflicts might cause consultants to attend to another organization's needs rather than the needs of your organization. For a more detailed discussion of outsourcing information security activities, see Chapter 17, "Outsourcing Firms."

Another serious consideration for smaller organizations is separation of duties. For example, in a medium-sized organization, the person who writes the checks based on purchase orders is generally not the same person who signs the checks. The involvement of more than one person reduces the chances of fraud and errors. This same perspective should be brought to the information security area. For example, programmers should not be the only ones to test their own code, just as information security administrative staff members should not be performing information security compliance checks. Of course, if the organization doesn't have enough people to support separation of duties, in some cases certain people will need to have several roles—roles that certain other organizations would consider incompatible. In this case, you should consider how separation of duties is going to be maintained even though the number of people involved is restricted. You can start by defining the areas in which separation of duties absolutely must be present. The roles and responsibilities documentation should then be compiled, all the while maintaining separation of duties in these same areas. The material provided in Chapter 11 and Chapter 12 already has separation of duties built into it.

Although not nearly as effective an option as having a single person who is designated as the organization-wide Information Security Coordinator, it is possible for small organizations to address information security by assigning specific tasks to a variety of existing personnel. While being concerned about conflicts of interest and separation of duties, you can, for example, assign information security administrative tasks to Systems Administrators, controls related consulting tasks to Internal Auditors, intrusion monitoring tasks to Computer Operators, etc. The important benefit of this approach is that the tasks have been clearly specified and assigned to individuals. Even with this approach, some additional effort will still be needed to coordinate the work of these individuals.

Another option for smaller organizations is to assign various information security tasks to department managers. For example, department managers may be responsible for the physical security of sensitive business information, and may be expected to ensure that all the people in their department are using paper shredders, anti-virus software, computer lock-down devices (to prevent theft), and locking file cabinets. With this approach responsibility is dispersed and localized, and only the bare essentials are covered. This approach still requires some coordination across the organization, and this coordination might be provided by an Information Security Coordinator or a Physical Security Manager.

Small organizations should also consider cross-training and back-up for their information security personnel. To an increasing extent, information security is coming to be appreciated as an essential organizational function, a function that must be present on a continuous basis. This trend argues persuasively for the existence of at least two people inside your organization who are trained and ready to take over essential information

security duties on a moment's notice. You can ask management, "What would happen if our Coordinator of Information Security took a job elsewhere and gave us one week's notice?" With the very strong job market in the information security field, this is not just a remote possibility.

While a formal Information Security Management Committee is something that very small organizations can do without, there needs to be a formal assignment of certain basic responsibilities. For most organizations, these basics include information systems contingency planning, systems access control, controls in the systems development process, and information security user awareness. These basic duties must be clearly and definitively assigned to various individuals such as user department managers and Systems Administrators. Tasks related to information security still need to be included in other related job descriptions, such as those of the Chief Information Officer, the Internal Audit Department Manager, and the Physical Security Department Manager (see Chapter 12 for job descriptions).

An uncomfortable topic for many people is the issue of *nepotism*. Having a family member such as a spouse or child work in the organization is common for small businesses. The same issues come up when two people who work together are having a romantic affair (although this is certainly not a special issue applicable to small organizations). You may wonder how to adjust the templates found in this book for those circumstances where nepotism exists. In general, no reporting relationships should exist for people who have family or other ties. Thus the Information Security Manager, who reports to the Chief Information Officer, should not be married to the Chief Information Officer. Likewise, where separation of duties is critical to the performance of a specific job, the two people supporting the separation of duties should not have a family or romantic tie. In response to nepotism problems, it is better to move people around the organization, rather than create a dysfunctional organizational structure that will linger even after the people in question have moved on.

While I am sympathetic to organizations that say they don't have the budget for a significant investment in information security, there is a grave danger that management will under invest in information security. This can lead to a variety of problems such as unwanted hacker intrusions, excessive system downtime, and privacy disputes with customers. To ensure that management is investing sufficiently in information security, a statistical barometer of information security staffing is included in Appendix A, "Staffing Levels." You should review this appendix to ensure that management is being realistic when they say, "as a small firm, we don't have the need, nor do we have the money."

This under investment in information security unfortunately in many instances means that those who do hold information security positions end up running around putting out fires, and otherwise attending only to those things that are the very most rudimentary (such as changing passwords when somebody leaves the organization). The Coordinator of Information Security will need to have enough time to be able to take the pulse of the organization's information security status, to plan the changes that need to be made, to evaluate the merits of new products, etc. Management needs to understand that information security is an exceedingly complex matter, not something that can be dealt with in a single afternoon one time per quarter. Additional tips that may be helpful when it comes to changing management's attitude can be found in Chapter 2, "Justification" and Chapter 3, "Persuasion."

Any specification of roles and responsibilities implicitly makes trade-offs that should be consistent with organizational culture, business objectives, available resources, and other organization-specific factors. You should engage top management at your organization in a discussion about the places where they wish to draw the line when it comes to these same trade-offs. The discussion in many instances will help top management to understand that they need to devote additional resources to information security. An example of such a discussion would entail the Information Security Department's ability to handle maximum demands, for example, during recovery from a hacker intrusion, but being underutilized much of the time, and placing a major emphasis on the ability to expediently handle contingencies. Taking a different perspective on this same issue, the Information Security Department could be fully utilized all the time, thus forcing certain departments to suffer occasional outages and delays, even if outsiders were used to handle occasional problems. There is no correct answer to this trade-off. A credit card processing firm would probably opt for the former approach, while a retail store chain would probably opt for the latter approach.

As another point of reference to make sure that organizations are spending enough on information security, consider the 1994 survey of Fortune 1000 companies performed by Forrester Research, a Cambridge, Massachusetts information systems research firm. According to the report, security represents 9.0% of information systems budgets. This represents an increase of two percentage points over a similar study

performed five years earlier. I think these reported figures are high, but they are provided to you as a point of reference. The percentage has undoubtedly been going up over time. By way of comparison, consider another report about the percentage of the information systems budget that is devoted to information security. In 1989, Computer Economics, a Carlsbad, California management research firm, found that 2.3% of the information systems budget is spent on information security. Every small firm should be somewhere in between 2.3% and 9.0%, but this will vary considerably based on the organization's industry (see Appendix A, "Staffing Levels" for more details). Note that as much or more of the budget for information security can come from the Physical Security Department as from the Information Systems Department. Also note that, as a general rule of thumb, between half to two-thirds of the information security budget is devoted to people (be they employees, temporaries, consultants, or contractors).

One erroneous idea that small organizations have held is that they can't afford information security and that, as a consequence, they can ignore information security. To a much greater extent than in recent years, a new baseline of minimum controls is evolving. For example, if an organization (no matter what size) is going to support Internet credit card orders, it needs to offer SSL (secure sockets layer, a type of encryption) to protect the credit card data as it travels over the Internet. Other standards such as the British Standard 7799 (entitled *Code of Practice for Information Security Management*) are defining a minimum set of controls that all organizations must subscribe to if they are going to participate in the modern computerized economy. This means that, as a percentage of total sales, smaller organizations may actually end up spending a higher percentage of their available cash on information security. You can think of this as the cost to play the game (of Internet commerce, of electronic data interchange, etc.).

While your management may still be complaining that they don't have the money for anything sophisticated in the information security area, you should not think that management is going to be converted all at once. It is unfortunately a slow and painful process to get management to wake up to the importance of information security. All too often, major security losses or other painful events will finally force management to pay attention to information security. This is, and will continue to be, frustrating for information security specialists. For example, in 1993, the Computer Security Institute (CSI), an educational firm based in San Francisco, California, conducted a survey that found that 60% of Information Security Managers consider their budgets to be inadequate to meet the challenges posed by security risks. Fully 47% said that senior management does not consider security as high a concern as other information systems priorities. This is changing, but all too slowly, so you should get used to having it this way for the next few years at least.

Small organizations also need to appreciate that information security is no longer a project that gets addressed periodically. At one time, an annual audit may have sufficed for those organizations that are not particularly information intensive. For example, a small manufacturing firm is not nearly as information intensive as a commercial bank, and as a result, the investment in information security in a small manufacturing firm will be a much smaller percentage of available funds. Instead of being addressed as an occasional project, information security has now become an essential and ongoing organizational function much like accounting and marketing. As such, for every organization with over 25 employees, it should be recognized in job descriptions as an ongoing activity.

Chapter 19 ORGANIZATIONAL STRUCTURE

In addition to offering some advice about how best to implement a centralized organizational structure for information security management, this chapter explores the pros and cons of such a centralized organizational structure. As you go through this chapter, you should consider how your organization could be changed to better exploit the advantages of a centralized approach to information security management. You should be aware that I am a strong supporter of a centralized approach to information security management.

A Few Critical Distinctions

With the move to decentralized and distributed systems (such as personal computers and the Internet), centralized management of information systems acquired an undesirable image. When people think of centralized systems, they often think of bureaucracy, mainframes, and slow response time. While this image may have, in some cases, been justified for information systems management, it is not rightfully applied to information security management. It is possible, and also desirable to have decentralized and distributed information systems management, and at the same time have centralized information security management.

As covered in Chapter 3, "Persuasion," I believe that the information security field has become too complex and time-consuming for any one department to realistically handle everything. Accordingly, this chapter urges the adoption of an organizational structure that uses centralized information security management but decentralized execution of information security activities. For example, the information security policies and standards for developing business application systems should be defined centrally, but these same policies and standards can be consulted by user department staff as they utilize a small database management system (such as Microsoft Access) to develop their own applications. Likewise, the popularity of Local Information Security Coordinators is further testament to the merits of having decentralized execution of information security activities.

To make this discussion more real and tangible, I have listed a variety of activities that should be performed on a centralized basis. The list is meant to be illustrative rather than comprehensive. The specifics of this list can be combined with the mission statement for the centralized information security function found in

"Information Security Department" on page 46. Note that just because these activities are done centrally doesn't mean that they should all be done by an Information Security Group. For example, monitoring network activity ordinarily would be done by a network operations group.

Activities That Should Be Centralized

- Defining information security roles and responsibilities
- Developing network security architectures
- Issuing network security standards (such as encryption algorithms)
- Writing information security policies and guidelines
- Creating information security training and awareness material
- Developing systems development process security requirements
- Ensuring systems acquisitions are compliant with security standards
- Negotiating volume purchase agreements with security vendors
- Compiling inventory of organizational intellectual property
- Performing contingency planning related business impact analysis (BIA)
- Issuing information systems contingency planning guidelines
- Conducting organization-wide risk assessments and EDP audits
- Interacting with the media about information security problems
- Organizing and training a computer emergency response team (alias CERT)
- Developing standardized confidentiality and non-compete agreements
- Coordinating computer virus eradication efforts
- Monitoring network security to immediately detect intruders

Why Centralized Information Security Management Is Advisable

While I may urge centralization of a wide variety of information security activities, I do not mean to imply that these same activities absolutely must be centralized. For example, consider the administrative process of updating user-IDs and fixed passwords on a local intranet server. Taking a decentralized view, the update process could be performed by a local Systems Administrator, a distributed Network Administrator, or a Local Information Security Coordinator. Taking a centralized view, the same update process could be performed by an Access Control System Administrator who is part of an Information Security Department. The update process could go either way, but the policies and procedures defining how to perform these updates need to be dictated on a centralized basis. Statements of organization-wide information security requirements should always come from a centralized group. Efforts to follow these same requirements can be distributed or centralized.

Some organizations have already gotten into trouble when they attempted to manage information security in a decentralized manner. For example, at a well-known semi-conductor manufacturer, the Research & Development Department was concerned about its latest chip designs "walking out the door." To protect the proprietary chip designs that the R&D Department developed, this local department evaluated encryption products and established a standard to which every employee working in the department must subscribe. At the same time, the Information Security Department was worried about the same risks and they too were evaluating encryption products. When the Information Security Department learned that the R&D Department had already done this work, a dispute ensued about who sets the standards. Executive management intervention was required to settle the dispute, and after many heated words had been exchanged, eventually the job was delegated to the Information Security Department. A centralized approach to information security can help prevent these disputes from occurring. A centralized approach can also prevent resources from needlessly being wasted on redundant tasks.

Left to their own devices, users are ordinarily not supportive of information security. Users, like local managers, often complain that they have other things to do, and that information security doesn't appear near the top of their to-do lists. Local managers will also complain that their people have no resources or time to attend to information security matters. To overcome these attitudes and anti-information-security pressures,

a centralized group that has top management support should issue information security directives. An example of such directives is the use of extended user authentication systems for all inbound access to internal networks (dial-up lines, inbound Internet connections, etc.). Without a centralized approach to extended user authentication, some departments will use it and some will not. If this departmental discretion approach is employed, because all departments share a network, the inevitable result will be that the security of every internal system will be needlessly jeopardized by those departments that refuse to adopt extended user authentication systems. Only through a centralized approach can across-the-board compliance be achieved.

One of the perverse aspects of the information security field is the disproportionate amount of effort required by the "good guys" and the "bad guys." Hackers and others bent on compromising security need only find one major weak spot to achieve their goals. This is another way of stating the often-heard maxim where intruders need only discover the "weakest link in the chain." In many cases, these intruders don't even need to come up with the attack method; all they need to do is find the method (or software that executes the method) described on the Internet. On the other hand, those who seek to secure systems must have adequately dealt with all major threats to achieve a secure information systems environment. Thus the level of effort that the good guys must expend is disproportionately large relative to the level of effort that the bad guys must expend. Unless the good guys are approaching information security with a centralized approach, these efforts will be uncoordinated, and as a result the likelihood that important areas are not being adequately addressed will be high. As information systems continue to get more complex, the amount of effort required by those attempting to ensure security will markedly increase. To manage the increasing amount of effort required to secure systems, only a centralized approach will prove effective. Modern automated information security tools, such as centralized access control system monitoring consoles, are a reflection of the efficiency and effectiveness that goes along with a centralized approach.

Networking is rapidly changing the nature of information security. Years ago, locking office doors, locking file cabinets, and shredding papers may have been sufficient for some departments. This is because the departmental collection of information was isolated from the rest of the world. Networks interconnect the world and in the process they create a shared information resource on which many people depend. For example, a single virus could damage software, hardware, and information used by all the people connected to a wide area network. To prevent these types of problems, organizations need to adopt a minimum set of controls to which all people must subscribe (this is often called a *baseline*). Virus detection and eradication software is often included in such a baseline. The most efficient way to define, publicize, and check compliance with a baseline is to use centralized groups such as an Information Security Department or EDP Audit Department.

Perhaps the most significant force driving the movement to centralize various information systems functions (including information security), is the growing reliance on integrated systems. Closer links between applications and databases means that previously stand-alone systems are increasingly part of a tightly knit web of data flows. Integration with the systems of outside companies, for instance via extranets, further accentuates this trend. The development of these integrated systems requires new roles to deal with organization-wide information systems that didn't exist before. An example is an organization-wide central point of contact for all emergencies or disasters related to information security (this person is also called a CERT team leader). Only through a centralized approach to information security can an organization ensure the security of the new integrated systems that are being established.

Another good reason to have a centralized information security organizational structure is to clearly show top management support. The fact that management has established a centralized organizational structure to formalize its communications related to information security shows a level of concern that will indirectly support information security efforts throughout the organization. A centralized structure will generally have greater control and influence than a decentralized structure, and this in turn will communicate in many subtle ways to the workers that management really is serious about information security. This seriousness can also be helpful when it comes to defending management against allegations of negligence and failure to live up to a fiduciary duty to protect corporate assets (and information is one such asset).

A centralized approach to information security can enable a variety of new and innovative controls that would not otherwise be available. For example, with a centralized approach, an organization can negotiate special deals with vendors, such as VPAs (volume purchase agreements). A centralized approach can also enable certain technological solutions, such as an organization-wide user-ID database. Such a database can be consulted when any worker leaves the organiza-

tion, and it can be used to quickly identify the specific computers on which this worker had been granted privileges. These privileges can then be quickly disabled. A centralized approach is also useful when adopting a variety of security tools such as software license management systems. Standards, such as a minimum password length standard, are additionally very difficult to promulgate and enforce unless a centralized information security management structure exists.

Local departmental management cannot and should not call the shots when it comes to information security. Departmental managers simply don't have the time or background to adequately research and weigh the many considerations involved. Specialists are needed to deal with the very complex information security field. Because these specialists are unlikely to be engaged full-time on information security issues if they are located in a user department, they should instead be situated in a centralized information security group. Only when the specialists are in a centralized information security group can their scarce time and attention be best devoted to the involved organization's information security problems.

Resolving a Variety of Implementation Issues

While some people can in theory agree that a centralized information security function should exist, they cannot specifically envision what this centralized group would do. The concept of a factory assembly line is apt here. As is the case in any manufacturing operation, a centralized group is needed to define the nature of the product, its quality, its specifications, its manufacturing process, and other specifics. There will always be a need for people to work on the assembly line, actually manufacturing the product. And these people, to get back to the information security field, could be Systems Administrators, Departmental Information Security Coordinators, users, local managers, and others. When confronted with a decision to centralize or decentralize a particular activity, you can think of how things are done in the manufacturing industry, and whether this analogy makes sense at your organization.

When some people encounter a proposal to centralize anything, they often get concerned about the development of an unresponsive and rigid bureaucracy. It is certainly possible for information security to evolve into such a bureaucracy, but in practice, I have seen it only in civilian government and military organizations. In most cases, an information security group is so strapped for funds and so overwhelmed with important work to do that it cannot act as a rigid bureaucracy. Instead, it must be accountable to many constituencies, and it must work out appropriate compromises on a variety of difficult issues. These constituencies include top management, legal, internal audit, user departments, and other functions. A better way to characterize a centralized information security group is an expediter or facilitator of desirable results. A few examples will clarify this role. If centralized systems development security guidelines exist, new applications can be written and tested more rapidly than they could without these guidelines. If information security roles and responsibilities documentation exists, the internal response to a break-in can be much more rapid and effective than it could ever have been in the absence of such documentation.

No matter what type of structure your organization employs, it should have a single manager or executive who is responsible for information security throughout the organization. Only through a centralized manager or executive can the organization obtain a broad overview of an organization's information security risks and the appropriate controls to address these risks. As mentioned, many organizations are realizing that local solutions to information security problems are not sufficient, especially in the age of interconnected networks. This is why many have recently attempted to put together a network security architecture for the organization as a whole. This type of effort is unthinkable without a single manager or executive in charge of information security.

In a *matrixed organization*, a single manager or executive responsible for information security could have only a few staff members in his or her group. The bulk of the staff working on information security matters could be found in other groups such as the Information Technology Department. This structure would be quite different from a traditional hierarchical organization, where a manager or executive could have many information staff members all working in his or her department. In terms of a matrixed organization, to which departments these people are assigned is much less important than to whom they report when it comes to information security activities. Regular status reports, plans of action, budget requests, and similar documents should regularly move between these people and the single manager or executive responsible for information security. In other words, it is the coordination and communication that is essential, not the specific organizational structure. Consequently, the nature of this coordination and communication needs to be clearly defined in effective information security roles and responsibilities documentation.

If the people actually doing the information security work are assigned to different departments, and physically located in different offices, it is important that formal coordination and communication structures be established. These structures go beyond the activities mentioned in mission statements, job descriptions, and reporting relationship diagrams. For example, at one high-tech firm, all the Systems Administrators got together once a month for a chance to share tools and techniques. An international consumer products company used encrypted video teleconferencing facilities to have meetings between a centralized group and the people working on information security matters who were located in different countries. A financial services firm used quarterly meetings to bring everyone working on information security together. Alternatively, restricted information appearing on special intranet web pages may be used to coordinate people working on information security matters. Likewise, telephone conference calls may be used to periodically discuss problems and the best solutions. Even paper or electronic mail newsletters can be used to facilitate this coordination and communication.

The technical support specialists working exclusively in the information security field should also be located in a centralized group. In even the largest of organizations, it is simply too expensive to have these individuals duplicated across business units. Typically these specialists will be reporting to the single manager or executive in charge of information security. These specialists include virus infestation computer emergency response team (CERT) coordinators, network security architecture specialists, applications development security specialists, and other relatively expensive staff. With this approach, business unit managers do not need to recruit, train, supervise, or evaluate these specialists—something that they may not know how to do anyway.

On the other hand, staff who are not specialists in information security, and who may have a designated information security role, will usually *NOT* be found in a centralized information security group. People falling into this category are Systems Administrators and Network Administrators. As the information systems work is increasingly being performed by user departments, it is not unusual to find Computer Operators, Application System Programmers, other traditional IT staff in decentralized user department groups. All of these staff members will typically spend most of their time addressing local needs, rather than organization-wide needs. If people are spending a significant amount of their time dealing with organization-wide needs, such as network security architectures, then they should be located in a centralized group.

The staff who are not information security specialists, who usually will not be located in a centralized information security group, should generally be trained by a centralized group. Likewise, users and others with some information security responsibilities should receive training from, or at least training developed by, technical specialists in a centralized information security group. This approach to training facilitates job rotation, that is, the movement of Systems Administrators and Network Administrators across groups thereby advancing their careers. More importantly, it fosters a consistent culture and set of tools for dealing with information security across the organization.

One important strategy that is relevant to information security role and responsibility specification involves minimizing unnecessary changes in the organization. The organizational structure that you develop should mirror the existing organization structure as much as possible. For example, if the organization is highly centralized, then the proposed roles and responsibilities for information security should also be highly centralized. If the organization is highly decentralized, then the proposed roles and responsibilities for information security should include a scaled-down centralized

group. Even in a highly decentralized environment a centralized group is still appropriate. Information security staff will have a difficult enough time working out suitable compromises on tough issues; you should not create unnecessary enemies by proposing roles and responsibilities that do not fit in with the existing organizational structure.

One way to make sure that information systems expenses are realistic and truly in the service of business needs is to adopt a *charge-back scheme*. Although widely used for IT services such as network connect time, charge-back schemes are not recommended for information security. This is because the people who pay the charge-back bills (local departmental managers) are often not supportive of information security, and generally very concerned about the financial results of their department. Instead, the budget for a centralized group should be organizational overhead, shared by all organizational units. Besides, other mechanisms can be used to make sure that the centralized information security group is doing what needs to be done; the most recommended of these mechanisms is an Information Security Management Committee (see "Information Security Management Committee" on page 52 for a definition). Appendix C, "Performance Criteria," includes other approaches for evaluating the performance of a centralized information security function.

Chapter 20 COMMON MISTAKES

This chapter covers common mistakes that you will want to avoid when putting together information security roles and responsibilities documentation. While some of these mistakes may seem foolish and unlikely, I have encountered all of them in real-life situations during my consulting engagements. Topics in this chapter move from general and conceptual to specific and operational. Before you read this chapter, I suggest that you skim Chapter 4, "Preparation," which deals with prerequisites to an information security roles and responsibilities project.

Management Has Not Been Sensitized to Information Security Risks

To start an effort to assign roles and responsibilities when management doesn't yet understand the need for information security is asking for trouble. If top managers aren't really concerned about information security, they will refuse to allocate the resources to develop specific roles and responsibilities documentation. If this sounds like your organization, you should back-up and deal with the basics first. In most cases, an organization-wide risk analysis (risk assessment) will be needed to clearly show how and where your organization is vulnerable. There is often merit to having an outside expert provide the risk analysis so that there can be no allegations of *empire building* (internal political advantage) or favoritism. An organization-wide EDP Audit, performed by the Internal Audit Department or an external consulting firm, can generate much the same results. A less desirable yet effective option is an intellectual property audit. In this process, trade secrets, patents, copyrights, trademarks, service marks, and the like are identified and inventoried. This type of an audit will naturally lead to discussions about the ways to protect the organization's intellectual property. When conducting this type of an audit, you should be sure to include intellectual property entrusted to the organization by other entities (such as business partners), as well as intellectual property owned by the organization entrusted to other entities (such as outsourcing firms). For further discussion, see Chapter 4, "Preparation."

No Executive Sponsor for Information Security Has Been Arranged

To be successful with a roles and responsibilities clarification effort, you will need the support and encouragement of a member of the top management team. This top manager must understand the need for information security and be willing to take a stand for the establishment of formalized roles and responsibilities. If you don't have a top manager who meets this billing, it's best for you to postpone the roles and responsibilities clarification project until such a manager can be located. This is because top management will eventually need to formally approve the roles and responsibilities that you document. If you know that you can count on the support of just one top manager, then the project will proceed a great deal more smoothly. Information security managers have been known to drop the name of this top manager when rounding-up support among the rank-and-file for a roles and responsibilities project. It should be noted that reference to a "sponsor" in the title to this paragraph has nothing to do with an information "owner" (sometimes called a "steward") who defines user access control privileges and who has additional duties described in Chapter 15, "Ownership."

Sufficient Management Approvals Were Not Obtained

Although an impressive information security roles and responsibilities document may have been developed, all too often this document doesn't go through the proper management approval channels. In some cases this is because the process is not clear to the persons who developed the document, while in other cases, they didn't want to risk a fight with certain members of the management team. Whatever the reason, anything less than full and complete approval by the very highest levels of internal management jeopardizes the future efforts of the information security function. If the proper approvals were not obtained, this fact will surface at the most inconvenient of times—when a hotly debated issue is forced up the management chain for resolution. Any effort on the part of information security to engage in activities that had not been fully approved by all members of the top management team will be a major reason not to support information security's position on the issue in question. At times like these, the information security function needs all the support it can muster, and this is not the time to have arguments about roles and responsibilities. The management approval process is discussed in Chapter 7, "Review and Approval."

Positioning of Information Security Conflicts with Organizational Objectives

For management to seriously support information security, it must clearly see the link between information security and the achievement of organizational goals and objectives. If information security is characterized (or "positioned" in marketing language) as adversarial or in conflict with organizational goals and objectives, a proposed roles and responsibilities definition effort is bound to fail. In most cases, this conflict in goals and objectives is implied or imagined, and never specifically articulated. In other instances, a promoter of information security is so forceful or strong-willed that he or she forgets that information security must play a supporting role, not a leading role (there are a few exceptions such as military and diplomatic organizations as well as information security consulting firms). For example, if management sees information security as an impediment to progress, perhaps an obstacle that may slow development of new applications, then it will be hostile to any efforts that appear to expand and clarify related roles and responsibilities. On the other hand, if management appreciates that a clear definition of roles and responsibilities will speed business application development, it will be much more supportive. It's worth your time to identify management attitudes like this through a few interviews before actually releasing a draft roles and responsibilities document. Only when you know the objections that management harbors can you then deal with them effectively. This matter is discussed in greater depth in Chapter 4, "Preparation."

Top Management Believes Its Duty Is Discharged by Appointing Someone

To have an effective information security organizational function, it is critical that the people who work in the information security area have relevant experience, training, and skills. All too often management thinks that the totality of its duty has been discharged by simply appointing someone to a newly-created position of Information Security Coordinator or Information Security Department Manager. To the contrary, as explained in Chapter 12, "Job Descriptions," there are a significant number of people throughout every organization who all have different roles to play on an information security team. Likewise, top management's responsibilities in the information security area are not handled just because a person who knows very little about information security, who has no relevant experience, is now supposedly handling the issue. Sending these people to classes and conferences, and perhaps sending them to observe what happens at other organi-

zations, in many cases will take too long to show significant results. When a new information security function is being created it is especially important to have seasoned and experienced staff who know what they are doing. Without this seasoned and experienced staff, a newly-appointed person is likely to make mistakes that significantly set back the information security effort, and it may take months or even a year to regain the ground lost in this way.

Other duties of top management include allocating sufficient funds, reviewing progress, setting policy, and other tasks; these duties are described at length in Chapter 11, "Mission Statements" and Chapter 12, "Job Descriptions."

Accountability Does Not Match Responsibility

In far too many cases, top management will blame and punish lower level managers for information security failings, when these lower level managers were never given the resources to properly address information security. Often this unfortunate scenario takes place after a major publicly-known security breach. Management may not know what to do; terminating a manager who they think should have been more diligent often looks like the only justifiable reaction. If top management is going to hold these lower level managers accountable for information security, they should formally assign responsibility and allocate sufficient resources as well.

The formal assignment of responsibility is best accomplished via mission statements, job descriptions, and the other documents described in this book (particularly those discussed in Chapter 11, "Mission Statements," Chapter 12, "Job Descriptions," and Chapter 13, "Reporting Relationships"). Statistics to help you determine an appropriate budget for information security can be found in Appendix A, "Staffing Levels."

Staff Assumes Revenue Producing Activities Overshadow Information Security

For far too long, people have thought that information security is just an overhead cost. As such, information security activities are something to be minimized, perhaps even dispensed with in tough times. Information security in reality is much more than that. It can be a source of competitive advantage, a way to polish the organization's public image, a source of new features for existing products and services, and even a source of new products and services. In some industries, such as Internet commerce consumer product sales, information security is something more than a way to achieve competitive advantage—it is a competitive necessity. In some other industries, such as financial services, customer confidence critically depends on an image of good information security. For example, if your bank regularly made random errors on your bank statement it wouldn't be long before you found another bank. Top management has to appreciate the contribution that information security can make to the business before they will be willing to specifically define information security roles and responsibilities. Likewise, management must appreciate this contribution before they will approve the budget for a wide variety of information security efforts.

Management Says Everybody Is Responsible

Some top managers will claim that every worker is responsible for information security, and that everyone must chip in. While it is true that information is handled by nearly every worker, and that every person must participate in one way or another, this approach can make it appear as though responsibility has been assigned when in fact it has not. If remarks like this are all that top management says about information security roles and responsibilities, it will invariably cause perverse results. For example, this approach can cause all serious information security work to be postponed. In response, workers may say things like, "it's not my job" and, "when management tells me to do something specific about it, I will." Accordingly, bland and vague statements from top management about information security responsibility are not sufficient—they need to be accompanied by explicit documentation that assigns roles and responsibilities. Such bland and vague statements can, nonetheless, be useful because they can underscore management's concern and reinforce the need for widespread participation.

Staff Takes a Reactive Approach to Information Security

You should ask whether your organization is primarily reactive or primarily proactive when it comes to information security. Most organizations have traditionally been reactive. Increasingly organizations are adopting a more proactive stance. The economics of information security clearly support a more proactive position. Recovering from the bad publicity and chaos surrounding an information security incident can take years and be much more expensive than correcting the immediate problems and thus preventing an incident. Similarly, research done at SRI Consulting (formerly Stanford Research Institute) indicates that it's ten times

more expensive to add controls to an application after it has gone into production than it is to build controls into the application while it is still in development. If management is thinking that information security should be primarily reactive, they will minimize the roles and responsibilities of the function. On the other hand, if management appreciates what information security can do for them, they will approve a considerably broader array of roles and responsibilities. In addition, one of the objectives behind a formal written definition of roles and responsibilities is to motivate staff to act in proactive fashion.

Management Relies on Voluntary Information Security Cooperation

Some things need to be dictated centrally, and information security roles and responsibilities are one of these things. Most users have no intention or motivation to understand the risks of information security, let alone what their role and responsibility is in terms of dealing with these risks. Most users are pressed by other objectives, rewarded for achieving results in areas other than information security, and likely to push information security projects to the end of their to-do lists. Reliance on the goodwill and voluntary cooperation of users and lower level managers is bound to lead to sub-optimal results. Even though an end-user empowerment approach is fashionable these days, workers still need specific instructions about roles and responsibilities related to information security. While information security decision-making can be pushed down the management hierarchy, in accord with the notion of empowerment, what's often missing is a clear description of the decisions that need to be made. That's where a clear articulation of roles and responsibilities is needed. Beyond clarifying the work to be done, there is a need to manage certain information security activities on a centralized basis. For example, network management systems, encryption standards, and dial-up user authentication standards all need a centralized organization-wide approach. Centralization is discussed in Chapter 19, "Organizational Structure."

Contribution Made by Information Security Is Not Regularly Reinforced

The information security function is caught between the proverbial "rock and a hard place." If there has been a recent security incident, then management feels that information security isn't doing its job. If there has been no recent incident, management feels that they can cut information security's budget to save money. Sometimes this is called "damned if you do, and damned if you don't" (in this case it refers to experiencing a security relevant event). While this may sound discouraging, there is a way to avoid either of these undesirable alternatives. The preferred approach is to regularly communicate the contribution made by the information security function as well as others working in the information security area (EDP Auditors, Systems Administrators, etc.). This often takes the form of quarterly written status reports, although many other approaches can be used. For example, if you can show how superior information security is a factor causing new customers to do business with your organization, this will significantly advance the information security group's image in management's eyes. Likewise, if the Information Security Department can show how the latest strategic alliance critically depended on strong information security measures to protect the business partner's proprietary information, this should be trumpeted to top management. If these types of reinforcement are not periodically provided, management may downgrade and minimize the roles and responsibilities of information security. Another way to look at this is that good Information Security Department Managers must always be selling the contribution that their group is making to the organization.

Management Does Not Reinforce New Roles and Responsibilities

All too often information security roles and responsibilities are defined and approved, and then that's the end of the discussion so far as top management is concerned. While these documents might be presented to outsiders like external auditors, they are often not periodically reinforced with insiders via staff training and awareness courses, information security manuals, system usage pamphlets, management memorandums, and the like. For many organizations, the establishment of a formal organizational structure in support of information security is a major cultural change. To be truly effective, this cultural change must be periodically reinforced, repeatedly justified, regularly altered to reflect new circumstances, and periodically reevaluated. The most common place to communicate the new roles and responsibilities of the information security function is in new employee orientation. An information security policies manual is another favorite tool used to reinforce these same roles and responsibilities.

Major Projects Are Initiated Before Roles and Responsibilities Are Defined

This problem is sometimes referred to as putting the "cart before the horse." If a cart with wheels is placed in front of a horse, things don't work right. The horse has to come first and then pull the cart. Similarly, in the realm of application systems development, requirements must be defined before programming code is developed. The same is true with information security roles and responsibilities. Roles and responsibilities should be defined before major information security projects like the installation of a password-based access control package are undertaken. Although management may say, "just go do it," they may be unaware of the difficulties associated with major projects if roles and responsibilities are ill-defined. In the absence of clear roles and responsibilities, staff will typically spend an inordinate amount of time trying to figure out who is supposed to do what, attempting to get these people to attend to information security tasks, assigning blame to people who had no idea they were supposed to be doing something, etc. To avoid these problems, you should make sure that roles and responsibilities are clearly defined before major projects like a network security architecture project get underway. If roles and responsibilities are presently defined in a loose or informal way, you should fix them up so people can work with focused effort and a clear understanding of who will do what. This topic and related dependencies are discussed in Chapter 4, "Preparation."

Scope of Information Security Duties Are Too Narrowly Defined

Information flows quickly and relatively inexpensively from internal unit to internal unit, and increasingly back and forth with outside organizations like suppliers. The widespread distribution of information makes security a pervasive concern that should be on the minds of virtually every worker at your organization. Developments such as Internet commerce and extranets further underscore the need for adopting a broad view of information security roles and responsibilities. Nonetheless, in far too many organizations the roles and responsibilities of an Information Security Department are defined too narrowly. As a result, the Department is hampered from contributing to its full potential. For example, in some organizations privacy is considered outside the Department's mission. Similarly, in other organizations, contingency planning is considered outside the Department's mission. Both of these areas can and should be addressed, at least in part, by the work of an Information Security Department. The full range of activities for an information security function is found in Chapter 12, "Job Descriptions." While not all of these duties will be relevant to your organization, the list can help you move well along towards a fully-rounded definition of information security roles and responsibilities.

Scope of Information Security Duties Are Too Loosely Defined

In many organizations, the roles and responsibilities of an Information Security Department are too loosely defined. A one-paragraph mission statement may be all that exists. Job descriptions may be missing. This loose and fuzzy approach causes several undesirable results including:

- excessive resources repeatedly consumed by role and responsibility definition work that could have been better spent actually doing project work

- surprise information security incidents because important duties had not been properly performed

- lack of results from the Information Security Department because the Department's authority to do certain things—such as block an application moving into production—was not clear

This book is intended to overcome this problem, and you should use the detailed mission statements and job descriptions to specifically define information security duties (see Chapter 11, "Mission Statements" and Chapter 12, "Job Descriptions"). The consequences of loosely defining information security roles and responsibilities are further discussed in Chapter 2, "Justification."

Inappropriate Person Prepares Roles and Responsibilities Documents

If someone with a general business background prepared roles and responsibilities documentation for an information security group, and if he or she did not have the benefit of the information in this book or comparable resources, the result will often be dysfunctional. Important topics are often left out and the thrust of the information security effort may be twisted to support another organizational function such as computer operations. The resulting documentation may need to be thrown out and a new version developed, or worse yet, the document may languish in an approving manager's in-basket forever. The person who writes information security roles and responsibilities needs to be a good writer, needs to have inside knowledge about

the business in question, and needs to be free of internal politics (a consultant is often advisable). This topic is further explored in Chapter 6, "Documentation."

Time Required to Get Top Management Approval Is Underestimated

In an effort to get management to approve a roles and responsibilities project, some people may underestimate the elapsed time required to get top management approval. While roles and responsibilities documents that are truly tailored to your organization generally sail right through the approval process with few if any objections, others may take up to six months to complete several iterations of a review and revision process. To minimize the involvement of top management, you should take a strong stand in favor of adequate up-front research to prepare a document that is truly customized to your organization. Whatever the up-front effort used to prepare the document, you should be sure to leave open the possibility that several time-consuming review and revision iterations may be required.

Additional details on this same topic, as well as a suggested schedule, can be found in Chapter 9, "Time Estimates." Factors associated with customization of the templates in this book are discussed in Chapter 14, "Customization Factors."

Roles and Responsibilities Are Not Periodically Updated

In many cases, information security roles and responsibilities were defined a long time ago but they have not been updated to reflect changes in information systems technology (such as telecommuting), nor have they been updated to reflect new business structures (such as outsourcing). At the very least, information security roles and responsibilities should be revisited every two years to make sure that they are still relevant. Likewise, when there are significant technological or business changes (such as a merger or acquisition), there should often be changes in the documents reflecting information security roles and responsibilities. This topic is discussed at length in Chapter 5, "Modification."

Staff Performance Reviews Do Not Include Information Security

In far too many situations, staff performance reviews do not consider whether workers carried out their jobs in compliance with information security policies, standards, and other requirements. For example, a systems administrator may be judged on technical knowledge, ability to manage multiple projects, problem solving ability, and other factors—but not on compliance with information security requirements. The most important thing that you can do to ensure that information security will be considered in the performance review process is to get it written into job descriptions. In most cases, only the job descriptions of workers directly involved with information security matters will include mention of information security. Over time, it is desirable to include it in the job descriptions of other workers including users. The second best thing that you can do to get information included in the performance review process is to get a question included in standard organization-wide performance evaluation questionnaires. These questionnaires can include questions like, "Does the worker deal courteously with customers?" If your organization does not use a set of questions like this, you may wish to have a conversation with the Director of Human Resources about the merits of adopting such a template. A template can be an effective way to reinforce corporate values and ensure that these values are considered by all workers. Performance review considerations are taken up in greater detail in Appendix C, "Performance Criteria."

No Disciplinary Process Exists

Having well-written roles and responsibilities documentation is going to do your organization very little good unless it also has a disciplinary process that is regularly applied as circumstances warrant. Without a disciplinary process, information security requirements will be "without teeth" and not worthy of worker attention. Any attempt to define roles and responsibilities relative to information security will be met with the same attitude. If you can do it, you should use the material that the Human Resources Department has already prepared rather than come up with a separate disciplinary process. Besides the Director of Human Resources, you may also wish to discuss the disciplinary process and related action-forcing mechanisms with people in both the Legal Department and the Internal Audit Department.

No Compliance Checking Process Exists

It doesn't matter how impressive the information security roles and responsibilities documentation happens to be if no one is checking to make sure that people are working in a manner that is consistent with this documentation. Most often *compliance checking* is performed by the Internal Audit Department, not the Information Security Department. This is because the Information Security Department is generally responsible for developing the documentation. To have the same department develop a control and also review its effectiveness would be a conflict of interest. Besides the Internal Audit Department, this compliance checking could be done by an external consultant as well as a government regulator. Increasingly, some software packages can be used to make sure that people are doing their jobs. For example, vulnerability identification software can determine whether Systems Administrators are applying the latest operating system patches.

No Clear Problem Reporting Process Exists

Managers in a position to actually do something about information security often do not hear about the problems that people elsewhere in the organization are having. For example, top management may not hear about a hacker intrusion that a group of Systems Administrators handled on their own. Problem reports may not be communicated for a variety of reasons, including middle management's desire to look good in the eyes of top management. This situation also occurs because roles and responsibilities for the problem reporting and management escalation process are not sufficiently defined. To get a good idea about the problem reporting and escalation process at your organization, you should attempt to identify who would be notified if there were to be a computer-assisted internal fraud at the organization. You can also attempt to determine who should be notified in the event of a computer related emergency or disaster. You can furthermore attempt to determine who should be notified about information security vulnerabilities as well as violations of information security policies. In a well-structured organization, both the people to be notified and the information that needs to be communicated will be clearly defined in writing.

Appendix A   STAFFING LEVELS

The following report, "Information Security Staffing: Calculating the Standard of Due Care," will provide you with a rough indication of the adequacy of an organization's current staffing levels. It is intended for use in so-called "back of the envelope" calculations that provide overall guidance, not precise and definitive results. The survey results should not be taken as a strict standard to which every organization should aspire. Instead, in every organization there will be special circumstances requiring either more or less information security personnel.

While many numbers are included in the following report, you should not be discouraged. The process for using the results is actually quite simple and is based on ratios. For example, the ratios given in the report can be multiplied by the total full-time equivalent workers at

your organization to come up with an anticipated average staffing level. This process is described in greater detail in the first few paragraphs of the report. The chapter is thus especially useful when preparing budgets, project plans, or requests for additional information security resources.

Although this survey was performed at the end of 1997, its results are still relevant to organizations in the United States and Canada. If anything, the average staffing levels will have increased in the years that have elapsed since the report was prepared. This is because information security is increasingly being appreciated by top management as an essential business function. Thus the numbers in this report can be used to indicate a conservative minimum staffing level below which organizations should not go.

INFORMATION SECURITY STAFFING: CALCULATING THE STANDARD OF DUE CARE

Annual Survey Objectives

Overwhelmed with the myriad of things that they are expected to accomplish, many information security practitioners wonder whether their organization has comparable staffing levels to other organizations in the same industry. For many years this question was destined to remain unanswered. But that has now changed with this staffing survey. This survey allows you to provide definitive quantitative reference points that management can use to determine whether an organization is falling behind, or whether it is out in front of the competition.

The idea behind this survey is basically a legal one: to avoid charges of negligence, computer professional malpractice, or breach of fiduciary duty (specifically the duty to protect assets such as information and information systems). To provide a credible defense against such charges, management needs to be able to show that they have exercised due diligence. In the information security arena, this means that management needs to demonstrate that they have deployed controls that are comparable to those found in similar organizations. It also means that management needs to have made a comparable investment in information security. In other

words, management needs to be able to show that they have been operating in a manner consistent with the standard of due care.

In response to practitioner claims that staffing levels are insufficient, management often says they don't believe it. Unfortunately, management is often disinclined to take any action until they see detailed quantitative evidence indicating that a change is appropriate. This chapter provides just such evidence compiled by independent parties. Intended primarily to answer budgeting and human resources questions, the numbers found below can also be useful in risk assessments, as well as in both internal and external audits.

Under some circumstances, the numbers appearing in this report can also be used to prevent information security staff from being laid off when management decides that it's time to cutback on expenses. This last suggested use is an especially important one because information security, EDP audit, and quality assurance are all areas that frequently bear disproportionately large reductions in staff when available organizational resources are especially tight.

Survey Structure

The survey used ratios as an expedient way to calculate the level of information security staffing. Ratios are used extensively in financial accounting. One example is the P/E (Price/Earnings) ratio, which indicates the reasonableness of a stock's current price. Rather than focusing on financial ratios, this survey focused on staff head-count. The use of *head-count ratios* eliminates conversion problems associated with different national currencies, location-related variations in the cost of living, different pay scales for the same job, and different duties for the same job. The use of head-count ratios also allows the results to be readily applied to organizations of any size. The usefulness of the ratios described below is furthermore enhanced because they fall into relatively narrow windows that then reduce decision-making uncertainty.

The questionnaire used to gather data for this survey was distributed in November 1997 to recipients of *Computer Security Alert*, a newsletter published by the Computer Security Institute (San Francisco). All responses were anonymous. Incomplete responses were excluded from the applicable ratios, but were otherwise used for calculations. Some 302 usable responses were received.

In general, this survey was not conducted with strict scientific statistical sampling procedures. Accordingly, the results provide only a rough approximation of the real world. The large sample size does, however, allow you to have significant confidence in these numbers.

The average organization responding to the survey had a total of 6,458 staff workers. Like the previous year, most of the respondents hailed from the Financial Services sector, with the Government sector coming in a close second. Unlike the survey conducted in the previous year, there were no respondents in the Retailing/Wholesaling industry in this survey. To provide a reference point for those working in this industry, we provide the 1996 figures in all the tables shown below. To remind you that the Retailing/Wholesaling industry figures are from a previous year, this topic is mentioned repeatedly in the first several tables. Separately, the "Other" category for industry was primarily pharmaceuticals, oil and gas, law enforcement, consulting, agriculture, and publishing.

Although a formal count was not made, approximately 90% of the responses were sent from American or Canadian locations. The numbers provided should be relevant to other industrialized countries as well.

Figure A-1: Distribution of Respondents by Industry

Definition of Information Security

To simplify computations, the study used the term *full-time equivalent* (FTE) to indicate the sum of both full-time and part-time workers. For example, one full-time and four half-time people would equal three full-time equivalent staff.

The study deliberately ignored organizational structures. Instead, it attempted to include all information security staff, whether they are permanent staff, temporaries, consultants, contractors, or outsourcing personnel. Likewise, the study attempted to include all personnel performing information security work, whatever their title or affiliated department. Only those staff members who have been specifically charged with information security responsibilities that are not expected of others were included in the tallies. Thus users who attend to their own information security tasks were specifically excluded from the tabulations. The survey was addressed to in-house information security practitioners; vendors, consultants, contractors, and other non-employees were told not to respond.

Information security was described broadly to include all activities that protect information and/or information systems. Thus information systems contingency planning, archival records management, and information systems access control are all considered to be information security activities. Staff in Information Systems, Electronic Data Processing (EDP) Auditing, Risk Management, Legal, and Physical (Industrial) Security departments are considered to be conducting other activities.

Information Security as a Percentage of Total Workers

For the survey as a whole, the staff (including contractors, consultants, temporaries, and outsourced workers) who work in the information security area made up 0.100% of total staff. This is a 64% increase over the prior year's survey (1996). This year's number also represented a 300% increase over the 1989 survey.

This ratio varied considerably by organizational size. Those organizations with fewer than 2500 full-time equivalent staff had 0.638% of staff devoted to information security. Organizations that had between 2501 and 5000 workers had 0.140% of staff devoted to information security. While organizations that had 5001 and more workers had 0.047% of staff devoted to information security. Clearly there are some economies of scale whereby larger organizations can leverage their information security staff better than small organizations can. This significant disparity between large and small organizations also implies that there are some basic things that must be in place no matter what the size of the organization; these include written policies, a user awareness program, and a secure systems development process. In larger organizations, these basic information security efforts can be spread out over more people and thus consume a smaller portion of the total cost for staff.

Looking still at the percentage of total workers devoted to information security, it is interesting to see that small organizations are changing much faster than larger organizations. Smaller organizations are increasing head-count at a 68% annual rate, while medium sized organizations are increasing at a 27% rate, and large organizations are increasing at only a 24% rate. This appears to be a reflection of catch-up efforts on the part of smaller organizations, which historically have not been as sophisticated in the information security area as large organizations.

The differences between large and small organizations when looking at this ratio are also illuminating. This year the difference between large and small organizations was a factor of 13, but a year ago it was a factor of 10, and back in 1989 it was a factor of five. This increasing disparity between large and small organizations may be a reflection of better risk assessments, which more finely tune the information security expenditures to the unique risks facing each organization. The more a risk assessment accurately reflects prevailing circumstances, the more management is likely to tailor the staffing levels to meet these unique circumstances. The increasing disparity may also be a reflection of more sophisticated information security tools, which often can be afforded only by larger organizations. These sophisticated tools, such as expert systems that help detect credit card frauds, will generally reduce the need for staff.

Continuing with an examination of the percentage of total workers devoted to information security, we found that the ratio was quite different when one looks at the number of years that an organization has had an information security function in place. If a function has existed for five or fewer years, then the ratio is 0.069%. The same ratio applies if the function has existed for six to ten years. But if the function has existed for eleven or more years, then the ratio jumps to 0.181%. The very much larger staffs found in those organizations with a long-standing information security function implies that management understands and supports information security in these organizations. This should be encouraging to all of us who have labored with awareness campaigns year after year, hoping that management will finally understand how important information security is. If you keep at it, management eventually does appreciate information security.

Taking another vantage point on this same ratio, we can examine the effect of military, defense, and diplomatic activities. Organizations that were involved with these national defense activities had 0.188% of their total staff devoted to information security, while those organizations that did not engage in national defense activities had only 0.089% of their staff working in the information security area. It is intriguing to note that the ratio for the national defense organizations increased 55% over the prior year's survey, but the ratio for those organizations not involved in national defense increased 71%. As these year-to-year changes indicate, information security is becoming a business issue to a much greater extent than it had in previous years. The expansion of Internet commerce is partially driving this trend to increased investment in the private sector information security area.

Table A-1 shows an industry-by-industry breakdown for this ratio. Health Care saw the largest year-to-year change, a whopping 564% increase. This makes sense given the US government's efforts to pass legislation to reform the industry, as well as the rapidly rising level of consumer concern about the privacy of health care information. Computers/Telecommunications saw the next largest annual increase at 66%. Education, Utilities, and Aerospace/Defense saw declines over the last year. Because this year had no respondents from the Retailing/Wholesaling industry, the specific numbers for that industry are from the prior year's survey. The specific numbers from other industries, from the prior year's survey, are not provided here in an effort to reduce the possibility of confusion.

Table A-1: Information Security as a Percentage of Total Workers

Business Activity	InfoSecurity Workers / Total Workers
Computers/Telecommunications	0.208%
Education	0.063%
Government	0.161%
Manufacturing	0.035%
Retailing/Wholesaling	0.020%
Transportation/Distribution	0.037%
Financial Services	0.138%
Health Care	0.093%
Utilities	0.092%
Aerospace/Defense	0.047%
Other	0.229%

EDP Audit as a Percentage of Total Workers

Similar calculations can be performed for the EDP Audit function. In overall terms, organizations in the sample had 0.058% of their total staff devoted to EDP audit. This represents a 49% increase over the prior year. As with information security, the relative number of people devoted to EDP audit was correlated with the information intensity of business activities. In other words, the greater the reliance on information and information systems, the greater the number of both information security staff and EDP audit staff. Table A-2 shows the ratio of EDP audit to total workers. Again, the figure for the Retailing/Wholesaling industry is from the prior year's survey. Similar to information security, the greatest increase in this ratio was in the Health Care sector, which saw a 285% increase. Relatively minor year-to-year declines were noted in the Education, Manufacturing/Production, and Aerospace/Defense sectors.

Table A-2: EDP Audit as a Percentage of Total Workers

Business Activity	EDP Audit Workers / Total Workers
Computers/Telecommunications	0.054%
Education	0.057%
Government	0.114%
Manufacturing	0.017%
Retailing/Wholesaling	0.014%
Transportation/Distribution	0.017%
Financial Services	0.102%
Health Care	0.050%
Utilities	0.060%
Aerospace/Defense	0.043%
Other	0.090%

Information Security Staff Relative to EDP Audit Staff

This year's ratio of information security head-count to EDP audit head-count was 1.75. This means that there are 1.75 information security staff members for every single EDP audit staff member. This ratio has advanced 10% over the last year. The prior year's ratio was a dramatic departure from the 1989 survey, when there were 1.55 EDP auditors for every information security person. In other words, information security continues to grow faster than EDP audit.

Table A-3 provides a set of ratios for information security relative to EDP audit. Major increases were noted in the Health Care area, with an 89% uptick, and in the Transportation/Distribution area, with an 82% upwards move. Decreases were notable in the Government sector as well as in the Aerospace/Defense area. The realignments of priorities in the two sectors experiencing a decline in this ratio are probably a function of the massive cut-backs that they both have suffered over the last few years.

Table A-3: Information Security Staff Divided by EDP Audit Staff

Business Activity	InfoSecurity Workers / EDP Auditors
Computers/Telecommunications	3.82
Education	1.09
Government	1.41
Manufacturing	2.11
Retailing/Wholesaling	1.42
Transportation/Distribution	2.11
Financial Services	1.36
Health Care	1.87
Utilities	1.54
Aerospace/Defense	1.09
Other	2.55

Physical Security as a Percentage of Total Workers

Measuring physical (institutional) security as a percentage of total workers, there has been a marked decrease of 52% since the last year. This year's ratio is 0.334%. The decrease in physical security may be in part due to increased automation of burglar alarms, CCTV, and other physical security systems. The decrease may also be affected by the declining crime rates experienced in many parts of North America. A dramatic decrease in the Government sector, and to a lesser extent in the Aerospace/Defense sector seems to have had a major effect in this overall ratio. Health Care saw a very substantial increase of 306% over the prior year.

Because physical security staff typically don't do much work in the information security area, no correlation with information intensity was found in the following industry ratios. As one might expect, the extent to which military, diplomatic, and other governmental activities were performed was a much more reliable predictor of physical security staffing levels.

In previous years, the ratio of information security to total workers was much more tightly constrained in a window than the ratio of physical security to total workers. This variability by industry seems to be decreasing in the physical security area; last year the ratios differed by a factor of 65 for physical security to total workers, but this year they differed only by a factor of 41. The industry ratios of information security to total workers differed last year by a factor of 10, but this year they differed by a factor of 11.

Table A-4: Physical Security as a Percentage of Total Workers

Business Activity	Physical Security Workers / Total Workers
Computers/Telecommunications	0.128%
Education	0.243%
Government	0.509%
Manufacturing	0.452%
Retailing/Wholesaling	0.933%
Transportation/Distribution	0.023%
Financial Services	0.207%
Health Care	0.414%
Utilities	0.148%
Aerospace/Defense	0.195%
Other	0.250%

Information Security Relative to Physical Security

In overall terms, the ratio of information security workers to physical security workers this year was 0.311. This means that for every single information security worker, there are about three physical security workers. This ratio has changed dramatically over the years. Last year the ratio indicated that there was one information security person for every eleven physical security persons, while in 1989 there was one information security person for every twenty physical security people. The increasing influence of information security relative to physical security is clearly showing up in these numbers.

As Table A-5 indicates, the ratio of information security staff to physical security staff is highest in the Computers/Telecommunications sector. Increasing concerns about industrial espionage in high-tech companies may be a significant cause of this high ratio. A relatively high ratio was also found in the Transportation/Distribution area. The latter may be caused by the increased reliance of these industries on high-technology such as satellite-based systems to track the location of vehicles. The lowest ratio of information security staff to physical security staff occurs in Retailing/Wholesaling (again, we used last year's number for this industry), which has significant concerns about shoplifting and cargo theft, both of which necessitate heavy investments in physical security.

Table A-5: Information Security Staff Divided by Physical Security Staff

Business Activity	InfoSecurity Workers / Physical Security Workers
Computers/Telecommunications	1.62
Education	0.27
Government	0.24
Manufacturing	0.08
Retailing/Wholesaling	0.02
Transportation/Distribution	1.58
Financial Services	0.70
Health Care	0.23
Utilities	0.59
Aerospace/Defense	0.24
Other	0.92

Information Services as a Percentage of Total Workers

Similar calculations can be performed for information services (alias data processing, information technology, or management information systems). In overall terms, this year information services made up 3.78% of total workers. In last year's survey, information services made up 3.51% of total workers. Thus information services gained only eight percent over the prior year, while information security gained 64% over the prior year.

This ratio indicates information intensity. In other words, it indicates the extent to which an organization is dependent on information systems. As we might expect, and consistent with the prior year's statistics, Financial Services is the most information intensive. The least information intensive sector was Retailing/Wholesaling (again, we used last year's data for this industry only because we had no respondents in this category this year). Industries that seem to be becoming relatively less information intensive include Aerospace/Defense and Manufacturing. Industries that seem to be becoming more information intensive include Financial Services and Health Care. These changes in information intensity may foreshadow changes in the information security effort for each industry.

Table A-6: Information Intensity by Industry

Business Activity	Information Services Staff Total Workers
Computers/Telecommunications	0.040
Education	0.024
Government	0.040
Manufacturing	0.016
Retailing/Wholesaling	0.013
Transportation/Distribution	0.059
Financial Services	0.078
Health Care	0.039
Utilities	0.039
Aerospace/Defense	0.017
Other	0.049

Information Security Relative to Information Services

In terms of information security staff relative to information services staff, the ratio this year was 0.027, whereas last year it was 0.017. This 58% increase means that now there are, on average, about 37 information services staff for each information security staff member. Last year there were about 81 information services staff members for each information security staff member. Nobody questions that information services is fast becoming an essential part of modern organizations; what they often fail to appreciate is that information security is moving ahead even faster.

The ratio of information security to information services staff can be broken down by the number of full-time equivalent staff found in the organization. For organizations having less than 2,500 staff members, the ratio is 0.054. For organizations with between 2,501 and 5,000 staff members, the ratio is 0.026. For organizations with over 5,001 staff members, the ratio is 0.019. Thus, as other ratios mentioned above have shown, smaller organizations have a considerably larger proportion of their staff devoted to information security than larger organizations do. This same pattern was evident in previous surveys, although the ratio for smaller organizations is zooming ahead faster than the rest.

The ratio of information security staff to information services staff can also be broken out by the number of years that a formal information security group has been in place. This ratio was surprisingly narrowly constrained no matter how many years an information security function has existed. For organizations with an information security function for five or fewer years the ratio was 0.019, for organizations with an information security function for six to ten years the ratio was 0.023, and for organizations with an information security function for eleven or more years the ratio was 0.019. There has been no appreciable change in this ratio since the prior year's survey.

Those organizations with national defense activities registered a significantly higher number of information security staff to information systems staff than those organizations without such activities. Those with national defense activities had a ratio of information security staff to information services staff of 0.069, while those without such activities had a ratio of 0.023. The ratio for those organizations involved in national defense activities has increased markedly over the prior year. This increase in the information security staff relative to information systems staff may in part be a reflection of recent highly publicized break-ins at these organizations.

As Table A-7 indicates, the ratio of information security staff to information services staff is highest in Computers/Telecommunications. In the prior year, the highest ratio was found in the Government category. This expanded emphasis on information security within Computer/Telecommunication organizations may reflect an increasing appreciation that good information security can be used to sell both information systems as well as communications systems.

Table A-7: Information Security Staff Divided by Information Services Staff

Business Activity	InfoSecurity Workers / Information Services Workers
Computers/Telecommunications	0.051
Education	0.027
Government	0.031
Manufacturing	0.021
Retailing/Wholesaling	0.015
Transportation/Distribution	0.006
Financial Services	0.018
Health Care	0.025
Utilities	0.019
Aerospace/Defense	0.028
Other	0.047

Part-Time Workers

In overall terms, some 14.60% of the information security workforce was part-time. This represents a slight decrease over the prior year's survey, which indicated that 17.27% of the workers were part-time. By far the most part-time workers are found in the Manufacturing/Production sector, while the least can be found in the Financial Services area. Because we received no usable responses to this question from the Transportation/Distribution sector, like the Retailing/Wholesaling sector, Table A-8 reflects the prior year's data.

Table A-8: Percentage of Part-Time Information Security Workers

Business Activity	Percentage of InfoSecurity Work Done by Part-Time Staff
Computers/Telecommunications	15.34%
Education	17.27%
Government	14.16%
Manufacturing	24.43%
Retailing/Wholesaling	12.31%
Transportation/Distribution	6.60%
Financial Services	7.87%
Health Care	15.91%
Utilities	16.06%
Other	11.42%

Use of Outsourcing

When asked what percentage of the information security workforce is outsourced, respondents indicated that, on the average, some 7.44% was outsourced. This is a moderate increase over the prior year, when the average was 5.83%. Like the prior year, the amount of outsourcing again varied considerably by industry, as Table A-9 indicates. A marked decrease in outsourcing took place in the Computers/Telecommunications sector since the last year, perhaps due to concerns about contractors and consultants being eligible for fringe benefits (as the court said they were in a notable Microsoft case). A significant decrease was also noted in the Health Care sector. A notable increase in outsourcing over the prior year took place in the Transportation/Distribution area, as well as in both the Government and Manufacturing/Production sectors. The increase in outsourcing, at least in the Government sector, can be partially explained by the increase in Y2K conversion work which some people consider to be an information security problem (rather than an information services problem).

Table A-9: Percentage of Information Security Work Outsourced

Business Activity	Percentage of InfoSecurity Work Outsourced
Computers/Telecommunications	5.24%
Education	1.50%
Government	11.21%
Manufacturing	10.61%
Retailing/Wholesaling	1.54%
Transportation/Distribution	18.33%
Financial Services	5.89%
Health Care	0.95%
Utilities	6.57%
Aerospace/Defense	4.83
Other	8.07%

In-House Information Security Staff and Total Budgets

When asked what percentage of the total information security budget is devoted to in-house staff, respondents indicated, in overall terms, that some 36.92% was for such staff. This was a slight decrease over the prior year, when they indicated that some 38.92% was devoted to in-house staff. Given the slight increases in the use of outsourcing, the total percentage of the budget devoted to staff of all types seems to be holding stable. There are, however, considerable differences from industry to industry. As Table A-10 shows, the Transportation/Distribution sector, as well as the Utilities sector, seem to be the most dependent on people to get the information security job done. One reason why Utilities may have the highest percentage of the information security budget devoted to in-house staff may be the fact that this industrial segment uses part-time workers more than most others (there may be more overhead associated with part-time rather than full-time workers).

Table A-10: Percentage of Budget Devoted to In-House Staff

Business Activity	Percentage of InfoSecurity Budget Devoted to In-House Staff
Computers/Telecommunications	32.56%
Education	27.50%
Government	39.67%
Manufacturing	20.58%
Retailing/Wholesaling	37.59%
Transportation/Distribution	52.66%
Financial Services	44.81%
Health Care	38.42%
Utilities	55.00%
Aerospace/Defense	30.56
Other	31.00%

Staffing Increases for Next Year

Respondents were also asked about the expected percentage increase or decrease in total information security workers anticipated for the next year. On the average, they anticipated a 14.86% increase over the prior year. This was slightly down from the 17.78% increase anticipated in the prior year. The increase or decrease expected varied considerably by industry as Table A-11 indicates. Major increases are expected next year in the Computer/Telecommunication sector, as well as in both the Health Care and Financial Services areas. The smallest increase is expected in the Transportation/Distribution area, where staffing levels are already high relative to other industries (see Table A-10). Government also has a relatively small-expected increase for next year (7.86%), but then again they had a very large expected increase in the prior year (42.62%).

Table A-11: Anticipated Increases in Next Year's Staffing Budget

Business Activity	Percentage Increase Expected in Staffing Budget
Computers/Telecommunications	21.27%
Education	11.00%
Government	7.86%
Manufacturing	8.90%
Retailing/Wholesaling	37.59%
Transportation/Distribution	3.33%
Financial Services	20.39%
Health Care	21.09%
Utilities	15.31%
Aerospace/Defense	14.00
Other	17.92%

Annual Budget for Information Security

This year's survey included a few new questions about budgets for information security. If a respondent organization did not use budgets, they were asked to indicate the total dollar amount spent on information security for a single year. Although there may be a difference in practice between budgeted spending and actual spending, for purposes of this study, no such distinction was made. The average annual figure provided was $976,697.

Respondents indicated that they expect the total budget for information security to increase, on the average, 20.42% over the next year. The largest expected increase was in the Education sector, which makes sense given the relatively low levels of staffing that Educational institutions currently have. The smallest expected increase in overall budgets was in the Utilities industry, which by the way now has the largest percentage of its budget devoted to staff of any industry. No numbers were available in the Retailing/Wholesaling area because these questions were not asked in the surveys for prior years, and because there were no respondents in this year's survey which hailed from that industrial segment.

Contrary to what one might expect, the number of years that an information security function was in place did not substantially increase the expected increases in next year's budget. Those organizations with a formal organizational unit in place for five or fewer years expected an increase of 17.67%, while those with a unit for six to ten years had an expected increase of 13.63%, and those with a unit for eleven or more years had an expected increase of 18.61%.

It is intriguing to note that organizations working in the national defense area had a substantially higher expected increase in next year's budget than those organizations not working in this area. Although military, diplomatic, and defense related organizations have been thinking about information security for decades, they have suffered major budget cutbacks in the last few years. Perhaps it is now time for them to catch up? The expected budget increase for those working in the defense area was 24.86%, while the expected budget increase for those organizations not working in this area was 17.90%.

Table A-12: Anticipated Increases in Next Year's Total Annual Budget

Business Activity	Percentage Increase Expected in Budget
Computers/Telecommunications	18.76%
Education	41.38%
Government	13.28%
Manufacturing	18.20%
Retailing/Wholesaling	not available
Transportation/Distribution	25.00%
Financial Services	17.45%
Health Care	14.24%
Utilities	10.71%
Aerospace/Defense	14.22
Other	54.91%

Average Budget Dollars per Information Security Staff Member

We also calculated the average dollars spent on information security for each information security staff person. This was calculated by multiplying the budget for information security at each organization by the percentage of the budget devoted to information security staff. This intermediate result was then divided by the number of information security staff members. This statistic allows an organization to go from the number of information security staff members to the expected budget, or vice-versa. Across all industries, the average was $88,424.

It's interesting that this statistic varies so much from industry to industry. A high average dollars spent per information security staff person could indicate that staff is very efficient, or that sophisticated tools are used to extend the influence of each staff member. On the other hand, a low average dollars spent per information security staff person could indicate that management is unwilling to empower information security staff members by giving them the tools that they really need. We recalculated the average for the Other category because it seemed so different from the other industry sectors, but it is correct. The Other category included a single respondent who claimed an $80,000,000 budget, and thus skewed the results.

The influence of experience in the information security field was profoundly seen in this calculation. Those organizations with information security functions in place for five or fewer years had an average dollars per information security staff member of $35,664. Organizations with information security functions in place for six to ten years had an average of $51,306. And notably, those with an information security function in place for eleven or more years had an average of $101,612. Evidently, as organizations gain more experience with information security, they are able to leverage their staff members much more efficiently. This might be due to the implementation of sophisticated security tools like network management systems, or it might be due to the cumulative positive effects of building information security infrastructure (such as an information security architecture document).

Looking at the same calculation in terms of involvement in national defense activities, we see that there again was a substantial difference. Organizations involved with national defense had an average budget for information security per information security staff member of $34,672. Meanwhile, those without this type of involvement, had an average of $99,398.

Table A-13: Average Budget per Information Security Staff Member

Business Activity	Average Dollars per Worker
Computers/Telecommunications	$20,820
Education	$12,622
Government	$17,893
Manufacturing	$38,896
Retailing/Wholesaling	not available
Transportation/Distribution	$24,552
Financial Services	$41,535
Health Care	$353,461
Utilities	$58,900
Aerospace/Defense	$44,305
Other	$1,166,843

Average Budget Dollars per Total Workers

The last calculation that we will discuss involves average budget dollars spent on information security per worker (for all types of workers). This was calculated by dividing the budget for information security at each organization by the number of full-time equivalent staff at that same organization. The ratios were then averaged by industry.

This ratio provides a way for an organization to quickly back-into an appropriate budget for information security. Simply start with the number of workers and then multiply by the average dollars per worker provided in Table A-14 to get the appropriate budget estimate. The average amount spent for each worker, for all industries, was $7,082.

It's particularly intriguing to see that this calculation provided numbers that varied by industry by a factor of 738. Like several ratios mentioned above, these dramatic differences from industry to industry also appear to be correlated with both information intensity and involvement in national defense activities. For example, as an indication of information intensity, the Computers/Telecommunications industry and the Financial Services industries both have high average dollars per worker. Similarly, as an indication of involvement in national defense, the Government and the Aerospace/Defense sectors additionally showed relatively high average dollars per worker. The average for all respondents with an involvement in national defense activities was $32,409, while the average for all respondents without such an involvement was $1,717.

Table A-14: Average Budget per Worker (All Types)

Business Activity	Average Dollars per Worker
Computers/Telecommunications	$14,766
Education	$671
Government	$12,992
Manufacturing	$660
Retailing/Wholesaling	not available
Transportation/Distribution	$20
Financial Services	$1,079
Health Care	$2,917
Utilities	$142
Aerospace/Defense	$3,100
Other	$1,072

Conclusion

Appropriate information security staffing levels have long been insufficiently-defined, even for many people working in the field. This survey provides specific numbers to characterize the prevailing *standard of due care*. Without question the information security field is expanding at a robust rate. As modern business increasingly relies more on information as an essential factor of production, information security is coming to be appreciated as an essential business function akin to marketing and accounting.

In spite of the trend towards the use of sophisticated technical tools rather than people to perform certain security functions, and in spite of the trend towards the empowerment of users and others to attend to their own information security needs, the relative number of staff with assigned information security duties is growing at a significant rate. Perhaps the most salient example of this is the statistic indicating that the number of information security staff as a percentage of total workers has grown approximately 64% in the course of a single year.

Special thanks are extended to the statistical analyst who helped with this survey, Richard Rohde. This report was originally published in the Computer Security Journal, published by the Computer Security Institute, San Francisco, California. It is reprinted here with appropriate permission.

Appendix B PERSONAL QUALIFICATIONS

When interviewing candidates for an Information Security Manager (or information security executive) position, it is important to consider the personality characteristics most relevant to the job. This appendix provides both a ranked list of these characteristics as well as the reasons why these characteristics are important. The most important factors appear at the top of the list. I suggest that you photocopy this appendix and distribute it to all those who will interview candidates (including a third-party recruiter working on the assignment). These people can then rank the candidates according to these criteria to quickly determine which candidates should proceed to the next step in the recruitment process.

Excellent Communication Skills

More than anything else, an Information Security Manager must act as a liaison between many different groups with different objectives and needs. The manager must be able to attentively listen, just as he or she must be able to clearly state what needs to be done. This manager must also be able to persuade management to adopt new and possibly unpopular courses of action. The manager will be required to write top management status report memos, risk analysis reports, security incident post-mortem analyses, vendor request for proposal documents, employee job performance evaluations, and many other documents. This manager may also be called upon to act as an organizational spokesperson with the news media and professional society standards setting committees. The manager may additionally be called upon to give presentations at industry and technical conferences.

Ability to Resolve Conflicts Between Security and Business Objectives

The Information Security Manager must be able to clearly see the pros and cons of certain courses of action, and then choose a compromise which best serves the organization. Information security is always a compromise because the only absolutely secure information system is an unusable one. The manager must be comfortable making compromises, and must know about the management tools that can be used to arrive at decisions of this nature (net present value, internal rate of return, payback, Monte Carlo simulation, automated testing tools, etc.). The manager must be able to withstand pressure from various groups with competing objectives, and be willing to take a stand for a course of action that is in the long-run best interests of the organization. The manager should not be overly concerned about being popular and well-liked; a manager concerned about popularity will soon be fired for getting nothing done.

Ability to See the Big Picture

The Information Security Manager must not be easily distracted by the fire-fighting that inevitably comes with the job. Taking care of virus infections is certainly important but this day-to-day work must not crowd out important but not urgent long-run projects such as compiling a network security architecture. The manager must be able to prioritize resources in a way that satisfies the organization's urgently pressing needs, but at the same time move the organization in the direction of implementing all generally accepted information security solutions. The manager must also be able to synthesize information from many different sources to come up with a plan for improving information security that is truly responsive to the organization's business needs. Furthermore, the manager must be able to read between the lines, identifying the true underlying causes of problems that the organization faces. The manager must additionally have the guts to tell the truth about these underlying causes.

Basic Familiarity with Information Security Technology

The Information Security Manager must be knowledgeable in information security technical areas such as encryption, smart cards, and system access control. Not only must the manager not be duped by technical specialists, he or she must know the best technology to apply in response to an organization's information security needs. Without this knowledge the manager will lose credibility, and thereby jeopardize current and future information security initiatives. Generally a manager will not have the luxury of learning a great deal about information security technology on the job, so organizations should not hire an incompetent person and expect that they will be able to pick up the technology as they go along. Familiarity with the technology does not mean that an Information Security Manager is expected to program a digital certificate user authentication system, but it does mean that the manager would know when such a technology should be used. In general, an Information Security Manager must be familiar with the methods used, the processes employed, and the business reasons cited to justify information security measures.

Commitment to Staying on Top of the Technology

The Information Security Manager must also keep abreast of recent developments in the information security field. Attending a conference or two each year will generally not constitute sufficient effort. The manager must read technical magazines, subscribe to online news services, and if he or she is located near a major city, attend an occasional professional society meeting as well. A familiarity with the latest developments is essential if the manager is going to be able to recommend appropriate responses to recently discovered vulnerabilities. If the manager doesn't possess this knowledge, the organization runs the risk that it will learn about these vulnerabilities because it was victimized. If the manager doesn't possess this knowledge, it is likely that the organization will be using information security solutions that are unnecessarily costly, burdensome, and/or antiquated.

Familiarity with Information Security Management

The Information Security Manager must know about the elements of an information security organizational infrastructure. These elements includes responsibilities, policies, standards, procedures, and the like (a list of these is provided in Chapter 10, "Current Documents"). The manager must also be familiar with, and know how to use generally accepted information security management tools such as risk analysis software and contingency planning software. This manager must additionally be aware of other information systems management tools that can be used to enhance information security; one commonly deployed example is a network management system. If the manager is not familiar with information security management tools and approaches, he or she will not be able to marshal the limited information security resources to the organization's best advantage. This in turn will lead to problems like unnecessary costs and delays in developing new systems.

Tolerance for Ambiguity and Uncertainty

Information security is very complex and full of interdependencies. In many instances, a viable solution to various information security problems has not yet been released as a commercial product. This means that the

Information Security Manager must be able to make do with the tools and techniques currently at his or her disposal. The manager must also be able to make defensible decisions when important or even critical pieces of information are unavailable or too costly to obtain. The manager must have a strong and tenacious personality that does not let these problems cause him or her to become overly cynical. At the same time, the manager must not live in a fantasy land where he or she does not see the realistic and serious nature of the information security issues facing the organization. A well-reasoned and level-headed manager who can adjust to a wide variety of situations will do best in this position.

Ability to Manage Many Important Projects Simultaneously

The Information Security Manager must be a good project manager and must be familiar with project management tools and techniques. He or she must be able to delegate work to, and later manage people outside an information security group (these people will typically include consultants and contractors). In an increasing majority of cases, the pressing information security projects that most organizations need to complete simply cannot be accomplished with the limited information security staff on hand. At the same time, the manager must stay on top of these projects, making sure that progress proceeds as top management intended. The manager must be able to put together organization-wide status reports that clearly show trends, problems, and areas in need of top management intervention. Separately, the Information Security Manager often has a dotted-line reporting relationship with a variety of staff that have information security related jobs (Systems Developers, Systems Administrators, etc.). The manager is thus indirectly responsible for obtaining results, but often not in a position where he or she can take direct action to force compliance with information security requirements. To get results in this environment, the manager must be a both a diplomat and a politician. An Information Security Manager must thus be both a team builder and a team leader.

Ability to Work Independently

The Information Security Manager must be able to work independently without direct supervision or encouragement. In many cases, top management will not know exactly what he or she is doing. At the same time the manager must be accountable to top management and the Audit Committee of the Board of Directors. The manager must be able to stay focused and get things done, even though the resources at his or her disposal are quite limited. The manager must also be accustomed to taking the lead and not waiting for users or other groups to tell him or her what to do. A deep and abiding commitment to improve the information security status of the organization must carry the Information Security Manager through the inevitable contentious and difficult situations that he or she will encounter. To work independently, the manager must be creative, proactive, and inspired by a vision of how things could be.

A Certain Amount of Polish

Although this may at first sound like an unnecessary characteristic of an Information Security Manager, it can be very important when it comes to dealings with both top management and representatives from external organizations. If the Information Security Manager does not take care to dress professionally and conduct him or herself in a professional manner, he or she may be judged adversely (just as we judge a book by its cover). The Information Security Manager is an important spokesperson who will be a role model and focal point for many new projects. This person needs to inspire respect and admiration. If the Information Security Manager is disorganized, unfocused, and poorly spoken, then people will discount what he or she says, and the projects that he or she promotes will fall on deaf ears. To even mention this point may seem to be an unwarranted emphasis on external appearance and behavior, but this is the way that the world works, and organizations that ignore it do so at their own peril.

Appendix C   PERFORMANCE CRITERIA

This appendix discusses both performance measurement metrics and incentive systems relevant to information security. The discussion of necessity involves both individual performance and the performance of groups such as the Information Security Department. A list of possible metrics for measuring individual performance and Information Security Department performance are provided. You will need to tailor these metrics to your organization because every organization has a unique collection of workers, a unique organizational culture, different societal norms, different human resources laws and regulations, and other situation-specific factors that should be taken into consideration.

This material is an appendix rather than a chapter in the book because the establishment of an information security related performance measurement system should generally be performed after information security roles and responsibilities have been clarified, documented, and approved by top management. You may find it possible to have an information security performance measurement project integrated with the roles and responsibilities clarification project. In most cases, however, it will be preferable to have two separate projects. Having two separate projects is desirable because the Information Security Department can recognize two separate successes. Using the two separate project approach is also desirable because the two projects are each quite large, and problems with a proposed performance measurement system will not delay the adoption and usage of documented roles and responsibilities.

It is through a formal performance measurement system that information security specialists will get letters of commendation, promotions, raises, bonuses, extra time off, and other acknowledgements that they deserve. In the absence of specific performance evaluation criteria, information security staff members are likely to suffer because management may employ traditional performance evaluation criteria. For example, management may look to see whether the individual gets along with his or her coworkers, considering confrontations to be evidence of poor performance. While diplomacy goes a long way in the information security field, there are many situations where confrontations are a necessary part of the job. For example, if a major new application has inadequate controls, but is about to be placed on an Internet web server, the Information Security Manager should object and take the matter to top management. If the Information Security Manager did not object and make a fuss, he or she would not be doing his or her job.

Having a discussion with top management about incentives to support information security is an essential part of any project to establish an information security performance measurement system. Such a discussion is an excellent opportunity to clarify what management really wants from an information security function. In this discussion, you should point out the many ways in which the current incentive systems encourage people to act in ways that compromise information security. While there are many other possibilities, the following list defines typical ways that organizations are structured to get people to ignore and downgrade the importance of information security:

- Piecework pay systems, such as those for data entry operators, typically pay a fixed amount per piece, and if workers subject to these systems are asked to take on information security tasks, such as checking for fraud, there will be strenuous objections.

- Sales commission systems encourage salespeople to reveal more information than they should to get additional sales, and this behavior may lead to the unauthorized disclosure of sensitive material.

- Short term financial results are stressed by management bonus systems and this in turn may discourage management from investing in information security because the payoff is long-term in nature.

- Standard industry practice may conflict with organizational policy, for example, stockbrokers may take the contact information about their personal clients with them when they leave their employer, even though this may be a violation of their employer's privacy policy.

- Politeness may conflict with good security practice, as is often seen at the entrance to computer data centers where individuals hold the door open for the person behind them regardless of the authorization of that person to enter the data center.

- Organizational culture may conflict with good security practice, for example, the organizational culture may foster an open and sharing attitude towards information exchange when this is likely to lead to unauthorized disclosure of sensitive information.

- Employees are often pressured to handle the things which management is immediately concerned about and if they don't receive ongoing information security training then security may be "out of sight and out of mind" and therefore be ignored.

It will not be enough for the people working in the information security area to have clear and rational performance measurement systems. As discussed in Chapter 3, "Persuasion," information security can only be successfully addressed if everyone on the organizational team is aligned with the goals of information security. Obtaining this alignment can take many forms such as putting a question in everybody's job performance evaluation form. Such a question could simply ask whether the individual has been doing their job in accordance with information security policies and procedures (yes or no). Other techniques to establish the appropriate new balance between conflicting objectives, like cost minimization and information security, include handing out $100 bills on the spot to people who detect and report information security violations. When designing or redesigning the performance evaluation system for those working in the information security area, you should not miss the opportunity to engage management in a question about incentive systems throughout the organization.

So much of the work in the information security field is negative in its orientation. For example, Information Security Consultants look for and try to prevent problems. Likewise, Investigators in the Physical Security Department investigate computer crimes. This focus on bad things has an unfortunate side effect which could impact the extent to which management believes that these people are doing their jobs. If there are problems, then management is upset and wondering whether the people in the information security area are doing their jobs. But if there are no problems, then management is wondering whether the people working in this area are really needed, whether they could be dismissed the next time that the organization needs to reduce expenses.

An excellent way to show management the contribution that people in the information security area are making is to adopt bonuses. It is also a great way to shift the attitude of the people working in this area from negative to positive. At this point in time, bonuses are already being used in many private sector Internal Audit Departments, but it is rare to find them in Information Security Departments. Credit card fraud investigations and penetration attack projects provide two good examples where bonuses are currently used in the information security area. In the next few years, bonuses will be increasingly used as a way to shift worker pay away from straight salaries and into incentive-based pay systems. Worker motivation is expected to increase with the increased reliance on these incentive-based pay systems. Of course, incentive-based pay systems shouldn't rely on bonuses alone; they should include salary increases, promotions, time off with pay, and other benefits.

To support incentive-based pay systems, organizations will need to create metrics that truly motivate the actions management intends. This can be done by adopting a holistic perspective and focusing on the critical drivers and dependencies needed to get the intended results. For example, if an organization has problems with the prompt establishment of new user-IDs and passwords, an investigation can be initiated. This investigation may reveal that the local managers hiring new workers don't notify the Information Security Department until the new worker is actually sitting at their desk. Accordingly, the issue is not so much a matter of Information Security Department response time as it is getting advance notification. Although a metric can be established to measure the response time to new user-ID and password issuance requests, redesigning the new worker arrival notification process would solve the problem better than a metric looking at response time.

Each of the metrics that management adopts for the information security function should also be tied in with specific results for the next year, or perhaps for longer time frames. For example, if the organization has, as one of its goals for the next year, the process of converting all user-IDs and fixed passwords to user-IDs and smart cards, then the percentage of users who are converted successfully might be an appropriate quantitative yardstick. If this type of performance indicator is employed, it will also be possible to measure how many information security people are needed to achieve specific results.

The following metrics are just a sample of the many potential ways to structure an incentive-based pay system for those workers with assigned duties in the information security area. Because it would be too complicated to administer and track, no real-world organization would have anywhere near all of these metrics. Instead you should choose a few that seem to be most aligned with current business objectives. The chosen metrics should also be periodically reevaluated to determine whether they are creating undesirable side-effects. For example, with a bonus for completing projects on time, employees can get the impression that an individual's ability to meet deadlines is more important than doing quality work.

Information Security Department Metrics

- Accomplished specific project goals as defined in an action plan

- Reduced actual information security losses (based on a reliable loss reporting system, usually managed by the Physical Security Department, to prevent a conflict of interest that might cause fudging of the statistics)

- Received positive comments from internal auditors or external auditors

- Increased the number of internal organizational units in compliance with information security standards

- Expanded the number of workers in compliance with policies by a certain percentage

- Trained a certain number of people (systems administrators, end-users, etc.) about information security with a predetermined curriculum

- Was under a threshold ratio calculated by the number of security violations (wrong password, etc.) as a percentage of attempted log-ins

- Was under a threshold ratio calculated by the number of users with privileges revoked for security violations as a percentage of total users

- Met a specific quantitative goal for the number of computer systems in compliance with information security requirements

- Cast the organization in a positive light through information security related publicity a certain number of times over the last year

- Kept the organization's name out of news stories that discussed information security [*in this case the lower the number of news appearances, the better*]

- Improved the organization's image a certain number of times by publicly showing that it has superior and reliable information security

- Shifted organizational culture related to information security so that information security is now perceived as a necessary business function as evidenced by a certain number of departments using line item budgets for information security (results from a staff survey may also be used to measure a shift in culture)

- Got involved in a certain number of systems development projects to ensure that adequate controls were included in the final production systems

- Created a certain number of new approaches (such as already tested and approved standardized encryption systems) that expedited the systems development process

- Enabled a certain number of business activities such as Internet commerce credit card sales that would not have been possible without new security technologies

- Developed and documented a certain number of new procedures that help ensure the security of Company X information

- Reestablished full information systems services within a certain pre-determined time frame after an emergency or disaster took place

- Converted a certain number of users from old and insufficiently secured systems (such as those which use shared fixed passwords) to systems that are sufficiently secured (such as those which employ personal smart cards with one-time passwords)

- Eliminated a certain number of insufficiently secure information systems (such as modems inside desktop computers) and replaced these with new and more secure technology (such as an inbound call modem pool which uses extended user authentication technology)

- Brought the organization into compliance with a certain number of new and externally-dictated information security requirements

- Reduced Internet commerce related credit card fraud to a certain dollar level over a defined time span

- Expanded the total number of users supported by a new access control system (such as a smart card with one-time passwords)

Individual Worker Metrics

These metrics apply whether or not the workers are in the Information Security Department.

- Achieved a specific desirable result in the information security area related to legal proceedings, whether civil or criminal

- Successfully concluded an investigation of information security violations and incidents

- Posted a certain number of changes to the access control privilege database

- Achieved a certain threshold average time to process a new user-ID requests

- Created a certain number of new user-IDs with new passwords and privileges

- Modified the privileges on a certain number of user-IDs to reflect new duties for the involved users

- Reset a certain number of lost or forgotten fixed passwords

- Reissued a certain number of smart cards, badges, or other access devices

- Answered a certain number of questions from users and others who are confused about information security

- Delivered a certain number of information security awareness training classes

- Reached a predetermined goal involving a certain number of users who viewed the computer based training program developed by the Information Security Department

- Reviewed a certain number of new or enhanced business applications to ensure that adequate controls were incorporated into these systems

- Evaluated a certain number of new information security technologies to determine whether they are suitable for your organization

- Assisted with the classification of a certain number of sensitive documents which had not been previously ranked with a data classification system

- Assisted with the ranking of a certain number of applications according to a previously established system criticality scale

- Eradicated a certain number of computer viruses, Trojan horses, or other malicious software infestations

- Screened at least a predetermined number of viruses and Trojan horses at the firewall, departmental server, or mail server level, and thereby prevented infestations and other problems

- Restored a certain number of systems to a trusted state following intrusion by hackers or other unauthorized outsiders

- Installed a certain number of security-related patches or fixes on existing machines for which this individual was responsible

- Configured and placed into service a certain number of new servers/systems

- Responded to a certain number of Computer Emergency Response Team incident alerts

While there are other possible metrics, these should get you thinking about the metrics that might be used at your organization. Before any of these metrics can be adopted, you will need to clearly see how the metric can be captured by someone or something other than the person or department whose performance is being measured. For example, the Systems Development Department could indicate the number of new applications that were reviewed by the Information Security Department within a calendar year. Likewise, an EDP auditor could determine the percentage of staff that are in compliance with information security policies now and one year ago, to see whether there has been a noticeable improvement. Alternatively, a help desk trouble ticket system can indicate how many virus infestations took place in a certain year, and how many were taken care of with less than $1000 of damage (or whatever other criteria the organization wishes to employ). Generally the person or department being measured should not keep track of the metrics themselves because they may be tempted to overstate their accomplishments or exaggerate the contribution that they have made. Likewise, as is the case with a trouble ticket system, whenever possible it is desirable to capture the metrics in an automated system as a by-product of doing other tasks.

Perhaps the best metric reflecting an information security function's success is that it saved the organization money. While at first you may scoff, thinking that information security is always an overhead item that only costs money, there are some exceptions. It behooves you to loudly trumpet these exceptions to help change management's viewpoint of information security. One example of such an exception involves software licensing; through the adoption of a new license management system, software costs can actually be reduced. Another example involves an uninterruptible power system (UPS); a power outage of a certain duration can be expected to cost an organization a certain amount due to lost business, and this may be considerably more than the cost of buying and maintaining the UPS. Yet another example involves file backup systems; the cost of recreating files lost in a virus infestation can be compared favorably to the cost of purchasing and operating the backup system. While showing that good information security saved the organization money will help with efforts to get a larger budget and greater number of people on the Information Security Department staff, it can also show that a specific individual is doing a good job, and therefore deserves a promotion, a raise, a bonus, etc.

Information Security Roles & Responsibilities Made Easy

Appendix D   PROFESSIONAL CERTIFICATIONS

With résumé fraud on the rise, one of the sure-fire methods for employers to be sure that the people they hire are indeed familiar with the essentials of the field is to insist that they have certain certifications. The certifications can then be checked with the issuing organizations to make sure that they have indeed been conferred on the applicant for employment. This chapter lists the major certifications relevant to the information security field. There are others, but these are the ones that the practitioner will encounter most frequently, and these are the ones that have the greatest credibility.

The following professional certifications are relevant primarily to centralized information security positions. They are not generally relevant to staff working in decentralized information security positions, unless these individuals intend to become information security specialists. You may also look for these certifications on the résumés of consultants and contractors working in the information security field.

You may wish to list these designations in help wanted advertisements, look for them on résumés, and ask about them during interviews. Automatic résumé scanning software can also be set up to search for these strings of characters. The certifications are listed below in order of relevance to information security activities (most to least relevant).

CISSP

Certified Information Systems Security Professional - intended for information systems security specialists, this credential covers topics such as system access control, cryptography, telecommunications security, computer risk management, data classification, computer operation security, and information ethics.

(ISC)2, Inc.

860 Worcester Road, Suite 101
Framingham, MA 01702 USA

voice: 508-875-8400
fax: 508-875-8450
web: www.isc2.org

CISA

Certified Information Systems Auditor - intended for EDP auditors, this credential covers topics such as systems development life cycle, operating systems software controls, computer application system controls, data integrity, computer product acquisitions process, risk analysis, and computer operational procedures.

Information Systems Audit & Control Association (ISACA)

3701 Algonquin Road, Suite 1010
Rolling Meadows, IL 60008 USA

voice: 847-253-1545
fax: 847-253-1443
web: www.isaca.org

CBCP

Certified Business Continuity Planner (also related designations known as ABCP or Associate Business Continuity Planner, and MBCP or Master Business Continuity Planner) - intended for business contingency planners and information systems contingency planners, this credential covers topics such as business impact analysis, emergency response, developing recovery strategies, testing recovery plans, and awareness training.

DRI International

111 Park Place
Falls Church, VA 22046-4513 USA

voice: 703-538-1792
fax: 703-241-5603
web: www.drii.org

CCP

Certified Computer Professional (with demonstrated specialty in systems security) - intended for technical specialists like programmers and systems analysts, this credential covers topics such as systems programming, data resource management, microcomputer networks, systems development process, software engineering, and systems security.

Institute for Certification of Computing Professionals (ICCP)

2350 E. Devon Ave., Suite 115
Des Plaines, IL 60018-4610 USA

voice: 847-299-4227
fax: 847-299-4280
web: www.iccp.org

CSM

Certified Software Manager - intended for systems administrators, help-desk personnel and information security specialists, this credential covers topics such as copyright law, software licenses, software inventory tools, software audit process, security awareness training, and virus infestation responses.

The Software & Information Industry Association (SIIA)

1090 Vermont Ave, NW, Sixth Floor
Washington, DC 20005 USA

voice: 202-289-7442
fax: 202-289-7097
web: www.siia.net

GCIA

GIAC (Global Incident Analysis Center) Certified Intrusion Analyst - intended for systems administrators and others who must respond to hacker attacks and understand operating system logs and intrusion detection software reports.

SANS Institute

5401 Westbard Ave., Suite 1501
Bethesda, MD, 20816 USA

voice: 866-570-9927
fax: 301-951-0140
web: www.sans.org

CFE

Certified Fraud Examiner - intended for internal auditors, forensic accountants, private investigators, academic researchers, and law enforcement personnel, this credential covers topics such as financial transactions, statistical analysis, fraud investigation tools, fraud deterrence, criminology, ethics, and the legal process.

Association of Certified Fraud Examiners

The Gregor Building
716 West Avenue
Austin, TX 78701 USA

voice: 512-478-9070 / 800-254-3321 (USA and Canada)
fax: 512-478-9297
web: www.acfe.org

CPP

Certified Protection Professional - intended for directors of Security Departments, this credential covers topics such as emergency planning, sensitive information protection, personnel security, investigations, loss prevention, physical security, and substance abuse.

American Society for Industrial Security

1625 Prince Street
Alexandria, VA 22314-2818 USA

voice: 703-519-6200
fax: 703-519-6299
web: www.asisonline.org

CIA

Certified Internal Auditor - intended for internal auditors, this credential covers topics such as the fraud detection, interviewing for investigations, reporting problems to management, control of information technology, mathematics of statistical sampling, managerial accounting, and financial accounting.

The Institute of Internal Auditors

249 Maitland Ave.
Altamonte Springs, FL 32701-4201 USA

voice: 407-830-7600, Ext. 1
fax: 407-831-5171
web: www.theiia.org

Appendix E   RESPONSIBILITY AND LIABILITY

This appendix explores a number of issues related to top management's ultimate responsibility for information security. Liability is a vast topic and this chapter is intended to provide only a few starting points for further investigation. The material is intended to be helpful to you in your efforts to gain management support for an information security roles and responsibilities definition/revision project. Consultation with legal counsel is strongly advised prior to having discussions with top management on any issue related to legal liability. I am not an attorney.

Modern information systems technology enables a variety of acts that were not possible in years gone past. For example, through e-mail, employees can unintentionally bind the organization to a contract, unintentionally libel another entity, or unintentionally trigger charges of a hostile working environment (via dirty jokes for example). E-mail provides a new and easy-to-use channel for the transmission of a wide variety of different types of information including strategic plans, employee performance reviews, as well as merger and acquisition plans. One of the areas where management (which includes the Board of Directors) can be held individually and personally responsible for the acts of employees involves e-mail communications.

Management may also be held liable for the actions of employees if these same employees do not properly handle intellectual property belonging to others. The Software Publishers Association and the Business Publishers Association (both now merged with the Information Industry Association) have conducted many high-visibility audits where they have proven the use of illegal software at major organizations. The resulting fines have been significant and the adverse publicity has been embarrassing. While these organizational risks are serious, management at your organization may not pay much attention unless the risks are to their own personal wealth and well-being. Many managers do not realize that they have a vicarious liability for acts of software piracy by their employees. Managers in the United States can be held liable under the Copyright Act for up to $250,000 in fines and up to two years in prison.

At the heart of the issue related to management's responsibility for information security problems lies the question "Is management legally responsible for the actions of the people who report to them?" In some

countries the answer is a definitive "yes," in others the answer is "yes sometimes," and in yet others it is "not so much." In the United States, the answer is "yes sometimes." For example, the False Claims Act, a federal statute that is normally used to prosecute fraud in military contracting, was used against the University of Utah and the University of California at San Diego. The federal government filed suit to hold management at these two universities responsible for research conducted on their campuses. It was alleged that two professors fraudulently obtained research grants by misrepresenting the results of their research. The suit also alleged that the management at these two universities recklessly certified the grant applications. Beyond the False Claims Act, other statutes such as the Major Fraud Act and the Truth in Negotiation Act can be used by the United States government to bring information security related lawsuits.

When a manager asks you why they should spend money on information security, perhaps the most engaging response is, "Because it will keep you out of jail." Depending on the jurisdiction where your organization operates, there are a number of statutes that attempt to assign greater accountability to management for the maintenance of internal control. And internal control is, of course, critically dependent on information security. One example of such a statute in the United States is the Foreign Corrupt Practices Act (FCPA), which incidentally applies only to companies listed on a stock exchange. Originally written as an anti-bribery statute, the FCPA requires the establishment and maintenance of an adequate system of accounting and management controls. Under the FCPA, top managers can lose their house, their boat, their car, and their savings because they are civilly liable for lapses in internal control. You are urged to investigate the specific statutes—that are relevant to your organization—and that make management personally liable for information security problems.

Perhaps the most likely type of lawsuit that management will encounter is a stockholder lawsuit. Stockholders may allege that management did not adequately protect their investment, that they breached their fiduciary duty to conserve and protect corporate assets. Even if there are no stockholder suits, the stock price declines related to information security problems can be severe. When one considers the stock options that management has at many organizations, talking about these price declines with management can often help obtain management support for an information security roles and responsibilities effort. For example, eBay, an Internet auction company, saw the market value of its stock decline $4 billion dollars in 1999 because it had a twenty-two hour outage on its auction site. Executives at eBay estimate that the impact included a loss of $3 to $5 million in sales. Likewise, in 1999, AOL saw its stock plunge $4.50/share because it was off-line for nineteen hours. In a similar vein, in the same year, E*Trade saw its stock decline $6.50/share because it had two software related outages that lasted a combined seventy-five minutes. All of these outages directly relate to systems availability, an important information security consideration.

There is a new type of exposure that management may not know about, and it's called computer professional malpractice. This exposure involves those events where computer professionals don't act with the due care that one would expect of a computer professional. In a landmark case involving Ernst & Young when they were still called Ernst & Whinney (in 1990), consultants failed to provide a T-shirt manufacturing company with the services needed to integrate a new computer system. The court relied on commonly practiced professional standards, just as is done in medicine, when establishing this notion as legal precedent. It is only a matter of time before this same notion is extended to the information security area, an area fraught with complexity where it's easy to make mistakes. While you may choose not to use this notion in discussions with top management, you can use it in discussions with the Chief Information Officer and others who are computer professionals.

The notion of exercising due care is also important to discuss with top management. If a person's conduct caused an unreasonable risk of harm to others, then that person can be held liable under common law. In many cases, the standard of due care is readily evident in the information security field. It can be determined, for example, in the area of Internet commerce credit card fraud prevention—credit card numbers should not be transmitted over the Internet in unencrypted form. To do so would subject management to liability for a tort or civil wrong. However, management must be shown to have acted negligently or with wrongful intent. The real issue as it relates to information security is determining what exactly is prudent and what is negligent. The courts will determine this on a case-by-case basis, but it's advisable to stay out of court altogether. Primary to the court's determination of negligence is the notion of a "prudent man," in other words, someone else who was acting diligently and who was facing the same circumstances. You can thus compare your organization to others in the same industry to get a sense for what constitutes the standard of due care. For example, if other firms in the same industry have clear roles and responsibilities documentation, then your firm should also have this same type of documentation. You may also wish to investigate relevant United States cases dealing with the standard of due care such as: *Palmer v. Columbia Gas Co.*, *Ford Motor Credit Corp. v. Hitchcock*, *Delbueck v. Manufacturer's Hanover Bank*, *US v. Simon*, *Adams v. Standard Knitting*, and *Price v. Ford*.

Another legal notion that may be helpful in discussions with top management is the notion of *legal notice*. When management has been placed on notice that there is an information security problem, they have a duty to correct the problem. If management fails to take adequate precautions, they can be held liable. This notion was used against the now-bankrupt Pan American World Airways. Pan Am had received a number of threats about a terrorist act before one of its jets exploded due to a bomb over Scotland in 1988. Because it knew and failed to take certain precautions, it could be and was held liable for damages to the passengers who died in the crash. In a like manner, if management has been put on notice by a hacker, then it needs to upgrade its network security. Worse yet, if management knew a hacker was on its network, and then this hacker went on to use the organization's network to attack another organization, then management might be liable for damages done to that other organization.

Many industries have regulations specific to the industry. For example, in the United States, all federally chartered banks are required to have a contingency plan that meets federal government guidelines. Several legal scholars have implied that management would be personally liable if disaster strikes and a bank did not have adequate contingency plans in place. Unfortunately these directives do not include objective standards, so in the absence of dishonesty or gross negligence, managers would be likely to be saved by the common law business judgement rule (which avoids liability on the basis that managers acted legally, honestly, and in good faith). You should check the laws applicable to your industry to determine the extent to which management is personally liable for failing to be in compliance with information security related regulations.

There are also laws that cut across industries, laws that pertain to certain activities, such as the handling of credit history information. In the United States, the Fair Credit Reporting Act mandates that organizations handling credit history data maintain the data so that it is complete and up to date. Willful failure to comply can result in actual and punitive damages, court costs, and attorney's fees. The key of this law is willfulness, and personal liability for failing to live up to the standard of due care is not directly addressed.

Beyond multi-industry laws within a certain country, there are certain laws that have been adopted by multiple countries. For example, countries in the European Union (EU) have adopted harmonized privacy laws. Although the privacy laws are more relaxed in the United States, there is still reason for management to be concerned. One such area involves e-mail monitoring. For example, at Epson America an e-mail administrator was dismissed for refusing to monitor the e-mail of other employees. This administrator believed that unannounced monitoring was unethical and that it violated the privacy of the other employees. She went on to file a wrongful termination lawsuit, and 170 employees then joined her in filing a California wiretapping statute violation suit against the company. Although not a part of that case, the California Constitution guarantees the right to privacy and gives any citizen standing to bring a lawsuit when they believe that their right to privacy has been violated. You should pay particular attention to the privacy laws of the states and/or countries where your organization operates, and you should be sure to communicate the extent of management's liability for failure to observe these same laws. You should also note that there are United States federal laws that govern privacy such as the Electronic Communications Privacy Act.

The prospect of management liability within a single jurisdiction should be disconcerting enough, but the widespread usage of the Internet compounds this problem many times over. While the legal notion of doing Internet business in a certain jurisdiction is still evolving, there have been cases where the more stringent standards of one state are applied to systems that were physically located in another state with more lenient laws. The area of pornography is particularly good example here, but there are many other laws related to information security that should be of concern to you. In the United States, at the federal level, these include: the Computer Fraud and Abuse Act, the Copyright Act, the Crime Control Act, the Privacy Act, the Right to Financial Privacy Act, the Privacy Protection Act, the Electronic Funds Transfer Act, and the ERISA Retirement Record Keeping Act.

In whatever country your organization happens to operate, it is customary to have management be personally responsible for problems which are so severe that they jeopardize the very existence of the organization. There are a number of cases on record where the organization went out of business as a result of information security problems. For example, in London, England, a printer who thought that his employer was trying to avoid paying him 2,000 pounds that he believed was owed, used a special password to lock up the computers of Ampersand Typesetting Ltd. The firm was accordingly unable to conduct business, and lost more than 36,000 pounds in sales. Subsequent prosecution under the Computer Misuse Act claimed that the printer's actions contributed to the firm's bankruptcy which followed immediately after this incident. In this case, apparently no contingency plan was in place. Beyond the failure to develop and enhance an adequate contingency plan, management may also be held liable for failure to use virus detection software, or failure to perform proper background checks (the latter is known as negligent hiring).

Management at many organizations is not yet sufficiently aware of its liability for undue reliance on computerized records. In a landmark case in the United States called *Ford Motor Credit Co. v. Swarens*, the defendant firm was told by the plaintiff that computerized data was incorrect. The data in question involved a loan for a car. The plaintiff provided cancelled checks indicating that the computer records, which said that the plaintiff was seriously in arrears on his loan, were incorrect. Management chose to disregard this evidence, and proceeded to repossess the car. The Kentucky Court of Appeals indicated that management had unreasonably relied on the computerized records and was therefore liable. The management at Ford said that they were not at fault because they relied on erroneous data, and that they had no bad intent. This was not sufficient in the eyes of the court to avoid liability. On this same note, it is useful to ask top management just how much they rely on computerized information when making key decisions related to the organization. Management should be asked whether they really know how often data is updated, who provided it, how it is processed, etc.

In the United States, managers should also be aware of the Federal Sentencing Organizational Guidelines. These 1991 regulations are aimed at white collar crime but they have sobering implications for Chief Executive Officers as well as other top managers such as Chief Information Officers. The regulations hold senior management responsible for crime involving their organization. Management is responsible even if the organization and its members are honest and the crime was perpetrated by outsiders. Organizations are exposed to liability of up to $290 million and the possible loss of a corporate charter. High level managers are exposed to fines and possible imprisonment. To prevent this liability, management must prove its good faith by establishing an effective security program that prevents and deters criminal conduct. While broader in scope than just information security, these regulations point to need for the establishment of clear roles and responsibilities.

Although many people in the information security field don't appreciate their jobs in this light, they have a key role to play when it comes to protecting management against personal liability. The human resources area, at least in the United States, has become a hotbed of litigation with allegations like racial discrimination, age discrimination, wrongful termination, breach of implied promise, and the like. Top management has come to appreciate that the human resources function, if done well, will help to avoid litigation and disputes. The information security function at many organizations has not made this same point clearly to top management, and that is one of the great challenges in the information security awareness field. To be successful with a shift in management attitudes, top management must come to appreciate that information security is not just a technical issue, that it is a management and people issue as well.

To quantify the exposure that management faces, and to determine how much it is prudent to spend to reduce this exposure, you should perform a brief legal risk assessment. By identifying the serious risks, the likelihood of loss, and the financial implications of each loss, you will be able to go to management with a proposal containing ways to address these exposures. Of course, one very important step that should be included in this proposal is clarification of information security roles and responsibilities. After management receives the legal risk analysis and a proposal about appropriate next steps, it can determine which exposures it wishes to transfer (with insurance), which exposures it wishes to mitigate (with additional controls), and which exposures it wishes to accept (that is, do nothing about).

After the major legal exposures have been identified, your organization should establish a solid compliance program to ensure that the organization is following the dictates of both laws and regulations. A documented compliance program has been shown to impress the court, and show a *bona fide* intention on management's part to operate in a manner that is consistent with all aspects of laws and regulations. This can help avert prosecution, not just fines. This opinion is supported by a 1995 report prepared by the U.S. Sentencing Commission, an independent agency of the judicial branch of the federal government. In addition, the United States government has also gone on record stating that the existence of a compliance program would result in reduced fines for firms that have been convicted of statutory violations. A compliance program should be included as one of the responsibilities of the Legal Department, and this topic is further discussed in Chapter 11, "Mission Statements" and Chapter 12, "Job Descriptions."

SAMPLE USER AGREEMENT

This form must be completely filled out and signed by the user before it will be processed. Modifications to the terms and conditions provided in this form are not acceptable to management, although additional remarks will be noted.

Please check the relevant categories from the three options shown immediately below and provide the additional information requested.

__ User seeks a new user-ID

     Provide reason: _____

__ User seeks reauthorization of an existing user-ID

     Existing user-ID: _____

__ User seeks additional privileges on an existing user-ID

     Existing user-ID: _____

     Specify privileges needed: _____

     _____

     _____

User's name printed: _____

User's department: _____

User's telephone number: _____

User's internal mail location: _____

I am the user whose name appears above. I understand that my continued employment by or contractual work with Company X is contingent on my diligent and consistent compliance with information security policies and procedures. I have read a copy of the Company X information security policies manual, and I understand my responsibilities as defined in that manual. I have been warned and I understand that violation of the rules contained in that manual, or failure to perform my responsibilities as defined in that manual, will be sufficient cause for disciplinary action up to and including termination.

I understand that information owned by or entrusted to Company X is valuable and proprietary, and that it needs to be protected. I understand that my access to this information makes me an important part of the team charged with protecting this information. Accordingly, I agree to take all security and privacy precautions, as I have been instructed by Company X, to protect the information to which I have been given access in the course of my work for Company X.

When I cease to work for Company X, no matter what the circumstances, I agree to turn over to Company X all Company X information which is then in my possession or otherwise under my control. I agree that I will not retain copies of or summaries of this information, in any form, for any purpose whatsoever.

I acknowledge that the information I obtain access to in the course of my work for Company X is the property of Company X or another organization that does business with Company X. I promise that I will not use this information for my own personal purposes, including operating my business, selling the information to other parties, or performing analyses of this information on behalf of other parties. I agree not to disclose this information to third parties without first obtaining the approval of the Company X owner of the information.

To support Company X business activities, I agree to do my best to maintain the currency, accuracy, and relevance of information which I have access to in the course of my work. This includes reporting known errors or inconsistencies in the information.

To maintain the security of the information that I have been granted access to, I promise to choose only those fixed passwords which are difficult for other parties to guess (several words strung together, a combination of characters and numbers, a combination of characters and punctuation, etc.). I understand that my fixed password must be known only by myself, and must not be provided to any other person. I additionally agree not to write my password down on anything, or store it in any computer, unless it has been transformed by a special process which makes it unrecognizable and unusable by unauthorized parties.

I understand that Company X authorizes me only to access that information which I need to perform my job. I agree that I will not seek to obtain access to Company X information beyond that which has been expressly granted to me through a formal request process. I additionally agree not to use Company X information systems to launch an attack on any other computers, whether they are inside Company X's network or outside this network. In this same vein, I agree not to use software which discovers passwords, uses brute force routines to decrypt encrypted files, or in any other way seek access to information which has not been expressly granted to me. I additionally agree not to download any software from the Internet or dial-up bulletin-boards which has not been properly licensed and paid for, unless it is an authorized demonstration copy. I furthermore agree that I will not perform any activity which might be expected to lead to damage to Company X information or information systems (writing computer viruses, overloading systems via network games, etc.). I furthermore agree not to use electronic mail or any other system resources to intimidate or harass other people.

I promise to immediately report all violations or suspected violations of information security policies to the Manager of the Information Security Department.

User's Signature and Date: _____

ABOUT THE AUTHOR

Based in the San Francisco Bay Area, Charles Cresson Wood is an independent information security consultant, researcher, and author. As part of his consulting work, he prepares and reviews standards, architectures, policies, codes of conduct, procedures, budgets, action plans, mission statements, job descriptions, and other parts of an organizational infrastructure to support information security. He also performs risk assessments and designs custom information security solutions.

Working in the field full-time since 1979, he has been a computer security management consultant at SRI International (formerly Stanford Research Institute) and lead data communications security consultant at the Bank of America. He has done information security consulting work with over 120 organizations, many of them Fortune 500 companies. His consulting projects have taken him to Australia, Austria, Belgium, Brazil, Canada, England, Finland, France, Holland, Ireland, Italy, Japan, Norway, Portugal, Saudi Arabia, South Africa, and Sweden.

Mr. Wood has delivered over 125 information security presentations at various conferences; he has also been a keynote speaker at several of these same conferences. He has been quoted as an expert in publications such as Business Week, Computerworld, Information Week, LA Times, PC Week, The Wall Street Journal, and Time. In 1996 he received the Lifetime Achievement Award from the Computer Security Institute (San Francisco) for "sincere dedication to the computer security profession."

Mr. Wood is the Senior North American Editor for the technical journals Computers & Security and Computer Fraud and Security Bulletin. For the last six years he has written a monthly information security policies column for Computer Security Alert. He has published over 225 technical articles and five other books dealing with information security. His best selling book is entitled *Information Security Policies Made Easy*. Mr. Wood's work has been or is now being translated into a number of foreign languages including Brazilian Portuguese, Finnish, French, Japanese, Hebrew, Portuguese, Spanish, and Swedish.

Mr. Wood holds an MBA in financial information systems and a BSE in accounting, both from the Wharton School at the University of Pennsylvania. He also holds an MSE degree in computer science from the Moore School of Engineering at the same University (birthplace of the ENIAC, the world's first general purpose electronic computer). In addition to passing the Certified Public Accountant (CPA) exam, he is a Certified Information Systems Auditor (CISA), and a Certified Information Systems Security Professional (CISSP).

Mr. Wood can be reached directly at the following address: ccwood@ix.netcom.com.

Information Security Roles & Responsibilities Made Easy

SOURCES AND REFERENCES

Abrams, M., and Podell, H., *Managing Information Security, Computer Education*, 1991 [out of print]

Alkemi, A., *Computer Security Manager*, Elsevier Science, 1989

Anonymous, *A Guide To Understanding Information System Security Officer Responsibilities For Automated Information Systems*, Diane Publishing, 1995 [out of print]

Anonymous, *COBIT: Governance, Control, And Audit For Information And Related Technology, Information Systems Audit And Control Association*, second edition, 1998

Anonymous, *Code Of Practice For Information Security Management*, British Standard 7799, British Standards Institute, 1997

Anonymous, *Computers - Crimes, Clues & Controls: A Management Guide*, Diane Publishing, 1993

Anonymous, "More Firms Add Security Managers," *Communications Week*, 14 April 1997

Anonymous, "Proposed: A Protection Committee At Management Level," *Security Management Bulletin*, No. 2215, 10 August 1993

Attaway, Morris C., Sr., "What Every Auditor Needs To Know About E-Commerce Outsourcing," *Internal Auditor*, pp. 48- 55, June 2000

Badenhorst, Karin P., Eloff, Jan H. P., "Framework of a Methodology for the Life Cycle of Computer Security in an Organization," *Computers & Security*, Vol. 8, No. 5, pp. 433-442, August 1989

Barbier, Etienne, "Audit Committes A La Francaise," *Internal Auditor*, June 1998

Beane, William F., "Computer Security: Who's In Charge?," *Security World*, October 1984

Bernard, Ray, "Computer Security: Nerd, Technie, Specialist, Guru or Expert Which Do You Need?," *Security Technology & Design*, pp. 76, 78-79, April 1997

Bernstein, David S., "Certification: For Professionals Only," *InfoSecurity News*, pp. 21-22, March/April 1997

Bound, William A. J., "Discussing Security with Top Management," *Computers & Security*, Vol. 7, No. 2, pp. 129-130, April 1988

Caelli, William J., Longley, Dennis, and Shain, M., *Information Security For Managers*, Groves Dictionaries, 1989 [out of print]

Campbell, Robert P., "Structuring The Information Security Program," *Data Security Management*, Auerbach Publications, 1992

Carroll, Glen, and Michael Hannon, *Organizations In Industry: Strategy, Structure & Selection*, Oxford University Press, 1995

Christmas, P., *Network Security Manager*, Elsevier Science Publishers, 1996

Dale, Ernest, *Management Theory And Practice* (3rd Edition), McGraw-Hill, 1973

DeMaio, Harry B., *Information Protection And Other Unnatural Acts: Every Manager's Guide To Keeping Vital Computer Data Safe And Sound*, Amacom Press, 1992

Dhillon, Gurpeet, and James Backhouse, *Information Security: A Management Challenge*, Inter Thompson Press, 1997

Drucker, Peter F., "Management's New Paradigms," *Forbes*, 5 October 1998 [addresses number of levels in management hierarchy]

Ecklund, Eileen, "Protecting Data Is A Demanding But Secure Career," *Infoworld*, 7 September 1998

Fine, Leonard H., *Computer Security: Handbook For Management*, Trafalgar, 1984 [out of print]

Forcht, Karen A., *Computer Security Management*, Boyd & Fraser, 1994

Fried, Louis, "Assigning Responsibility For Security In Distributed And Outsourced Environments," *Data Security Management*, Auerbach Publications, 1993

Fried, Louis, "Distributed Information Security – Responsibility Assignments And Costs," *Information Systems Management*, Summer 1993

Gaskin, James, *Corporate Politics & The Internet*, Prentice-Hall, 1996

Gilbert, Dennis, and Nickilyn Lynch, *Sample Statements Of Work For Federal Computer Security Services: For Us In-House Or Contracting Out*, US Department Of Commerce, National Institute Of Standards And Technology, 1991

Greenia, Mark W., *Security In Computing: A Sourcebook For Security Officers & Managers*, Lexikon Services, 1990 [out of print]

Isaacson, Gerald I., *MIS Information Security Resource Manual*, MIS Training Institute, 1986

Jacques, Elliott, and Stephen D. Clement, *Executive Leadership: A Practical Guide To Managing Complexity*, Cason Hall & Co., 1994

Kovacich, Gerald, "Establishing A Network Security Programme," *Computers & Security*, Vol. 15 (1996), No. 6, pp. 486-498

Kovacich, Gerald, "Establishing An Information Systems Security Organization (ISSO)," *Computers & Security*, Vol. 17 (1998), No. 7, pp. 600-612

Kovacich, Gerald L., *Information Systems Security Officer's Guide*, Butterworth Heinemann Publishers, 1998

Krogstad, Jack L., Anthony J. Ridley, and Larry E. Rittenberg, "Where We're Going," *Internal Auditor*, October 1999 [about the future of the Internal Auditing profession including responsibilities]

Lowenthal, Jeffrey N., *Reengineering The Organization: A Step-By-Step Approach To Corporate Revitalization*, ASQC Quality Press, 1994

Madron, Thomas W., *Network Security In The Nineties: Issues & Solutions For Managers*, Wiley, 1992

Maglitta, Joseph, and Mehler, Mark, "Executive Report—Power Shifts—The New Centralization," *Computerworld*, pp. 85-87, 27 April 1992

Mansfield, Roger, *Company Strategy And Organizational Design*, St. Martin's Press, 1986

McClelland, Samuel B., *Organizational Needs Assessments: Design, Facilitation, and Analysis*, Quorum Books, 1995

Moulton, Rolf T., *Strategies And Techniques For Preventing Data Loss Or Theft*, Prentice Hall, 1986

Nadler, David, Gerstein, Marc, and Shaw, Robert, *Organizational Architecture: Designs For Changing Organizations*, Bass Publishers, 1992

Nakatani, Iwao, "How Competitive Are We?," *World Press Review*, August 1988, p. 64 [addresses organizational unit coordination]

Oppenheimer, David, Wagner, Avid, and Crabb, Michele D., *System Security: A Management Perspective*, USENIX Association, 1997

Palmer, Ian, *Computer Security Risk Management*, Van Nostrand Reinhold, 1990

Parker, Donn B., *A Manager's Guide To Computer Security*, Prentice-Hall, 1983

Peltier, Tom, "Who Should The Information Protection Staff Report To?," *Computer Security Alert*, No. 131, February 1994

Perry, William E., *Management Strategies For Computer Security*, Butterworth-Heinemann, 1985 [out of print]

Pfeffer, Jeffrey, *Organizations And Organizational Theory*, Putnam Publishing, 1982

Pine, Evelyn, and Jeff Johnson, "Cyber-Responsibilities," *Computer Professionals For Social Responsibility Newsletter*, Vol. 16, No. 3, Summer 1998

Pinkerton Service Corporation, *Top Organizational & Professional Issues For Today's Security Director*, 1997 (survey results)

Power, Richard, "How Should You Structure Your Information Protection Unit?," *Computer Security Alert*, April 1998

Power, Richard, "Is Your Job Description Out-Of-Date?," *Computer Security Alert*, March 1997

Power, Richard, "Job Descriptions: Excuse Me, Could Anyone Tell Me What I Do?," *Computer Security Alert*, September 1998

Power, Richard, "Where Should Information Security Report?," *Computer Security Journal*, Vol. XIII, No. 1., 1997

Robbins, Stephen P., *Organizational Theory – Structure, Design, And Applications*, Third Edition, Prentice-Hall, 1990

Ruthberg, Zella, and Tipton, Harold F., *Handbook Of Information Security Management*, Warren Gorham & Lamont, 1993

Schweitzer, James A., *Protecting Business Information: A Manager's Guide*, Butterworth-Heinemann, 1995

Serpico, Philip A., "What Is Security's Duty To Report?," *Security Management*, pp. 121-122, March 1997

Shapiro, Andrew, *The Control Revolution: How The Internet Is Putting Individuals In Charge And Changing The World We Know*, Security Foundation, 1999

Sherwood, John, "Managing Security For Outsourcing Contracts," *Proceedings Of The COMPSEC97 Conference* (London, England), Elsevier Advanced Technology, 1997

Smith, Martin R., *Commonsense Computer Security: Your Practical Guide To Information Protection*, McGraw-Hill, 1993

Straub, Detmar W., Jr., "Organizational Structuring Of The Computer Security Function," *Computers & Security*, Vol. 7, No. 2, April 1988

Talbot, J. R., *Management Guide To Computer Security*, Halstead Publishers, 1985 [out of print]

Tipton, Harold, and Elliott, Robert, *Data Security Management*, Warren Gorham & Lamont, 1992

Tipton, Harold F., "Liability Of Corporate Officers For Security Problems," *Computer Security Journal*, Vol. X., No. 1, pp. 59-69 (1991)

Van Tassel, D., *Computer Security Management*, Prentice-Hall, 1981 [out of print]

von Simson, Ernest M., "The Centrally Decentralized IS Organization," *Harvard Business Review*, pp. 158-162, July-August 1990

Watt, Steve, *Computer Security Manager*, Elsevier Advanced Technology, 1989

Weisul, Kimberly, "CSOs Become Indispensable," *Inter@active Week*, p. 94, 17 April 2000 [a CSO is a chief security officer]

Williamson, Oliver E., *Organizational Theory: From Chester Barnard To The Present And Beyond*, Oxford University Press, 1995

Wood, Charles Cresson, "A Policy For An Information Security Management Committee," *Computer Security Alert*, No. 115, October 1992

Wood, Charles Cresson, and Saari, Juhani, "A Strategy For Developing Information Security Documents," *Journal of Information Systems Security*, pp. 71-78, Auerbach Publishers, Vol. 1, Issue 2, Summer 1992

Wood, Charles Cresson, "Clarifying Responsibility For Network Security," *Computer Security Alert*, No. 152, November 1995

Wood, Charles Cresson, *Effective Information Security Management*, Elsevier Science Publishers, 1991

Wood, Charles Cresson, "How Many Information Security Staff People Should You Have?" *Computers & Security*, pp. 395-402, Vol. 9, 1990

Wood, Charles Cresson, "How To Achieve A Clear Definition Of Responsibilities For Information Security," *Datapro Information Security Service*, IS115-200-101, April 1993

Wood, Charles Cresson, "Information Security Staffing Levels: Calculating The Standard Of Due Care," *Computer Security Journal*, Summer 1998 [provided as Appendix A in this book]

Wood, Charles Cresson, *Information Security Policies Made Easy*, Baseline Software (Sausalito, California), 7th edition, 1999

Wood, Charles Cresson, "Mandating The Information Security Management Function," *Computer Security Alert*, No. 126, October 1993

Wood, Charles Cresson, "Shifting Information Systems Security Responsibility From User Organizations To Vendor/Publisher Organizations," *Computers & Security*, Vol. 14, No. 4, October 1995 [a revised version provided as Chapter 16 in this book]

Wood, Charles Cresson, "The Information Security Profession: Evolutionary Career Paths," *Information Security*, November 1999

Wood, Charles Cresson, "Why Have Decentralized Information Security Coordinators?," *Computer Fraud & Security Bulletin*, August 1992

Wylder, John O. D., "The Life Cycle Of Security Managers: New Responsibilities For A Distributed Environment," *Information Systems Management*, Vol. 9, No. 1, Winter, 1992

Yoder, Stephen Kreider, "When Things Go Wrong—The Main Strength of Networks, Giving Control to Individual Users, Is Also Its Greatest Weakness," *The Wall Street Journal*, p. R16, 14 November 1994

CD-ROM Files

All of the material found in this book is available on the accompanying CD-ROM in PDF and html format. To view the PDF version, open the **R&R.pdf** file using Adobe Acrobat Reader. If you need Adobe Acrobat Reader, you can download a free copy from the Adobe web site at www.adobe.com.

You can also use your web browser to access this book in html format by accessing the CD-ROM and opening the **Index.htm** file. For best results, you should use Microsoft® Internet Explorer 5.5 or Netscape 6.

To search the entire book for a certain word, click the Search tab and enter the word. As an example, suppose you wanted to get some insight into "separation of duties." In that case, you would type `separation duties` (do not type common words like *of, the, and, are, is*) and click **Search**. The Search tab displays all of the topics in the book that contain these words.

If you are ready to write a mission statement, you will want to open Chapter 11, "Mission Statements." Copy the desired text and paste it into a document to tailor the material to the needs of your organization. Likewise, if you are ready to write job descriptions, you should open Chapter 12, "Job Descriptions." If you are interested in reporting relationships, you should open Chapter 13, "Reporting Relationships." All other material can be easily located via the Contents and Index.

If you have trouble opening any of these files, if you have questions, or if you have suggestions for enhancing the next version of this product, please e-mail them directly to infopolicy@pentasafe.com. There is also a Feedback form provided at the back of this book. If you thought that this product was useful, please tell your business associates about it.

FEEDBACK

This book is intended to be a work-in-progress that will be updated as additional information security research is published and as generally accepted practices in this same field are clarified. Input from readers is greatly appreciated and is wholeheartedly solicited. The author pays a great deal of attention to reader feedback, and comments will be used when the next edition is prepared.

Using this page found on the accompanying CD-ROM, please copy and paste this text into an e-mail message and send your responses to infopolicy@pentasafe.com.

1   On a scale from 1 to 10 (1 is worst and 10 is best), how would you rate the usefulness of the information contained in this book?

2   Using the same scale, how would you rate the extent to which the information in this book is accessible, readily understood, and clear?

3   Using the same scale, how would you rate the way the information in this book is presented?

4   What could the author do to improve this book in future editions?

5   Were there any important roles and responsibilities related to information security that the author forgot to mention?

6   Using the material found in this book, how many hours did it take you to prepare information security related mission statements and job descriptions?

7   What is your job title?

8   To what industry does your employer belong?

9   Roughly how many full-time equivalent employees work at your employer (includes consultants, contractors, temporaries, and outsourcing staff)?

10   How did you first find out about this book?

Roles & Responsibilities Process Integration

Use the following checklists as a guideline to help you integrate roles and responsibilities into your information security process:

If You are Just Getting Started...		If You have Already Begun...	
	Perform Information Security Risk Assessment		Perform Information Security Risk Assessment
	Write Information Security Roles and Responsibilities		Revise Roles and Responsibilities, as Needed
	Establish Information Security Budget		Review Adequacy of Information Security Budget and Staffing Allocations
	Write Information Security Policies		Revise Information Security Policies, as Needed
	Hire Staff and/or Outsource Information Security Work		Hire More Staff and/or Outsource Other Information Security Work, as Needed
	Write Information Security Architecture and Standards		Identify Information Security Organizational Functions that are Not Being Adequately Performed
	Purchase, Install, and Run Appropriate Information Security Tools		Purchase, Install, and Run Appropriate Information Security Tools
	Write Information Security Procedures		Revise Information Security Procedures, as Needed
	Develop Information Security Training and Awareness Program		Revise Information Security Training and Awareness Program, as Needed
	Develop Incentive Systems and Compliance Checking Process		Revise Incentive Systems and Compliance Checking Process, as Needed
	Develop Performance Measurement Systems		Revise Performance Measurement Systems, as Needed

Information Security Roles & Responsibilities Made Easy

Index

Symbols

(ISC)2, Inc., 169

A

ABCP, 169
Access Control System Administrator, 59
Accounting & Finance Department, 104
acquisition, 22
action plan, 39
Adams v. Standard Knitting, 172
Administrative Services Department, 98
Adobe Acrobat, 115
Adobe Acrobat Reader, 183
American Institute of Certified Public Accountants, 124
American Society for Industrial Security, 170
AOL, 172
Application Service Provider, 119
application system requirements document, 41
approval, 27
architecture document, 39
archival records, 48
Archives Manager, 73
ASP, 119
Associate Business Continuity Planner, 169
Association of Certified Fraud Examiners, 170
Attorney, 86
Audit Committee, 52
author, 177
awareness pamphlet, 38
awareness reminder memo, 39

B

backup storage media, 49
badge readers, 46
baseline, 131
batch jobs, 49
bibliography, 179
bonuses, 22
books, 179
British Standard 7799, 127
budget percentage, 127
Building and Facilities Guard, 83
Buildings & Grounds, 105
business application systems, 47
Business Applications Programmer, 69
Business Contingency Planner, 92

C

career paths, 51
Carnegie-Mellon University, 63
CBCP, 169
CBT, 90
CCP, 169
CD-ROM, 183
centralized information security management, 129
centralized manager, 132
CEO, 94
CERT, 51
Certified Business Continuity Planner, 169
Certified Computer Professional, 169
Certified Fraud Examiner, 170
Certified Information Systems Auditor, 169
Certified Information Systems Security Professional, 169
Certified Internal Auditor, 170
Certified Protection Professional, 170
Certified Software Manager, 170
CFE, 170
CFO, 93
characteristics, 159
charge-back scheme, 133
checklist, 187
Chief Executive Officer, 94
Chief Financial Officer, 93
Chief Information Officer, 68
Chief Information Security Officer, 57
Chief Operating Officer, 105
Chief Security Officer, 57
CIA, 170
CIO, 68
CISA, 169
CISO, 57
CISSP, 169
clean desk policy, 84
code of conduct, 40
Code of Practice for Information Security Management, 127
comments, 185
Commerce Site Administrator, 77
communication skills, 159
communications links, 49
Company X, 11
compliance checking, 140
compromise, 52, 159
computer based training, 90

Computer Economics, 127
Computer Emergency Response Team, 51
Computer Operations Manager, 70
Computer Operations Unit, 49
Computer Operator, 71
Computer Security Alert, 142
Computer Security Department, 46
Computer Security Institute, 127, 142
conduct code, 40
confidential, 111
confidentiality agreement, 42
consulting agreement, 42
Contents tab, 183
contingency planning manual, 40
Contingency Planning Unit, 50
contracts, 51
contractual relationships, 51
cost, 31
   incremental, 31
   opportunity, 31
   sunk, 31
CPP, 170
credentials, 177
criticality scale, 111
CSM, 170
CSO, 57

D

Data Administration Manager, 80
Data Administration Unit, 50
data mart, 80
Data Processing Department, 96
Data Security Department, 46
Database Administration Unit, 49
Database Administrator, 79
database development, 48
databases, 49
DBA, 79
decentralized information security management, 129
deferrable, 111
Delbueck v. Manufacturer's Hanover Bank, 172
denial of service attacks, 51
Departmental Information Security Coordinator, 67
diagnostic software, 49
disaster, 50
disputes, 51
distributed information security management, 129
Divisional Information Security Coordinator, 67
documentation, 23
documents, 37
draft, 27
DRI International, 169

Drucker, Peter F., 95
due diligence, 124

E

E*Trade, 172
eBay, 172
EDP Audit Unit, 47
EDP Auditor, 85
Electronic Data Processing (EDP) Audit Unit, 47
Electronic Data Processing Auditor, 85
electronic vaulting, 78
e-mail system, 31
emergency, 50
empire building, 135
Ernst & Young, 172
ethical, 47
Ethics and Compliance Unit, 47
External Auditing Firm, 47
external information resources, 48

F

Facilities Management Department, 105
Facilities Management Outsourcing Firm, 53
Fair Credit Reporting Act, 86
False Claims Act, 171
feedback, 185
financial records, 47
firewalls, 49
Ford Motor Credit Co. v. Swarens, 173
Ford Motor Credit Corp. v. Hitchcock, 172
Foreign Corrupt Practices Act, 86
forms, 39
Forrester Research, 127
Fortune 1000, 127
full-time equivalent, 143
further reading, 179

G

GCIA, 170
GIAC, 170
Global Incident Analysis Center, 170
Gradient Technologies, 115
Guard, 83
guidance, 51

H

H.R. Manager, 87
hacker intrusions, 51
head-count ratios, 142
Help Desk Associate, 73
Help Desk Department, 103
Help Desk Unit, 48

170
software license management systems, 131
SOP manual, 40
sources, 179
SPRINT, 115
SRI Consulting, 137
staff function, 98, 108
staffing, 51
standard of due care, 158
standard operating procedures (SOP) manual, 40
standards document, 39
Statement on Auditing Standards 70, 124
storage media, 49
Strategy & Planning Department, 101
sunk cost, 31
system usage agreement, 175
systems administration procedures manual, 40
Systems Administration Unit, 49
Systems Administrator, 75
systems development process manual, 41
Systems Programmer, 69
Systems Security Department, 46
systems usage responsibility agreement, 42

T
technical support, 48
Telecommunications Manager, 74
telephone assistance, 48
third-party software, 47

time estimates, 35
Toll Fraud Prevention Committee, 115
trained incompetence, 22
Trainer, 90
trans-border data flow laws, 86

U
updates, 22
US v. Simon, 172
user agreement, 175

V
vehicles, 46
virus infections, 51
volume purchase agreement, 131
VPA, 131

W
WAN, 49
web browser, 183
Web Master, 77
Web Site Administrator, 77
Wheatley, Margaret, 9
Wood, Charles Cresson, 177
workstations, 49

Z
zombie computer, 78